OUR EARTH IN ACTION

MOUNTAINS

Chris Oxlade

W
FRANKLIN
LC

This edition published 2014 by Franklin Watts

Copyright © 2014 Franklin Watts

Franklin Watts
338 Euston Road
London NW1 3BH

Franklin Watts Australia
Level 17/207 Kent Street
Sydney, NSW 2000

A CIP catalogue record for this book is available
from the British Library.

Dewey number: 551.43' 2

ISBN 978 1 4451 3198 6

Printed in China

Franklin Watts is a division of Hachette Children's Books,
an Hachette UK company. www.hachette.co.uk

Artwork: John Alston
Editor: Sarah Ridley
Design: Thomas Keenes
Editor in Chief: John C. Miles
Art director: Jonathan Hair
Picture research: Diana Morris

Picture credits:
Bryan & Cherry Alexander/Alamy: 21. Mikhail Basov/Shutterstock: front cover, 1.
Bruce Block/istockphoto: 27. Rob Brock/istockphoto: 11. Bryan Busovicki/Shutterstock: 12t.
EVRON/Shutterstock: 30b. Justin Horrocks/istockphoto: 29t. Dave Logan/istockphoto: 19.
Jennifer London/istockphoto: 4-5b. NASA: 5t, 12b, 14. Andrew Penner/istockphoto: 17.
Piskunov/istockphoto: 16b. Igor Plotnikov/istockphoto: 25. Rest/istockphoto: 18.
Ashok Rodrigues/istockphoto: 13. Pupo Celso Rodrigues/istockphoto: 16t.
Noah Srycker/Shutterstock: 22. Stone/Getty Images: 20. Visuals Unlimited/Getty Images: 9.
Ingmar Wesemann/istockphoto: 23. Gary Yim/Shutterstock: 28. *Every attempt has been made
to clear copyright. Should there be any inadvertent omission please apply to the publisher for
rectification.*

CONTENTS

ABOUT MOUNTAINS

Mountains are places on the Earth's surface where rocks rise high above the surrounding landscape. They are built up by colossal forces that squash, stretch and fold the Earth's crust. The world of the high mountains is very different from the world on the plains below.

THE MOUNTAINOUS EARTH

Mountains cover about a quarter of the Earth's surface. Some mountains are 'free-standing', which means they are single mountains in a flat landscape. But most mountains are part of mountain ranges. The world's great ranges, such as the Himalayas and the Andes, stretch for thousands of kilometres and contain hundreds of towering, snow-covered peaks.

CHANGING THE LANDSCAPE

Mountain ranges are built up over hundreds of millions of years. They are pushed thousands of metres upwards as rocks are slowly folded or lifted on a huge scale. Mountains are also built up by eruptions of molten rock from underground. Just as the forces of nature build mountains, they

▼ *A typical mountain scene – snow-capped rocky peaks rising above the plains.*

knock them down again. The rocks of mountains are slowly worn away by the actions of wind, flowing water, and especially ice. This cycle of building and wearing away has been going on for billions of years, and there are remnants of vast mountain ranges all over the Earth. Most of the mountain ranges we see today have formed in the last 250 million years.

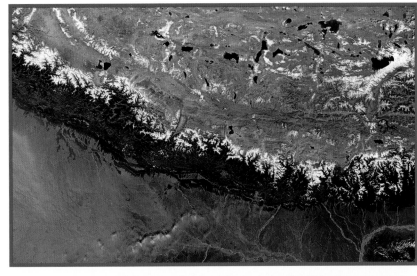

▲ A satellite image of part of the Himalayan mountain range. The white areas are snow.

IN THE MOUNTAINS

The environment on mountains is different from the environment around them, perhaps only a few kilometres away. The climate is colder, wetter and more windy than below on the plains, and on the peaks the ground is rocky and icy, so no plants can survive. These conditions make it challenging for people to live in the mountains. Mountains also affect the weather around them, making some places wetter and others drier.

When is a hill a mountain?

There is no official height at which a hill becomes a mountain. Whether a hill is called a mountain depends on the local landscape and traditional names. A hill 2,000 m high might be thought of as a tall mountain in one area of the world, but merely a foothill in another.

EARTH'S STRUCTURE

Mountains are built up by the slow, gradual movements of the rocks that make up the Earth, and by new rocks being formed. To see how these processes work we have to understand the structure of the Earth and what is going on deep under the surface.

THE CRACKED CRUST

The Earth has four main layers — the inner core, the outer core, the mantle and the crust, which is the outer layer. The Earth's crust is up to 70 km thick under mountain ranges and as little as 6 km thick under the oceans. The crust and top layer of the mantle form a layer called the lithosphere. It is cracked into many giant pieces called tectonic plates. These move around slowly, at just a few centimetres a year.

▼ *The internal structure of the Earth, showing the layers.*

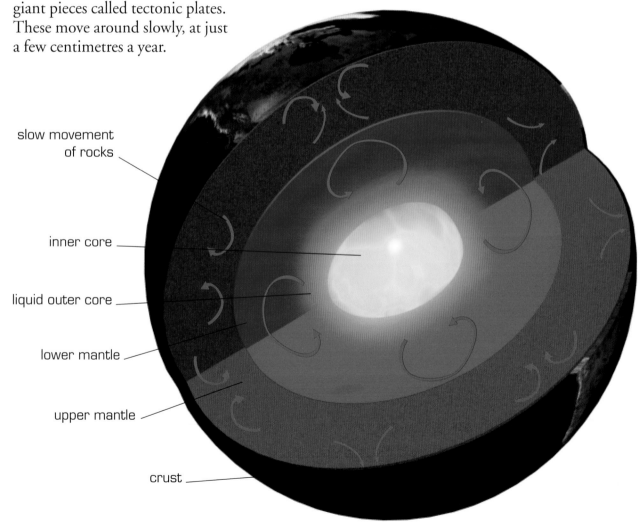

slow movement of rocks

inner core

liquid outer core

lower mantle

upper mantle

crust

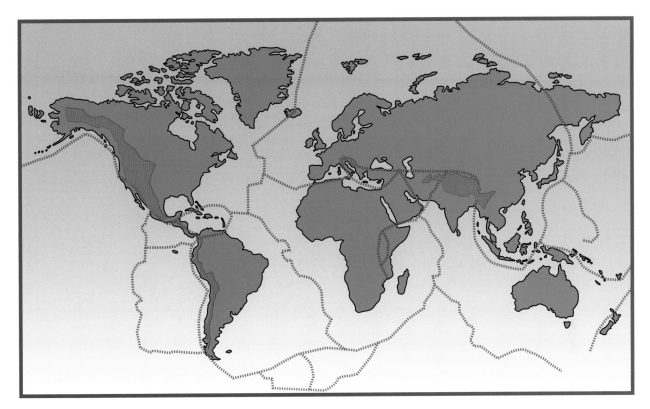

PLATE BOUNDARIES

A plate boundary is a line where one plate meets another plate. There are three types of boundaries — conservative, constructive and destructive. At a conservative boundary, the two plates slide past each other in opposite directions. At a constructive boundary the two plates move apart. At a destructive boundary, the two plates move towards each other. Here the plates can be two thin ocean plates, two thick continental plates, or one of each.

▲ The Earth's major mountain ranges (red areas) lie along boundaries between tectonic plates (red lines).

WHERE MOUNTAINS FORM

The location of mountain ranges is closely linked to tectonic plate boundaries. Most mountains form at destructive plate boundaries. Here, the collision between the plates crumples the edges of the plates, pushing up mountains. Volcanic mountains form along destructive and constructive plate boundaries. Where a volcano remains active, the mountain can be pushed up relatively quickly by the magma that forms deep beneath the Earth's crust. Finally, the movement of the tectonic plates can break up the Earth's crust, to form huge blocks of rock that thrust up to become mountain ranges.

Types of rock

All mountains are made up of three types of rock. Igneous rocks are made where magma (molten rock) cools and solidifies. This can happen underground or on the surface at volcanoes. Sedimentary rocks are made from layers of sediment (small particles of rock) that are deposited on sea-beds or river-beds. Metamorphic rocks are made when other rocks are changed by immense heat and pressure, often deep under mountains.

FOLD MOUNTAINS

There are three main types of mountain, named after the way they are formed. They are fold mountains, block mountains and volcanic mountains. Here we look at fold mountains. You can find out about block mountains on pages 10-11 and volcanic mountains on pages 12-13.

FORMATION OF FOLDS

All the major mountain ranges on Earth, such as the Alps and the Himalayas, are fold mountains. Fold mountains form where layers of rock are squashed by the movement of tectonic plates. This happens at destructive boundaries. As the plates move towards each other, the rocks at their edges crumple up, forcing them to fold. The tops of the folds are forced upwards, building mountains. Because tectonic plates move very slowly, it takes millions of years for a mountain range to be formed.

SUBDUCTION AND COLLISION

Where one of the plates at a destructive boundary is an ocean plate, this plate slides under the much thicker continental plate. It moves down into the mantle below and eventually melts. This process is called subduction. Sedimentary rocks from the ocean plate and rocks from the continental plate crumple to form fold mountains.

Mountains and earthquakes

Earthquakes occur frequently in mountain ranges formed at destructive plate boundaries, such as the Himalayas. They happen because the plates' edges are cracked by the huge forces; the cracks are called faults. As the plates move, the rocks each side of the faults tend to move in jerks rather than smoothly, causing earthquakes.

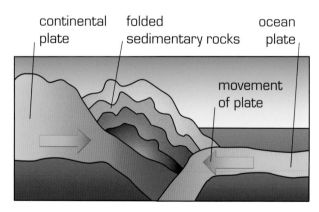

▲ Fold mountains being formed at a destructive boundary between continental and ocean plates.

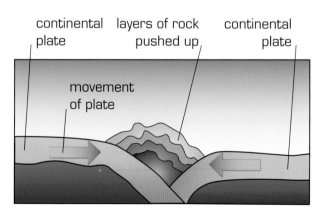

▲ Fold mountains being formed at a destructive boundary between two continental plates.

Where both plates are thick continental plates, there is no subduction. Instead, the plates collide head on, pushing rock both up and down. The mountains grow upwards, and rock pushes downwards, forming huge roots that support the mountains. The crust can be twice its normal thickness where plates collide like this.

▲ *Layers of rock folded by immense forces. Folding like this on a giant scale creates mountains.*

EVIDENCE OF FOLDING

There is plenty of evidence that rocks are folded to form mountains. Sedimentary rocks are formed in flat, horizontal layers, but in many places we find sloping layers and even vertical ones. Sometimes we see layers of rock in giant folds in cliff faces, bending up and down. Each fold can be many kilometres across or just a few metres across.

BLOCK MOUNTAINS

A block mountain is a mountain that is a giant block of rock. Block mountains are formed where blocks of rock rise or fall because the crust is stretched or squashed by the huge forces generated by the movement of tectonic plates. The Harz Mountains in Germany and the Sierra Nevada in North America are good examples of block mountains.

FAULTS AND MOVEMENTS

A fault is a weak area or crack in the rocks of the Earth's crust. Forces from the movement of tectonic plates create faults and make the rocks on each side of existing faults move. There are several different types of fault. For example, a normal fault is where the rocks on each side of a fault move up and down because the rocks are stretched apart. And a reverse fault is where the rocks along a fault move up and down because the rocks are squashed together. In most cases, faults are complex, with rocks moving up and down, from side to side and twisting as well. A fault may only move once every hundred years, and the size of each movement is normally only centimetres or metres. But over millions of years the total movement can add up to hundreds of metres.

RIFTS AND HORSTS

Block mountains normally form where a block of rock with a fault on each side falls or rises. A rift valley forms where stretching causes a block to fall, leaving higher blocks on each side. These higher blocks form mountains on each side of the valley. A horst block forms where rocks fall on each side of another block. This leaves a mountain standing above the ground on either side.

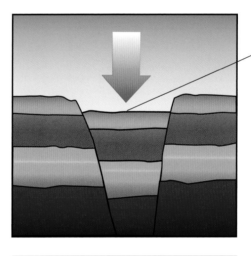

rift valley

◀ *Formation of a rift valley, with mountain ranges on each side.*

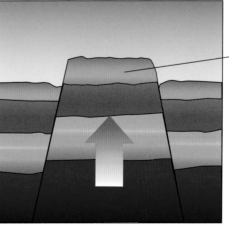

horst block mountain

◀ *Formation of a horst block mountain, where a block of rock rises or where blocks of rock on each side drop.*

The Great Rift Valley

The Great Rift Valley in Africa stretches nearly 5,000 km from Mozambique to the Red Sea. This rift valley has formed over the past 50 million years where the crust is being stretched, and is still growing. There are mountains up to around 5,000 m high on each side. There are also volcanoes, such as Mount Nyiragongo and Mount Kilimanjaro, where magma has leaked through the broken crust.

▼ *Mountains of Africa's Great Rift Valley.*

VOLCANIC MOUNTAINS

▲ *An explosive eruption at a destructive boundary, in this case in Hawaii.*

A volcano is a place where magma (molten rock) from deep under the crust comes to the Earth's surface. Volcanic eruptions build mountains from the lava and ash that is erupted. Volcanoes can be part of mountain ranges, or single, isolated peaks.

VOLCANOES AT PLATE BOUNDARIES

The majority of volcanoes form at the boundaries between the Earth's tectonic plates. At constructive boundaries, magma rises where plates are moving away from each other. The magma forms lava on the surface, which builds up in layers to form mountains. The volcanoes of Iceland and the Great Rift Valley have grown over constructive boundaries. At

Hot spots

A hot spot is a place where magma from the mantle pushes its way up through the crust far from any plate boundary. The magma is thought to come from huge pockets of magma called mantle plumes. The most famous hot-spot volcanoes are those on the Hawaiian Islands. These have grown over a hot spot under the Pacific tectonic plate. Over millions of years a whole chain of mountains has formed as the plate has moved slowly over the hot spot. The islands are actually the tips of enormous mountains that have grown up from the sea-bed (see page 15 for more about undersea mountains).

▶ *An aerial photo of some of the volcanic Hawaiian Islands.*

destructive boundaries, magma is formed where an ocean plate sinks into the mantle and partly melts. The magma forces its way upwards through the crust and creates volcanoes. These volcanoes are often part of ranges of fold mountains along the plate boundary.

VOLCANO SHAPES

Volcanoes come in various shapes and sizes, but most are either composite cone volcanoes or shield volcanoes. A composite cone volcano (or stratovolcano) is a steep-sided, cone-shaped mountain, made up of layers of ash and lava. Composite cone volcanoes form at destructive plate boundaries. They are made of loose material and are often unstable, and their tops can be blown off during violent eruptions. Shield volcanoes have gently sloping sides. They are built up from layers of lava that flow down their slopes. They are called shield volcanoes because they are shaped like an upturned warrior's shield.

▼ *Lava flowing into the sea and solidifying, slowly building up a new volcanic mountain.*

MOUNTAIN RANGES

Most mountains are part of large collections of mountains called mountain ranges, mountain chains or mountain belts. Some ranges contain just a few peaks, but others contain thousands. Large ranges are often divided into sub ranges and groups. The Himalayas is a mountain range that is still growing; other ranges are ancient and are being eroded away.

BUILDING MOUNTAIN RANGES

A map of the world's major mountain ranges and tectonic plates (see page 7) shows that most mountain ranges follow the line of plate boundaries. Large mountain ranges are normally long and thin in shape. This is because they form along the boundaries. The same folding movements or block movements happen right along a boundary, so that mountains are built right along it, too.

▲ The Caucasus mountain range (top-right) in eastern Europe, seen from space.

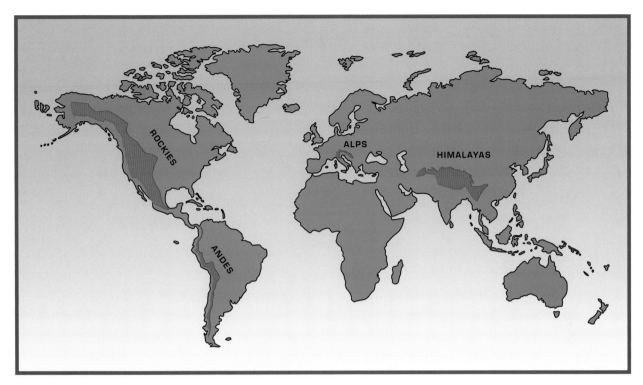

THE WORLD'S GREAT RANGES

Here are some of the world's major ranges and how they were formed.

▲ *The world's major mountain ranges.*

- **Himalayas, Asia** Formed by a collision between the Eurasian and the Indian tectonic plates. The world's highest mountain range.
- **Andes, South America** Formed along a destructive boundary between the Nazca and South American plates. The world's longest mountain chain.
- **Rockies, North America** Formed at a destructive boundary between the Pacific and the North American plates.
- **Alps, Europe** Formed by a collision between the African and Eurasian plates.

MOUNTAIN RANGES AS BARRIERS

The world's mountain ranges form physical barriers between the parts of the world on either side. In the distant past, they prevented people from migrating to populate new areas of the world. The Himalayas can still only be crossed in just a few places. They have kept Mongolian and Chinese people to the north separate from Indian people to the south, so the two groups of people have very different languages and customs.

Ranges under the sea

Many volcanic mountains are under the sea. Long mountain ranges form at constructive boundaries. The Mid-Atlantic Ridge under the Atlantic Ocean can be thought of as the world's longest mountain range. At some destructive boundaries and hot spots, volcanoes called seamounts grow from the sea floor. Mauna Kea in Hawaii rises 10,203 m from the sea floor, so some call it the world's tallest mountain.

WEARING DOWN MOUNTAINS

As mountains are slowly built up, so they are slowly worn away again. In the distant past, vast mountain ranges have been formed and then worn down into today's gentle hills.

Some of today's mountain ranges are remnants of once higher mountain ranges that have stopped growing and are now being destroyed by weathering and erosion.

WEATHERING

Weathering is the breaking down of rocks into small pieces, and is the first stage in the wearing away of mountains. Ice weathering is the most destructive type of weathering on mountain tops. It happens when water trickles into cracks in rocks and then freezes. The water expands slightly when it freezes, and this opens up the cracks. If the ice melts and then freezes again, the cracks enlarge.

▲ Sugar Loaf Mountain in Rio De Janeiro, Brazil, is the core of a volcanic mountain that has been eroded away.

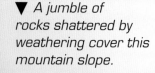

▼ A jumble of rocks shattered by weathering cover this mountain slope.

Eroding folded rocks

The rocks in fold mountains are weak because they have been folded and broken as the mountains were formed. This allows them to be weathered and eroded more quickly than if they were made of solid rock, and is why mountain peaks are often made up of shattered heaps of loose rock.

Other types of weathering in mountains include onion-skin weathering, where surface rock expands and contracts because of alternating hot and cold temperatures, chemical weathering, where rainwater slowly dissolves rocks, and biological weathering, where plant roots split up rock. Weathered rock is easily eroded.

▲ *The turbulent water of mountain rivers carries rocky particles down from the mountains and onto the plains below.*

EROSION

Erosion is the wearing away of rocks by wind, flowing water and ice. High winds may move loose particles, allowing them to roll down slopes. Flowing water carries material with it into streams and rivers. Fast-flowing river water pulls loose rocks from the river-bed and banks, and particles in the water knock out more loose rock. Gradually streams and rivers erode gulleys and steep-sided valleys in mountain slopes. The rivers carry the rocky material away to the plains below. Erosion by water is greatest when snows are melting and rivers are flooding. Glaciers also erode mountains (see pages 18-19). On mountains, loose material on cliffs and steep slopes is also carried downhill by gravity.

GLACIERS

Glaciers are slow-moving rivers of ice. They form over thousands of years from layers of snow that fall in high mountains. Over many years the weight of snow at the top squeezes the snow below into a thick sheet of solid ice. Gravity forces the ice to creep down the mountainside.

GLACIER FLOW

Glaciers flow downhill in valleys, as rivers of water do. They continue flowing until they reach a level where the air temperature is warm enough to make the ice melt. This lower end of a glacier is called its snout. Glaciers can be hundreds of metres deep and more than a kilometre across. They flow at any speed from 1 or 2 cm per day to 2 or 3 m per day. As glaciers turn corners or flow onto steeper ground, cracks called crevasses appear in them.

▲ *Underneath this glacier, ice is gouging away at the rocks, eroding a valley.*

GLACIAL EROSION

Glaciers erode away the rocks they flow over. The ice itself pulls the rock apart as it flows over them, but most erosion is caused by rocks dragged along the ground by the ice. In high mountains, glaciers are responsible for more erosion than wind and water together. Rocky material is carried along under the glacier, inside it and on top of it. When the ice melts at the glacier's snout, the material is dumped on the ground, forming mounds of rubble. This is then washed away in streams that carry water away from the melting glacier.

Retreating glaciers

Measurements of glaciers worldwide show that many glaciers are getting shorter, or retreating. For example, the Khumbu Glacier on Mount Everest has shortened by 5 km since the 1950s. Most scientists think that the glacial ice is melting because of global warming, which is causing milder weather conditions in mountains.

GLACIAL LANDFORMS

Over thousands of years, glaciers erode U-shaped valleys in the landscape. We can see these valleys if the glaciers melt away. There are many U-shaped valleys in the northern hemisphere that were formed thousands of years ago during the last ice age. Then much of the northern hemisphere was covered with a thick layer of ice. Other glacial features include cirque (or corries), which are armchair-shaped dips in mountain slopes, arêtes and sharp peaks.

▼ A typical glacial valley. The glacier that created it has long since melted away.

MOUNTAIN WEATHER

Typical mountain weather is wet, cold and windy. It makes high mountains dangerous places to be. Even on a day when it is warm and sunny in the valleys around a mountain, it can be freezing cold with gale-force winds on the mountain tops thousands of metres above.

DROPPING TEMPERATURES

The temperature in the atmosphere falls by about 1°C for every 100 m you move up. That means if the air temperature is a warm 20°C on the valley floor it will be 0°C on the mountain 2,000 m higher up. On the summits of the world's highest mountains, the temperature never rises above freezing. Most rain starts life as snow, which melts as it falls through warm air. In mountains the snow lands before it reaches the warmer air below, so snow regularly falls in mountains. There is always a visible snow line on high mountains, above which snow always falls instead of rain.

▼ *Freezing temperatures and high winds are a serious threat to mountaineers.*

MOUNTAIN WINDS

Wind is squeezed as it rises to flow over mountains, which means its speed increases. Winds also increase in strength as they blow through gaps between mountains. The summits of the world's highest mountains can be buffeted by high-level winds called jet streams, which can blow at hundreds of kilometres per hour.

CLOUD AND RAIN FORMATION

Mountains create their own weather because of the way air moves over them. Clouds form when humid air (air that contains water vapour) rises. As it rises, it cools, and the water vapour turns to droplets of liquid water, which make up clouds. When winds carrying humid air hit mountains, the air rises up the mountain slopes, which makes clouds form. This is why there are often clouds over mountains when the rest of the sky is clear, and is also why mountains get plenty of rain.

▲ *These clouds have formed as humid air is forced up and over the mountains.*

Rain shadows

Because humid air forms clouds and rain as it rises over mountains, it loses much of its water vapour. When the air descends down the other side of mountains, it is quite dry, and so the land here gets very little rain. This effect from the mountains is known as a rain shadow.

MOUNTAIN CLIMATES AND ZONES

Climate is the pattern of weather a place experiences over a long period of time. There are different climates at different places on a mountain. For example, the base of a mountain may have warm summers and cool winters, but its summit may experience cool summers and very cold winters. Different plants and animals live in these climates.

CHANGING CLIMATES

The climate is generally cooler, wetter and windier on mountains than on the plains and in the valleys below. This does not mean it is cold, wet and windy every day, but on average, the temperature is lower, rainfall (or snowfall) is higher, and winds are stronger. Winters are also longer, and summers shorter. On the summits of the highest mountains the climate is similar to polar climates experienced in the Arctic and Antarctic. Even in summer, temperatures are sub zero, and storm-force winds and snow storms are common.

▼ In tropical regions, forests grow on the cloudy, wet mountain slopes.

PLANTS AND ANIMALS

Mountain slopes can be divided into three different climate zones, called, from bottom to top, montane, sub-alpine and alpine. The position of the zones depends on the plants that live there. The plants that live in one zone cannot survive in the harsher conditions in the zone above, and so there is a line where vegetation changes that shows the boundary between one zone and the next. These are the typical plants found in each zone:

- **Montane zone** Conifer forests (pines, firs and spruces), with trees shaped so that snow falls off them. They have needles instead of leaves, so they can survive being frozen.
- **Sub-alpine zone** No forests, but stunted conifers because of high winds, or low shrubs that are not damaged by winds.
- **Alpine zone** No trees. Small flowering plants that survive on little water, and cope with the cold. Above a certain altitude, nothing can survive.

▲ *In the alpine zone, flowering plants come to life during the short spring and summer.*

Thin mountain air

As you move up through the atmosphere, the air becomes thinner and thinner, and so there is less oxygen for animals to breathe. Animals that live high in the mountains (in the sub-alpine and alpine zones) are adapted to survive with less oxygen. See also page 28.

CASE STUDY: THE HIMALAYAS

The Himalayas form the world's tallest mountain range. It contains nine of the top ten world's tallest mountains, including Everest, the tallest, at 8,850 m. The range stretches nearly 2,500 km from northeast India to Pakistan, and is up to 400 km wide from north to south. The word Himalayas means 'abode of the snow' in the Sanskrit language.

▲ *Location map of the Himalayas.*

HIMALAYAN WEATHER

The Himalayas lie between the north Indian plains to the south and the Tibetan Plateau to the north. There is a huge range of climates, from sub tropical (warm with heavy seasonal rains) in the southern foothills to polar in the high peaks, where there is permanent snow and ice. The Himalayas have a huge effect on climates around them. They trap warm, humid southerly winds blowing up from the south, causing heavy monsoon rains. Their rain shadow lies to the north, and keeps the Tibetan Plateau very dry. They also keep northern India warm by stopping Arctic winds from the north. The Himalayas are drained by several major rivers, including the Indus, the Ganges, the Brahmaputra and the Yangtze.

▶ *A view across the Himalayan foothills to the spectacular lofty peaks.*

FORMATION OF THE HIMALAYAS

The Himalayas were formed by the collision between the Indian and Eurasian tectonic plates. These are both continental plates, and their rocks have been pushed up into fold mountains. The collision started about 70 million years ago, where there was originally a sea, and the mountains began to rise about 50 million years ago. This makes the Himalayas among the youngest mountains on Earth. The Indian plate is still moving northwards, so the Himalayas are still growing, but only by a few centimetres per year. Earthquakes set off by the movement of the plates are common in the Himalayas.

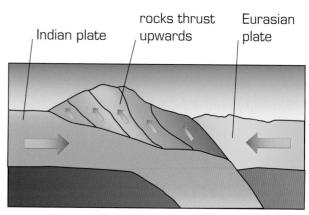

Indian plate

rocks thrust upwards

Eurasian plate

▲ *The Himalayas were built up as two tectonic plates collided, piling rocks on top of one another.*

Himalayan people

Very few people live in the high valleys, where the winters are long and cold. However, the southern foothills are densely populated. Deforestation is a problem here, and causes frequent landslides. Travel is slow, despite some modern roads, and there are only a handful of mountain passes through the range.

CASE STUDY: THE ANDES

The Andes is the world's longest mountain range. It runs 8,000 km along the west coast of South America, starting near the Caribbean Sea and finishing in the south of Chile. The Andes contains the highest mountains outside Asia, along with several active volcanoes.

▲ Location map of the Andes.

ANDEAN FEATURES

The Andes is generally about 300 km wide. At the northern end it divides into three distinct chains, parallel to each other. In the central area it is wider and there are two plateaus that lie between mountains to the west and east. These are called the Andean plateaus. Lake Titicaca, 190 km long, is on one of these plateaus. The highest mountain in the Andes is Aconcagua, in Argentina, at 6,962 m high. There are more than 200 active volcanoes.

ANDEAN CLIMATES

Because the Andes stretches from the tropics nearly to Antarctica, it experiences a wide range of climates. At the northern end there are tropical forests on the mountain slopes, and the peaks are free of snow for some of the year. At the southern end there is permanent snow at low levels and glaciers flowing down from the summits. Humid winds blowing from the east dump their rain when they hit the Andes. Much of it flows back to the sea through the Amazon river basin. The Atacama Desert lies in Chile in the rain shadow of the Andes. It is the driest place on Earth.

FORMATION

The Andes mountains began forming between about 140 and about 65 million years ago and are still growing. They lie over a destructive boundary between the South American and Nazca plates. They are a combination of fold mountains and volcanic mountains formed by subduction of the Nazca plate.

▶ Spectacular rock towers in Patagonia, at the southern end of the Andes. Erosion has worn away softer rock, leaving the hard core exposed.

Life on the plateau

The Andean plateaus, at between 3,600 m and 4,000 m above sea level, are some of the highest inhabited places on Earth. People grow crops and raise animals such as the llama. Lake Titicaca is the world's highest navigable lake. It has towns and villages on its shores and islands. Close by is La Paz, the largest city in Bolivia, and the highest major city in the world.

LIFE IN THE MOUNTAINS

Even though the world's mountains are sparsely populated compared to the plains, millions of people choose to live in them. Most make their lives here because generations of their families have done so, and often because they are part of ethnic groups that have lived here for hundreds of years. They have learned how to survive mountain life.

MOUNTAIN FARMING

Most mountain people survive by farming in high mountain valleys. Only some crops can grow in mountain areas because of the harsh climate. Animals adapted to the climate, such as sheep, goats, llama, and yak, are raised for meat, fur, milk and transport. They are normally moved to lower ground during winter.

▲ Farmers build terraces on the mountain slopes to increase land area and trap water.

MOUNTAIN RESOURCES

We make use of mountains for more than just farming. Tourism is a major industry in many of the world's mountainous regions. People travel to the mountains to enjoy the scenery, to walk and climb on the mountains, and to ski on their slopes. Mountain areas are also a good source of hydroelectric power, as the climate is often wet and rivers flow through steep-sided valleys suitable for dams.

DRAWBACKS AND DANGERS

Life in the mountains brings many problems. Mountain towns and villages are normally remote, and mountain roads are twisty, and often

▼ Ski resorts rely on heavy winter snows to keep their customers satisfied.

closed during winter because of snow or landslides. After heavy snow fall, avalanches threaten places at the foot of mountain slopes. Altitude sickness (or mountain sickness) is another problem for people visiting the mountains. This is caused by the lack of oxygen in the thin mountain air, and causes sickness and headaches. People who are raised at high altitude in the mountains are adapted to cope with low levels of oxygen. Volcanoes bring their own dangers of lava flows, ash avalanches (called pyroclastic flows) and mud flows, but people live around them because they offer excellent soil for growing crops.

MOUNTAINS IN THE FUTURE

The mountains that people live in and play on today are only temporary features on the Earth's surface. In tens of millions of years even the vast mountain range of the Himalayas will have been eroded away. But the world's tectonic plates will keep moving for billions of years to come. So entirely new mountain ranges, perhaps even higher than the Himalayas, will take their place.

▼ Dams in the mountains provide water and hydroelectricity for people in towns and cities on the plains below.

GLOSSARY

ash tiny particles of solidified magma

block mountain a mountain formed where huge blocks of rock rise or fall

climate the long-term pattern of weather that a place experiences

conservative plate boundary a line along which the edges of two tectonic plates slide past each other

constructive plate boundary a line along which two tectonic plates are moving apart

continental plate part of a tectonic plate under a continent, which is much thicker than an ocean plate

crust the rocky top layer of the Earth

deforestation the cutting down of forests for fuel and to create space for farming

destructive plate boundary a line along which the edges of two tectonic plates are moving towards each other

erosion the wearing away of the landscape

eruption the emission of lava, ash or gas from a volcano

fault a crack in the rocks of the Earth's crust

fold mountain a mountain formed when rocks are squeezed together and folded up

foothill a hill or mountain between the plains and the tallest mountains of a mountain range

glacier a slow-moving river of ice

global warming the gradual warming of the Earth's atmosphere

gravity the force that attracts all objects to the Earth

hot spot a place far from any tectonic plate boundary where magma forces its way to the surface

hydroelectricity electricity generated by water power

ice age a period of time in the past when the climate was colder than today and thick ice sheets covered much of the northern hemisphere

lava the name given to the molten, rocky part of magma when it comes out of a volcano

magma molten rock underground

mantle the thick layer of rock inside the Earth under the crust

mountain a place where the Earth's surface rises high above the surrounding landscape

mud flow a fast-flowing mixture of volcanic ash and water

northern hemisphere the part of the Earth's surface that lies north of the equator

ocean plate part of a tectonic plate under the ocean, which is much thinner than a continental plate

plain a broad flat area of land

plate boundary the line along which two tectonic plates meet

plateau an area of flat land in a mountain range

range a collection of mountains

seamount a volcano that grows up from the ocean floor

sedimentary rock rock formed when layers of sediment are laid down on top of each other over millions of years

tectonic plate one of the huge pieces that the Earth's crust is cracked into

volcanic to do with volcanoes

volcano a place where magma emerges onto the Earth's surface from under the crust

weathering the breaking up of rocks into smaller particles

Further information

EVEREST
Lots of information on Everest from the US Public Broadcasting Service.
www.pbs.org/wgbh/nova/everest/

GLOBAL VOLCANISM PROGRAM
Information on active volcanoes around the world.
www.volcano.si.edu/

GOOGLE EARTH
Downloadable software that displays the world in 3D — great for exploring the world's mountain ranges.
www.google.com/earth/

BBC NATURE
Videos, news and facts about mountain habitats.
www.bbc.co.uk/nature/habitats/Mountain

HOMEWORK HELP
Masses of facts about mountains from this school homework website.
www.primaryhomeworkhelp.co.uk/mountains.htm

NASA
Use the search function on NASA's Visible Earth website to look at photos taken from space of mountain ranges.
www.visibleearth.nasa.gov/

NATIONAL SNOW AND ICE DATA CENTER
US organisation site pages all about glaciers.
www.nsidc.org/cryosphere/glaciers

NOTE TO PARENTS AND TEACHERS:
Every effort has been made by the Publishers to ensure that the websites in this book are suitable for children, that they are of the highest educational value, and that they contain no inappropriate or offensive material. However, because of the nature of the Internet, it is impossible to guarantee that the contents of these sites will not be altered. We strongly advise that Internet access is supervised by a responsible adult.

INDEX

From the Chicken House

I was actually *thrilled* when I read this book for the first time. It's exciting, unexpected and *wild* – with brilliant creatures and extraordinary fantasy folk. But it also made me smile – I love the way the characters take on fearsome adventures while gently teasing each other – and sometimes make us laugh out loud in the face of danger! I certainly care about Felix and his friends – and I'm busy persuading Elizabeth Kay to write a sequel!

I hope you enjoy it, too.

Barry Cunningham
Publisher
The Chicken House

THE DIVIDE

ELIZABETH KAY

ILLUSTRATED BY TED DEWAN

Chicken House

2 Palmer Street, Frome, Somerset BA11 1DS

For Zackary Feliks

This paperback edition published in Great Britain 2005

First published in Great Britain in 2003
The Chicken House
2 Palmer Street
Frome, Somerset BA11 1DS
United Kingdom
www.doublecluck.com
Text © Elizabeth Kay 2003
Illustrations© Ted Dewan 2003

Cover design by Ian Butterworth
Cover illustration by Ted Dewan
Designed and typeset by Dorchester Typesetting Group Ltd
Printed and bound in Great Britain

1 3 5 7 9 10 8 6 4 2

British Library Cataloguing in Publication data available.

ISBN 1 905294 20 4

www.elizabeth-kay.co.uk

FELIX'S VOCABULARY NOTEBOOK
Tangle/English

Brazzle - Griffin
Brittlehorn - Unicorn
creepy-biter - No parallel
  (parasitic invertebrate)
cuddyak - No parallel
  (yak-buffalo with rhino horn)
Diggeluck - Gnome
Fire-breather - Dragon
Flame-bird - Phoenix
Humungally - Elephant
Japegrin - Pixie
Lickit - No parallel
  (elvish cookery experts)
No-horn - Horse
Ragamucky - Brownie
River-fatty - Hippopotamus
Shreddermouth - No parallel
  (crocodile with longer legs)
Sinistrom Devil-hyena
Small-tail - Faun
Tangle-person - Elf
Triple-head - Roc
Vamprey - Vampire
Wise-hoof - Centaur
Worrit - No parallel
  (dog with comic appearance)

I

The rat-tat-tat of the helicopter's rotor blades scattered the humming birds across the Study Centre garden as though someone had thrown a handful of jewels into the air.

Felix watched as the stretcher was carried across the lawn. The man lying on it had been bitten by so many insects that his face was puffed up like a toad's. His skin was an angry copper colour, and it was peeling away in little patches.

"It took us a week to find him," said Miguel. "He strayed off the path into the jungle. That is forbidden, of course. It is so easy to get lost."

"Does this happen a lot?" asked Felix's mother.

Miguel smiled. "No. Is only the third time since I work here. He saw an armadillo, so he followed it. A very foolish thing to do."

The man on the stretcher let out a brief cry of pain as he was loaded into the helicopter.

"I'm not so sure about doing this walk after all," said

7

Felix's mother. "You have taken your tablets, haven't you, Felix?"

Felix sighed. "Yes."

"And you did fill up your water bottle?"

"Yes."

"And you've got the map?"

Felix opened his bag and showed it to her, nestled between the book he was currently reading, his torch, his notebook, and his biro.

"And the compass?" queried his father.

Felix patted his chest. The tiny instrument was hung round his neck, but it was inside his T-shirt.

The helicopter door slammed shut and the stretcher-bearers made their way back across the lawn, shaking their heads and talking animatedly in Spanish.

Felix looked at Miguel. "Is that man going to die?"

Felix's parents glanced at one another.

Miguel ruffled Felix's hair. "What a question. He is dehydrated. He will be all right once he gets to hospital."

"I don't think we'll do the whole walk," said Felix's mother. "Felix isn't up to four and a half hours in this heat."

"But you have to go as far as the Continental Divide," said Miguel. "How old are you, Felix – eleven, twelve?"

"Thirteen," said Felix.

"He's not like other boys," said Felix's mother. "He has a very rare heart condition and an unusual blood group. Sometimes he passes out. We have to be careful."

"Oh," said Miguel. And there *was* something a bit differ-ent about Felix, a sort of greyness under the tan. He was small for his age – and thin, too. But his eyes were a deep, startling blue, and they seemed too old for the rest of his face.

"But I pestered them and pestered them to take me some-where exciting before I died," said Felix.

There was a horrible silence. Then Felix's father said, "You mustn't think like that, Felix. You've held up surpris-ingly well for the last few days."

Yes, thought Felix, I'm always better when I'm not think-ing about it. And Costa Rica has been brilliant – volcanoes, mangrove swamps, lizards, parrots. I don't want to go home. If I do have to die, I'd rather die here than anywhere else.

The helicopter took off, and the humming birds returned to the sugar-water feeders that were hung around the outside of the Study Centre. They used their beaks as rapiers, fenc-ing in mid-air as they tried to knock one another away from the rim. The ones that won looked smug, and the ones that lost zoomed around the garden pretending they didn't want a drink after all.

"Come on, then," said Felix's father. "Before it gets too hot."

They started out along the path. The canopy closed above them like the roof of a cathedral, and when they looked up they could see flowers growing between the branches. It was as though they'd been made of tissue paper and stuck on with glue.

"What pretty trees," said Felix's mother.

"The flowers are epiphytes," said Felix, who had read far more than most boys of his age. He did a lot of reading, because for a lot of the time he couldn't do much else, and he particularly liked things about science. "Epiphytes are parasitic plants," he added.

"Oh," said his mother.

"Like that strangler fig," Felix went on, pointing to a tangle of aerial roots. "The tree inside dies, in the end." Then he felt a little ashamed of himself. When his parents became too protective he always hit out the only way he knew how: by mentioning death.

They walked along for a while in silence. There wasn't as much to see as he'd expected, but he could hear the strange ringing call of a bellbird, which made him think of the little church in the village where they were staying. There were plenty of insects, though. A *Morpho* butterfly the size of a tea-plate, its wings the most astonishing metallic blue. An ants' nest, full of hollowed-out chambers.

"Don't go any closer," said Felix's mother. "They probably have a nasty sting. How are you feeling, dear? Tired?"

"No," said Felix. And he wasn't. He wanted to get as far as the Continental Divide. Wanted to say he'd stood with one foot on either side.

They were going uphill all the time now. The view was going to be magnificent when they reached the top – jungle on one side, and jungle on the other, right the way down to the Pacific. And then he did begin to feel tired. He could see from the map that they didn't have very far to go, but his mother was looking at him with that worried expression that irritated him so much.

And then, predictably, she said, "I think we should turn back now," and his father nodded.

"No," said Felix.

"Don't argue," said his father.

"But I want to get to the Divide."

"What's so special about it?" said his mother.

"It's the watershed," Felix explained. "All the water on one side goes into the Atlantic, and all the water on the other goes into the Pacific."

"So?"

Felix gritted his teeth. She didn't understand. It was such a cool idea. Bodies were seventy per cent water; if he could separate himself out the way he separated things out in the laboratory at school, half of him would go one way, and half of him the other.

"It's just an imaginary line," said his father. "There's nothing to see."

Felix glanced back at his mother. She was wriggling her shoulders, and then she turned her head to look behind her. Felix followed her gaze. There, on her back, was an insect the size of a pencil.

"Get it off me!" she shrieked.

Felix grinned. It was a stick insect; even though it was

much bigger than the ones at school, it wouldn't hurt her.

"David!" she yelled at his father. "*Do* something!"

Felix knew his father wouldn't kill it – he would try to lift it off, and it wouldn't be easy. He edged away. Just for once, he was going to do what *he* wanted.

He saw his father grasp the stick insect round its middle, and try to pull it off. The legs clung to the fabric like *Velcro*. Felix edged a bit further. Neither of his parents had noticed. His father lifted one of the insect's feet off the blouse, then another and another. By the time he reached the fourth leg, the first foot was back on the fabric again. Felix was nearly at the bend in the path; a few more steps and he'd be out of sight. "What are you *doing*?" yelled Felix's mother. "Asking it nicely? It won't work!"

The moment Felix reached the bend, he ran. It was hard work, running uphill – but suddenly, there it was; the top. It hadn't been very far away at all.

The view was just as breathtaking as he'd imagined. The Pacific stretched into the distance, shining silver where the sun caught it. He turned his attention to the ground. The line of the Divide had been marked out, and there was a notice next to it explaining about catchment boundaries and water conservation. He walked over to the line and stood with his feet on either side of it, exactly the way he'd wanted to.

And that was when the dizziness returned. He knew he really *had* done too much, and he was going to pass out. The feeling was so familiar, the ringing in his ears, the slight sickness in his stomach. And although he was able to recognise the sensations, the recognition always flashed through his mind like lightning, and there was never anything he could do about it.

And then … blackness.

Squelch. The pond-hopper jumped half a metre to the left, and glared at her. Betony sighed. Why couldn't she get this right? She'd placed the goblet of water in the middle of the circle, and she had the salt in her left hand. She tried again, trickling the salt through her fingers and muttering the incantation. *Squelch.* This time the pond-hopper jumped right out of the circle, and scuttled behind the statue that had once been Betony's mother. Betony scowled; she'd done everything right – why hadn't it worked?

"Betony!"

"What?"

"We're off now."

Betony scuffed the circle into oblivion as quickly as she could, and hid the salt in her pocket. Then she walked across the yard to the rope ladder, and peered up into the tree. "Off? Where to?"

"Tiratattle."

"*Tiratattle?* How long are you going to be gone?"

"A week or so," said Betony's elder sister Tansy. "We did tell you."

"No, you didn't," said Betony.

"I'm sure we did," said Tansy.

Tansy always reminds me of a stabber-bird, thought Betony, with her long nose and her snaky neck. "Who's going to look after me?" she demanded.

"Ramson!" called Tansy. "Did you ask Grisette if Betony could stay with her?"

"I thought you had," said Ramson, trying to cram some herbs into a bag and spilling them on to the ground. Ramson had to be the clumsiest brother ever; it was as though his body had suddenly become too big for him over the last year or so, and he couldn't control all of it at once.

"Honestly, Ramson, it was *your* turn to sort all that out," said Tansy.

"There isn't time to go and see her now, the flight leaves in ten minutes."

"Look," said Tansy to Betony. "Tell Grisette we'll make it up to her when we get back. We're going to make some real money with this tooth potion, it's perfect."

I doubt it, thought Betony, our parents never managed to. What makes you think that a couple of teenagers living in a rickety wooden treehouse on the edge of nowhere are going to do any better?

She climbed up the ladder, avoiding the wobbly rung, and stomped up the spiral staircase. The steps were made from sawn-off branches on the main trunk, and only a few of them had been sanded down. The house always reeked of sawdust and resin – apart from the dispensary, which smelt

14

of dried herbs and magic. She went into her room, and packed her rucksack. It wasn't the first time she'd done this; it wasn't even the third or fourth time. She hated staying with Grisette. Grisette's daughter, Agrimony, seemed to think that having the latest of everything made her a better person somehow. That was a laugh, really, because they all lived here in Geddon, one of the most isolated communities of all. The children in the nearest town regarded them with contempt.

As an afterthought, Betony retrieved her secret hairbrush from under her bed, took off her cap and brushed her pale blonde hair until it gleamed. That would annoy her sister. She hefted the rucksack on to her shoulders, and climbed down.

"You've forgotten the sickle," Ramson was saying.

"The sickle's *your* responsibility, dimwit," Tansy snapped. She glanced round. Then she did a double take. "Betony!" she shrieked. "What *do* you look like! Your hair!"

"It feels really nice," said Betony provocatively, "it swings when I shake my head."

"You've got a hairbrush hidden somewhere, haven't you? Honestly, kids. Agrimony never brushes her hair, it's beautifully knotted."

"I don't care," said Betony. "I like it like this. Have a good time then, and don't forget to come back."

"Oh, honestly," said Tansy, resorting to her favourite word again.

Betony could have reminded them of the time they went

away for two days and stayed away for two months, but she thought better of it. She settled her rucksack more comfortably on her shoulders, and walked off down the track towards the village.

It was a beautiful day. She dutifully identified all the plants as she walked along – then she thought, *fangs and talons*, I don't want to end up doing the same thing as my parents did. Ramson and Tansy seem to enjoy making infusions to cure people, but it's not what *I* want to do. I want ... I want ...

But she didn't know quite what it was that she wanted. Something different. She didn't want her life mapped out for her, the way everyone else's was. Go to school, study boring subjects like nuts and berries, follow your parents into their chosen speciality. And where had it got them? *Nowhere.* She remembered the incident as though it had been yesterday, although it was three years ago now.

The five of them had been standing in the yard, talking about the latest spell her father was testing. "It's going to be a real winner," he said. "Knits bones together and makes them as strong as stone. Lasts twenty years."

As he spoke there was a rumbling sound from the top of the lane. They all looked round. The family cart was trundling down the slight incline, and gathering speed.

"You forgot to put the handbrake on again!" yelled Betony's mother.

There was nothing anyone could do. As they watched, the cart passed the gate and hit a tree. The tree toppled across the well, and knocked the bucket from its hook. The bucket bounced across the yard, and dislodged a pile of logs. The logs rolled in all directions, and as Betony's father tried to stop them he lost his footing and fell into the pond. When he climbed out, he was holding his arm and his face was creased with pain. "It's broken," he said.

"We'll use the spell," said Betony's mother.

"But you haven't tested it properly yet," said Tansy. "And you haven't worked out the counter-charm if it goes wrong."

"It'll be fine," said Betony's mother. She put her hand on her husband's arm, and recited the incantation.

And as the three children watched, their parents turned to stone.

Ramson looked at Tansy, a horrified expression on his face. "What on earth do we do now? They're going to stay like that for *twenty years*."

"They'd look quite nice either side of the rope ladder," said Tansy. "Garden furniture, you know?"

Ramson gulped.

"Come on," said Tansy, always the practical one. "We can use the logs as rollers."

And that was how Betony ended up being brought up by her brother and sister. It seemed a bit odd to begin with, passing her parents every time she went up and down the ladder. She did miss them, of course, but after a while she got used to it. It wasn't as if they'd died.

As Betony carried on walking she suddenly thought:

Grisette isn't expecting me; no one will know if I go exploring. She glanced round. There were dangers in the woods – worrits, brazzles, vampreys – but there were flame-birds and brittlehorns as well. Agrimony said that she had seen a brittlehorn the previous week, but Betony didn't believe her. Brittlehorns were shy creatures, and they only spoke to the elders. Agrimony had a little notebook, in which she jotted down the names of all the creatures she'd seen and scored points for the more unusual ones.

With a little tingle of excitement Betony left the path, keeping the stream on her left so she wouldn't get lost. In the distance she could see the peak of Tromm Fell. It was said to be very beautiful in a stark, rocky sort of way – but nobody went there because of the brazzles. Brazzles were meant to be very clever; they hoarded gold, and rumour had it that there was a treasure trove up there on the peak. No one who lived in Geddon had ever tried to find out – brazzles were supposedly extremely fierce, and no one wanted their eyes pecked out. A song-merchant had passed by once, and said that brazzles were a common sight in far-off Andria, but nobody really believed him.

Betony started to sing. Brightly coloured toadstools littered the forest floor, and she had to force herself not to tick their names off in her head. "I'm not going to be a herbalist," she said to herself out loud, "I'm *not*. I'm keeping my options open. Why don't we do interesting things at school, like learning about the past? No one seems to care about the past all that much, only the song-merchants." The stream tinkled in a friendly sort of way, and after a while she realised that its source must be somewhere on Tromm Fell, for she was going uphill. From time to time she thought she saw hoof-prints, but she wasn't very good at tracking and she couldn't be sure. Supposing she really did see a brittlehorn? That would be one in the eye for Agrimony.

And then she did.

Betony stopped dead in her tracks, and rubbed her eyes. Perhaps Agrimony hadn't been fibbing after all. It was lying down under a tree, and lifted its head when it saw her. She expected it to leap to its feet and dash off through the under-growth, but it didn't. She took a tentative step forwards. The brittlehorn laid its head back down on the ground, and just watched her. She took another step forward, and saw its white flank twitch as a fly landed on it.

Betony swallowed. This wasn't the way things were meant to go. She walked right over, and knelt down beside it. The brittlehorn sighed and said, "I'm sick, tangle-child."

Betony didn't know what to do. Finally, she said, "Can I get you a drink of water, or something?"

The brittlehorn nodded. Betony went over to the stream, and filled her cap with water. Then she went back to the brittlehorn and held its head so that it could drink.

"Thank you," it said.

"What's your name?"

"Silvershank. Yours?"

"Betony."

"You're a herbalist then, aren't you, tangle-child. But even your knowledge cannot cure me now."

Betony felt dreadful. She didn't have any knowledge worth speaking of. She neglected her homework, didn't pay attention in class, and even played truant from time to time.

"I'm not very good at medicines," she admitted.

"Maybe that's just as well," said Silvershank.

He wasn't making sense. After a moment or two all she could think of to say was, "What are your symptoms?"

"My horn aches, and when that happens you know your time is up. Do something for me."

"What?"

"Go further upstream, to where my people are. Tell them not to take ... not to take ..."

But Silvershank never finished what he was going to say. His body shuddered, as though some powerful thread were being stretched to breaking point. Then his eyes closed, and the breath left his body in one last sigh.

He's dead, thought Betony. *Dead.* How *awful.* I couldn't do *anything*, I was absolutely *useless.* I find a brittlehorn, and I let him die. What do I do now? It's going to get dark in a couple of hours. If I took that unfinished message to his people, would it mean anything to them? But if they *do* know what he was talking about, it might stop the same thing happening to another one of them. On the other hand, the only tangle-folk the brittlehorns talk to are the elders, and I'm just a kid. If they saw me they'd probably run away. I'd be stuck out here overnight, and that's when the worrits are on the prowl. Oh *blazing feathers*, what a mess.

She sat and looked at Silvershank, the ivory spiralling horn in the centre of his forehead, the delicate cloven hooves, the white silk of his mane. She couldn't let his death go for nothing.

She stood up, and heaved her rucksack back on to her shoulders. Then she realised she had no proof that she'd seen Silvershank, apart from knowing his name, so she took out her knife, cut a few strands of hair from his mane, and put them in her rucksack. After that she whispered goodbye, and started back along the path. It was going up more steeply now, and the shadows were lengthening. She was frightened, there were no two ways about it, but she was good at climbing trees, and worrits were ground-dwelling beasts. If she couldn't find Silvershank's people before dark she would choose a nice big tree, and make herself a nest in it.

Felix came to in the way he always did — a slow, dawning awareness of the surface of his body. He thought his way round his limbs, checking to see if anything hurt. His brain always took a while to get going on these occasions, it didn't do to rush things. There was a dream-like quality about everything, as though his senses needed to wake up one by one. There was a pain in his knee that hadn't been there before. He opened his eyes.

Everything was dark. Where was he? The memories filtered back, taking their time, coming gradually into focus. He'd been standing across the Divide, that's right, one foot on either side. But it had been mid-morning, the sun had been shining. And where were his parents? Usually they were fussing round him, making sure he was in the recovery position, asking him if he was ready for a drink of water yet. He tried closing his eyes, and then opening them again. It was still dark. He realised that he was lying on his stomach, not on

23

his side, which was odd. No one had rearranged him. He rolled over on to his back, and looked up at the sky. The stars seemed impossibly brilliant. No cars, he thought, no exhaust fumes. The air's clear up here, and there's no light pollution from cities either. Then he noticed he was cold. He'd obviously been out for far longer than usual. But where *was* everyone?

He sat up. Something was pricking his shoulder, but when he brushed at it with his hand he realised it was only the pointed shaft of a feather that had somehow managed to penetrate his T-shirt. He looked round. He was completely alone. It didn't make sense, any of it. He got gingerly to his feet, and winced when he first put his weight on his knee. But actually the knee wasn't too bad, he would be able to walk. He felt a bit light-headed and other-worldly, the way he always did when he came round.

Nevertheless, things looked different. It was tempting to put it down to the change from sunlight to moonlight – things always did look different at night-time. But although he was on a ridge, the way he had been when he passed out, it didn't seem to be quite the same ridge. There was less vegetation, for one thing, and he could no longer see the sea. The hill dropped just as steeply as it had before, but there seemed to be a forest where the Pacific Ocean had twinkled at him earlier. This was ridiculous. How could you move an ocean?

He looked around for the path. And there *was* a path, but it wasn't the same path that had led him there. This one was criss-crossed with shapes that looked like the imprints of bird-feet – and big birds, at that – but they, in turn had paw-prints superimposed on top. He shivered. He'd never heard of a jaguar attacking a human being, but that didn't mean it had never happened. And there *were* jaguars in the reserve, he'd heard Miguel talking about them. And what were the birds? Cassowaries? No one had said anything about cassowaries. Then he remembered the compass round his neck, so he took a reading. The path went downhill in the right direction. And what about the notice-board that explained all about the Continental Divide? There would be a *You Are Here* symbol on it, of course there would. But when he looked for the notice-board, it wasn't there any more.

Now he really was frightened. This was all too weird by far. It was as though someone had moved him whilst he'd been unconscious, and put him somewhere else. He took a deep breath. Panicking wasn't going to get him anywhere. Maybe he should call out, maybe there was a search party looking for him. He tried to shout, but he had to clear his throat several times before his voice would work. Then he yelled as though his life depended on it, thinking that perhaps it did. He'd wanted the experience of a lifetime, and, by God, he'd got it.

Silence. He yelled again. And then, somewhere in the distance, a voice. But the voice had an unusual quality to it, earthy and metallic at the same time. It didn't sound human at all. He listened. The words gradually sorted themselves

25

out, and he realised that the voice was calling, "Who are you?"

"Felix!" he screamed.

There was a long pause. Then, "Helix? Did you say *Helix*?"

"*Felix!*" yelled Felix. "Felix Sanders!"

Another pause.

Then, "That's the most bizarre name I've ever heard! What do you want up here, Felix Sanders?"

What did he want? What a very peculiar thing to ask. Didn't whoever it was realise that he was missing? Well, it didn't really matter – all he wanted was company on the way back, someone who knew the area. "I've lost my parents!" he yelled.

Another pause. Then, "Happens to all of us, sooner or later! I lost mine twenty years ago ..." It wasn't the response he'd hoped for; in some way he couldn't quite define, it had gone off at a tangent.

Suddenly, Felix didn't want to meet the owner of the voice after all. He decided to make his own way back; the path had to lead somewhere. He remembered his water bottle, and had a drink. Then he had a pee, left the ridge as quietly as he could, and made his way downhill.

There were plenty of rocks and boulders, but very few trees. The plants were thorny little bushes, and it only took a couple of scratches for him to learn that he had to push them out of the way with his elbow. He glanced up, and saw something pass across the face of the moon. It was huge, and it definitely wasn't a bat. He blinked, but it had gone. Perhaps it had been a night-flying insect, one of those big beetle-things with strangely shaped wing-cases, magnified to pterodactyl size because it was closer to him than he'd thought. But it hadn't looked like a beetle. Even the most fleeting of glimpses had shown him that it didn't look like anything he'd ever seen before. His knee was loosening up, and the pain had nearly gone. That was *one* positive thing. He was trying to come up with a second when he rounded a rocky outcrop, and came face to face with the owner of the voice.

"*Well, peck me where it hurts!*" said the voice. "What in the world are *you*?"

Felix stared. I'm dreaming, he thought. That's it, I'm dreaming.

"You're not a tangle-child," said the creature, "your ears are the wrong shape."

The beast was enormous. It towered over him, like a misshapen grizzly bear. He couldn't see what colour it was as the moonlight turned everything to black and white, but he could work out that it had the head of an eagle, only five times the size, and feathery ears, like an owl. Its front legs were those of a raptor, and it had wings. But its back legs were those of a lion, and it had a lion's tail. Felix suddenly remembered the footprints he had seen. There hadn't been any jaguars or cassowaries after all. There hadn't been two creatures – just the one. This one.

As he was obviously dreaming Felix became bolder. "I'm a boy," he said. "A human being. *Homo sapiens*. What are you?"

"A brazzle, of course."

There was something familiar about the shape after all. Something heraldic. That was it, he'd seen one before – but it had been in the garden of a stately home, and it had been carved out of stone. "You look more like a griffin to me," he said.

The brazzle looked thoughtful. "No, I'm definitely a brazzle. My name's Ironclaw. And you're a human being, you say?" It shook itself, and ruffled its feathers. "I *feel* awake," it said. "That doesn't mean I'm not dreaming, though. You see, I don't believe in all that supernatural stuff. Very down to earth, I am – except when I'm flying." It chuckled at its own joke, as though it were the funniest thing ever. Then it shook its head and said, "Human beings are *mythical* beings. They don't really exist. They use science, for goodness' sake. Invent vehicles that run on their own, and fly around in balloons. How ridiculous is that?"

"Not as ridiculous as this conversation," said Felix, and he laughed.

"Aren't you frightened of me?" asked Ironclaw.

"No. Why should I be?"

"I'm very fierce," said the brazzle, with some pride. "*All* brazzles are fierce. They have to be, they guard hoards of

28

gold. And they peck people's eyes out. Only when necessary, you understand."

"Have *you* ever pecked someone's eyes out?"

Ironclaw looked sheepish. "No. But I could if I wanted to."

Felix smiled. "I thought griffins – brazzles – were fiercely intelligent, as well."

"I am," said the brazzle, affronted. "I can recite trifles to thirty places. Three point one four one five nine two six five ..."

"That's pi," said Felix.

"Pie, trifles, call it what you will."

"This is all very silly," said Felix. "I'm dreaming."

"No, no, *I'm* the one who's dreaming."

There was a moment of silence, when they just looked at one another.

"We could always test if we were dreaming," said the brazzle. "Magic doesn't work in a dream. Got any poison on you?"

"*Poison?* No."

"Pity. If I dip my talon in poison, it turns red."

Felix had read a book about dreams, and he suddenly remembered something strangely similar. "Electrical things don't work in dreams," he said. "Light switches, hair dryers ..."

The brazzle looked sceptical. "What on earth's a hair dryer?"

"Never mind," said Felix, remembering his torch. "I've got something in my bag that's just the job."

He took out his torch and twisted the end of it, expecting no response. The beam of light hit Ironclaw on the end of its beak, and the creature hopped backwards as though it had been stung. "It doesn't hurt," said Felix. "It's just light." Perhaps the book had been wrong about electrical appliances not working. He let the beam travel over the brazzle and was surprised at its beauty, although it looked a bit dishevelled. Its breast feathers were scarlet, the wings a sort of metallic blue. The back half of its body – the lion half – was the traditional tawny.

"I'm impressed," said Ironclaw. "Is that how *you* got here, then? Science?"

"I've no idea how I got here," said Felix, and he told Ironclaw about passing out on the Divide.

"Fascinating," said the brazzle.

"I think *you* should try something now," said Felix. "The poison test – are any of these shrubs poisonous?"

"Hmm," said Ironclaw, "it's the tangle-folk who know all about that sort of thing. Oh – hang on. What about the bloodwort?"

Felix shrugged. "Never heard of it."

"There's some in the forest," said the brazzle, as it clambered to the top of the outcrop. "I'll be two shakes of a worrit's tail. Don't go away." Then it stood on its hind legs and flapped its wings a few times until it generated enough lift for take-off. After a couple of false starts it finally rose into the air, and flew away.

This is the coolest dream I've ever had, thought Felix. He

switched off his torch. Then he switched it on and off again, several times. It behaved perfectly. He pinched himself. It hurt. He pinched himself again. It still hurt. He remembered times when he'd had nightmares – usually about hospitals – and he'd forced himself to wake up. He knew he could do it – all he had to do was to say *bingo* to himself. But this dream was a bit too good to leave straight away, so he decided against it. He sat down with his back against the rock, and waited. After he'd been waiting for what seemed like a very long time he came to the conclusion that either the brazzle had forgotten all about him, or it had found something more interesting to do, like trigonometry or calculus. He got up, and carried on walking down the path towards the forest.

Betony had managed to find a fork in a very big tree, and she'd woven some smaller branches together to make a nest. Her rucksack made a good pillow, and a few more leaves on top gave her a sort of quilt. She lay down, and closed her eyes.

Although she went to sleep quite easily, when she woke up it was still night-time. There was a full moon, and everything was bathed in silver. The branches looked like funny old people, with long twisted fingers. She smiled. The moon smiled back, and winked at her. That seemed so priceless that she laughed out loud. The leaves were giggling as well now, and even the stream sounded as though it were bubbling with glee. She sat up, fighting the urge to start laughing again. Why was everything so funny all of a sudden? She glanced down.

The worrit was standing at the foot of the tree, looking up at her. Its thick black coat was matted with burrs, and its paws were too big for it – the size of both her fists put together – but it looked like a bad joke. Its mouth was open in the silliest grin imaginable, and its huge tongue lolled out like a pink sausage someone had stamped on. One ear was cocked; the other flopped across its forehead, and kept getting in its eyes. The hair on its head wouldn't lie flat, and curled up in a silly little topknot. It was the most ridiculously soppy creature she'd ever seen. But the eyes were the eyes she'd seen illustrated in her children's book of shadow-beasts – one green, one yellow, and both gleaming with mischief.

Her arms and legs seemed to have turned to water, and she could feel a fit of the giggles coming on, exactly the way the book of shadow-beasts had said they would. She sat there, silently begging it to go away. The worrit gave a little whine and put its head on one side, as if it were asking her to come and play with it. Then it stood on its hind legs, and walked a few paces before tripping over its own feet and falling flat on its back. It looked up at its paws as though they were strange new appendages that had been put there when it hadn't been paying attention.

"Don't," she said, struggling to keep a straight face.

"Oh whoopee," said the worrit, scrambling to its feet. "You're talking to me. Where do vampreys go fishing?"

Betony shook her head, determined not to rise to the bait.

"In the blood stream! Go on, laugh, you know you want to. What sort of soup do brazzles like? No? All right, I'll tell you. One with plenty of body in it."

Betony started to giggle, she just couldn't help herself. The worrit suddenly spun round, and started to chase its own tail. When it finally caught it, it yelped with surprise and fell over again. It looked so silly, lying there on its back waving its legs in the air like an up-ended insect, that Betony began to laugh in earnest. This wouldn't do. Her ribs were starting to ache, she couldn't stop, it was hurting. She'd been stupid, coming out here on her own. She should have gone back to Geddon, explained about the brittlehorn, and one of the elders would have taken the message to them.

"What's a brittlehorn's favourite dance? Come on, have a go, this one's a goodie. You don't know? The hornpipe!" The worrit stood up on its hind legs again, and started to dance.

It looked totally absurd, a huge hairy creature taking mincing little steps and trying to pirouette. Betony was laughing so hard now that the tears were running down her face; it was scary, she couldn't stop, couldn't stop, it was getting difficult to breathe, as though someone were tickling her to death. And then it became quite terrifying; she really *was* going to die laughing, for that was how worrits killed their prey. They turned their noses up at anything that had passed away *not* laughing.

"Did you hear the one about the sailor on the sinking ship who grabbed a bar of soap to wash himself ashore?" chortled the worrit, trying to do a cartwheel and falling flat on its face when its feet got in the way again.

Betony shut her eyes tight, and put her fingers in her ears. After a while, she managed to get herself under control – and then a picture of the worrit tossing its ear back as it danced flashed into her mind, and she split her sides again. It was only when she found herself reflecting, *Agrimony hasn't got a worrit in her horrible little book*, that she realised she was thinking straight again. She opened her eyes, and looked down. The worrit had gone. She heaved a sigh of relief, and then she smiled. A normal, ordinary smile that wasn't going to lead to terminal hysterics. She'd survived. She was pretty hot stuff, really. She'd be totally wasted as a herbalist. And then she was asleep again, and dreaming about mythical beasts with grey bodies and long noses and great flapping ears.

Felix needed his torch now. The trees grew more thickly here, and he swept the beam from side to side as he followed the path – but there were no strangler figs any more, and no epiphytes. Oaks, sycamores, silver birches. Other trees he couldn't identify, but they didn't look tropical. This is one hell of a long dream, he thought to himself. And it's consistent – I don't suddenly find myself in a supermarket, or the cinema, or at home. One thing succeeds another, exactly the way it would in real life.

He came to a clearing, where the moonlight had turned the grass to one great sheet of rippled silver. Around the edge, the shadows of trees and bushes assumed strange and wonderful shapes. He stood there for a moment, imagining that one was a crouching giant, and another a dwarf. That one was definitely a dog. A big dog, a Bernese Mountain dog, or something like that.

The dog took a pace forwards.

Hey, thought Felix, it *is* a dog. It isn't a griffin or a giant or a dwarf, it's a real live dog. That must be a good sign; maybe there's a house around here somewhere. He peered into the gloom, in the forlorn hope that it was a proper rescue dog with a little barrel round its neck.

The dog took another pace forward, and suddenly it was out in the moonlight. It wasn't even wearing a collar. Felix stared. It was a cartoon dog, surely. That ridiculous little topknot, and the lop-sided ears. He couldn't help it; he laughed. The dog grinned back.

"Here, boy," said Felix, trying to keep his voice steady. It was the most absurd creature he had ever seen, even its eyes were different colours. All he wanted to do was have hysterics.

The dog trotted over and said, "Have you heard the one

about the brazzle, the fire-breather, and the brittlehorn?"

Felix shook his head, his smile so wide it hurt his face. A dog that told jokes? He was still dreaming, obviously.

"Neither have I," said the dog.

Felix burst out laughing.

The dog grinned again, and its left ear flopped across its left eye. It tossed its head back like a woman shaking back fly-away hair, its nose in the air, its eyes half-closed. The ear fell back in exactly the same position. Felix doubled up. The dog tossed its head again, as though it had just emerged from the hairdresser's, and once more the same thing happened.

"Washed my ears and now I can't do a thing with them," said the dog.

Felix couldn't stop laughing, no way could he stop. He couldn't help picturing the dog trying out a new shampoo and admiring itself in a mirror. Tears were streaming down his face, he was being mentally tickled to death. All of a sudden it got scary. His body felt like rubber, bendy and unreliable. He had no control over himself, none whatsoever; his chest was beginning to hurt, and he was gasping for breath. He had to get a grip on himself, stop laughing. He needed to think of something that wasn't funny at all, something real and terrifying ... his own death. His not being *anywhere* any more, and the world going on without him.

He sobered up immediately, and all of a sudden the dog didn't look like a joke any more. It looked sly and calculating. "What goes ha ha bonk?" it asked.

Someone laughing his head off, thought Felix. This isn't a dream, it's a nightmare. I want out, and I want out *now*. I have to wake up. He took a deep breath and shouted *"Bingo!"*

Nothing happened.

And then the dizziness. He knew he was going to pass out again, and as usual the thoughts flashed so quickly through his brain that they didn't seem to be composed of words at all. He'd never passed out in a dream before; it just didn't happen. He was frightened; no, it was more than that, much more. He was absolutely terrified. This wasn't a dream. It wasn't even a nightmare. It was some sort of twisted reality, and he was going to die here.

And then blackness.

Well, muddy my paws, thought the worrit. That was a waste of time, wasn't it? There isn't even a hint of a smile on his face, he'd taste like ditchwater. I needed him to die laughing; I can't eat something that refuses to co-operate.

He gave Felix one last prod with his nose, just to make sure there wasn't a giggle lurking there somewhere, but there was no response. He sighed, and trotted off into the forest to look for more obliging game.

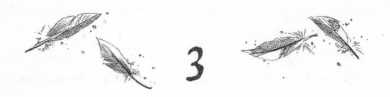

3

When Felix came round this time, his cheek was pressed against something cool and soft – grass, probably. The slow recapture of his body went on as usual, along with the gradual recovery of whatever had been in his mind just before he went down. A moonlit clearing. Shadows. A *dog*.

He opened his eyes. It was daylight. Someone had put him in the recovery position; he was on his side, staring at blades of grass. How weird. Perhaps all that dog stuff *had* been a dream, a dream he'd had whilst he was unconscious. He must still be on the ridge; everything was explained now, his parents would ask him if he was ready for a drink of water in a moment, and they would make their way back down the path to the Study Centre.

He sat up. A girl of about his own age was sitting opposite him on the grass, cross-legged, and his parents were nowhere to be seen.

"You've been out for ages," she said. "I was quite worried."

He stared at her. She had a tanned skin, and white-blonde hair that was tucked into some sort of cap. Her eyes were green – really green, like the grass, and they slanted upwards at the corners.

"I found you here early this morning," she went on. "There were worrit prints all over the glade. I didn't know what to think."

He shook his head. He didn't know what to think either.

"I saw a worrit myself, last night," she said. "First time I've seen a shadow-beast, actually. Apart from vam-preys, but every-one sees those. Anyway, I shut my eyes and stuck my fingers in my ears, so I was OK."

He shook his head again. "You're not making sense," he said. "What's a worrit?"

"A *worrit*," she said, as if he were a bit thick. "Big hairy black thing, four legs and a tail."

"Oh," he said. "The dog."

"Are you trying to be funny or something?" she said, a slight edge of annoyance creeping into her voice. "A dog's a mythical creature. It doesn't really exist." She regarded him for a moment, her head slightly on one side. Then she said, "Oh, *I* see. You *are* having a laugh. You want me to think you're a human being, because of the accident to your ears."

Felix immediately put his hands up to his ears. They felt just the same as ever. He took his hands away again and looked at them, wondering if they would be covered in blood. They weren't. "There's nothing wrong with my ears," he said.

She laughed. "Good try."

"Really. There isn't."

"If you've got a problem about having mutilated ears, you should get them seen to. The elders will probably know a spell that works."

This conversation was even stranger than the one with the brazzle. He studied her more closely. She was wearing a green top and green trousers, neither of which could have been bought in the average shopping centre, and the cap that covered her blonde hair had obviously been stitched by hand – one of the seams was coming apart. Her shoes were green, too, although they were scuffed and dirty.

"What's your name?" he asked her.

"Betony. What's yours?"

"Felix."

"What an odd name."

"It is unusual," said Felix, remembering that the brazzle had called it bizarre, "but it's not *odd*. Felix means fortunate." He allowed himself a grim little smile. Ironic, that's what it was. He was the least fortunate boy he knew.

"You don't come from round here, do you?"

"No," said Felix, a faint suspicion growing ever stronger, "I don't think I do. Can I see your ears, please?"

Betony took off her cap. The blonde hair cascaded over her shoulders like a waterfall. She pushed it back. Her ears were as pointed as a Vulcan's.

"You're an elf," said Felix.

"I'm a tangle-child," said Betony, looking confused. "What's an elf?"

"A tangle-child, I suspect," Felix replied. "Just as a brazzle's a griffin."

"Have you seen a brazzle?"

He nodded. "Last night. Look, I think I'd better tell you what happened, and see if you can make any better sense of it than I can. If I'm not dreaming I think I must have died, and this is the afterlife."

"Well, *I'm* not dreaming," said Betony. "And I'm most certainly not dead."

Felix told her how he'd passed out on the Divide. Betony listened attentively, although her eyes widened now and again and she gave him the occasional old-fashioned look, as though she were wondering whether this was all some huge practical joke.

When he'd finished she said, "Fair enough. Now show me the science thing, and if it works I suppose I have to believe that I really have met a flesh and blood human being." She laughed suddenly. "*Fangs and talons*, I really need a notebook.

Eat your heart out, Agrimony."

Felix didn't ask her what she meant — but he had his notebook in his bag, so he handed it to her, along with a biro. She immediately tried to put the biro in her mouth, and he had to stop her.

"How does it write if you don't lick it?"

"It just does," he said. "Try it."

She wrote down *brittlehorn* and *human being* in rather untidy writing. Then she tried the torch, and after that Felix showed her how to take a reading from the compass.

"Well," she said. "You didn't use a circle, nor did you recite any incantations, nor did you scatter any herbs. That light thing obviously can't be magic; it has to be science. I don't know what to say."

"Can *you* do magic?"

"Not much," Betony confessed. "I hate school."

"Isn't there anything you can show me?"

"I come from a family of herbalists, and that's what I'm meant to become when I grow up. It's really *boring*. I can cure bruises."

"I've got one on my knee," said Felix, remembering.

"Oh, right," said Betony. She glanced round the glade. Then she spotted a plant with little yellow flowers, and she went over and picked it. After that she took a candle out of her rucksack, and lit it with a wave of her hand.

Felix leaned across and blew it out.

Betony scowled at him. "Why did you do that?"

"Because what you just did is impossible in my world. Do it again."

Betony lit the candle again, then she crushed the leaves and held them above it, muttering something. After that she put the green mush on Felix's knee, and five minutes later the bruise had completely gone.

"Wow," said Felix, "that's really useful."

"Listen," said Betony, "I can't just sit around here all day, I've got an important message to pass on to the brittlehorns. You can come with me if you like – that compass thing could come in handy."

"I've got to get back to my own world," said Felix. "My parents will be worried sick."

"What about?"

"Me disappearing."

"I disappear all the time," said Betony. "No one even notices."

"Well, my parents will," said Felix.

"We use my parents as boot-scrapers these days," said Betony. "I live with my brother and sister."

Felix thought he must have misheard. "Boot-

43

scrapers?"

Betony explained about her parents being turned to stone as though that sort of thing happened all the time, and said how useful they'd been as an anchor for the bottom end of the rope ladder. Then she said, "I've got no idea how you got here, let alone how to get you back. We could ask the brittlehorns. They're very wise. I've seen some hoof-prints, so they can't be far away."

"Brittlehorns," said Felix thoughtfully. "Do they have a single horn in the middle of their foreheads by any chance?"

"Yeah," said Betony. "Do you have them in your world as well, then?"

Felix shook his head. "I think you mean a unicorn," he said. "It's a mythical beast, the same as you are." He grinned. "And yes, I'd love to meet one."

Tansy glanced in the mirror, and messed up her hair. The flight had been delayed as the fire-breather had had a stomach upset, and another one had to be found at short notice. She and her brother had arrived at Tiratattle with only half an hour to spare.

"Have you got the sickle?" she asked Ramson.

"*Yes.* How many more times?"

They climbed down the ladder of the cheap treetop hotel, and started out for the conference centre. Tansy had never been to Tiratattle before, and Ramson was pretending to be more familiar with it than one school visit could possibly have made him. He refused point-blank to ask directions, and denied outright that they'd been past the chalice stall three times. The shops were full of candles and incense burners, their designs quite unlike anything Tansy had ever seen in Geddon. There were cuddyak carts everywhere, diggelucks carrying pickaxes, lickits balancing trays of cakes on their heads. And japegrins, with their red hair and their garish purple clothes; thousands of them. Every so often she saw one wearing black, which was extraordinary, and the passers-by always got out of their way.

"They're the militia," Ramson told her in his most annoying know-all voice. "See the badges?"

The conference centre was situated underground, and they had to take a flying carpet down to the sixth level. The main cave was lit with chandeliers, the candles flickering like fireflies, and there was a low buzz of voices. The audience was made up of tangle-folk like themselves, wearing green; a few ragamuckies, in brown, and some diggelucks, dressed, of course, in grey. There was even a handful of lickits, their white robes smelling faintly of vanilla. Tansy and Ramson sat down, and waited.

Once the hall was full, someone shut the main door. Then, from somewhere behind the stage, a couple of musicians started to play a dance tune. A gasp went up as a worrit pranced on-stage, dressed in a silly little skirt, and started to do the star squirm. A few people tried to leave immediately, but the door was locked. The ragamuckies in the front row began to snigger – the worrit was always half a beat behind the musicians, and it kept forgetting the steps and tripping over its own feet. Tansy felt herself go stiff with fright, but at the same time she was smiling as though her face would split in two. She fleetingly wondered if she'd fallen prey to an illusion spell – but illusion spells were party tricks for children, she ought to be immune to them by now.

A little moan went up from the person in front of her; the audience seemed glued to their seats. The music got faster; the worrit tried a few high kicks, and fell flat on its face. Everyone was laughing now. As the music reached a frenetic crescendo the worrit attempted an arabesque, which went completely wrong. It tried desperately to retain its balance, skidded across the stage and ended up in a heap against the wings. The music stopped. The worrit got to its feet and bowed, its ridiculous ears falling across its eyes – and then it seemed to split in two. Its black furry coat fell to the floor, revealing a japegrin.

"I bet that had you worried!" chuckled the japegrin.

The audience shifted uneasily, and a few people giggled nervously. Then someone started to clap. The rest followed suit, and after a moment or two the japegrin held up a hand for silence. "I'm just the entertainment," he said. "We all like a laugh, don't we? But now I want to introduce Snakeweed, who's going to make sure that laugh stays with you."

He held out a hand, and another japegrin walked on to

the stage.

"Fellow beings," he began. "Life isn't just a bowl of toad-stools these days, is it? You never get that crock of gold, do you? And why is that? Because although many of you have made interesting discoveries you don't have the means to publicise your inventions. This is an opportunity for you to present your ideas to GP, the biggest healing organisation in the world. GP is short for Global Panaceas, folks — some of you may already have heard of us, and we're going to give you the means to carry on with your research, secure in the knowledge that not only will you be able to afford that new talisman you've had your eye on — you'll be helping the whole world to better health."

There was something about Snakeweed that Tansy didn't like. He was wearing the regulation clothes — but the purple pointed hat had magenta stars on it, which clashed rather violently with his bright red hair, and the tight-fitting tunic was almost violet. His green eyes did squint the way they should, but there was a wicked little glint in them that made you think that his sense of humour might be more malicious than amusing. He talked for a while about the difficulties of working in a small community, where it could take weeks to get the right ingredients, and the advantages of working for a large organisation.

"Fellow beings," he concluded, smiling broadly, "don't think we can't see each and every one of you. We've got dozens of experts backstage who are just dying to meet you, and they'll be here tomorrow, as well. *All* of you will get the chance to discuss your ideas. Just line up down the aisles, and start thinking about how you're going to spend that crock of gold."

Tansy and Ramson joined one of the queues. Tansy felt uneasy, although she couldn't quite say why. Every single GP representative was a japegrin. No ragamuckies, no diggelucks, not even a lickit. A long row of pointed purple hats dipped up and down as they talked to people, and scribbled things on to their slates.

Eventually they reached the head of the queue. Ramson opened his rucksack, pulled out a bundle of herbs, and dropped them. He bent down to pick them up, seeming, as usual, to have too many knees and elbows.

"No, no," smiled the rep, "I don't want a demonstration. I just want to know what you're working on."

"Something to repair teeth," mumbled Ramson, and Tansy winced. She'd told him over and over again to call it dental reconstruction.

"Ah," said the japegrin, and he glanced at his slate.

"You're the sixth. Tell us what herbs you use, and the procedure, and we'll get back to you."

"It's *been* tested," said Ramson. "We do things properly in
Geddon."

"Geddon?" The japegrin raised a ginger eyebrow.

Tansy could have died. To anyone from Tiratattle,
Geddon was the back of beyond. She wished Ramson would
try using his brain before he opened his mouth. "We'd like
to think about it, if you don't mind," she said. She wasn't
going to hand over the spell just like that.

"Suit yourself," said the japegrin. "Next."

A lickit elbowed his way in front of them, and started to
tell the rep about a remedy for wing-rot. Fire-breathers were
big business, and the rep looked very interested indeed.

"Why did you do that, Tansy?" demanded Ramson. "I can
hardly believe it, an opportunity like this and you throw it
away."

"I haven't thrown anything away, you idiot," said Tansy.
"We can always come back tomorrow."

Ramson glared at her.

"I want to check that Betony's OK."

"Betony's always OK," said Ramson. "I suppose you're
going to suggest we go to one of those crystal ball places."

"Thirteen out of thirteen, for once," said Tansy.

Felix and Betony were following a path that ran along the
bank of a stream. The ground was softer here, and every so

49

often he could see hoof-prints. Although they never stopped talking, Betony wasn't nearly as interested in his world as he was in hers. She thought it sounded extremely dull – and when Felix described the grey buildings of London that stretched for miles in every direction, he could see her point.

Felix, on the other hand, couldn't get enough of her stories – even if it did take him a while to catch on to things.

"The last spelling test we had was brilliant," she told him.

Brilliant? A spelling test? Betony didn't look the swotty type.

"Agrimony was the only one who managed to make her twig burst into flower," Betony explained. "The rest of us ended up with creepy-biters, a pond-hopper, and a stabber-bird. The pond-hopper ate the creepy-biters, and the stabber-bird ate the pond-hopper. The teacher was ever so cross." She giggled. "Do you have fire-breathers in your world?"

"Are they all leathery, with wings?"

Betony nodded.

"Dragons," said Felix.

"I think dragon's a stupid name for a fire-breather," said Betony. "Have you ever been on one?"

"Dragons are mythical in my world."

"Oh," said Betony, "fire-breather flights are incredible." In actual fact she'd only been on a fire-breather once, when she was little – a short flight over the town during a summer fair, just to give her a taste of it. She'd screamed her head off and been sick, but she didn't tell Felix that.

They were crossing a clearing when Felix saw a movement in the trees. Was that a pale ghostly shape in there, or just his imagination?

"What?" asked Betony.

Felix shook his head. "I thought I saw something, but I'm not certain."

Betony stiffened. "What colour was it?"

"Silvery."

She smiled. "Good. None of the shadow-beasts are silver. They're usually black or brown." She pulled a handful of white hairs out of her rucksack, and laid them on the ground in the middle of the clearing. "Come on," she said, "let's climb a tree and wait."

She was much better at climbing than Felix, and she shinned up the tree as though it were a staircase. It took Felix rather longer, and he noticed that he was getting short of breath again. Once they'd settled themselves in a comfortable fork, he checked in his pocket – how many of his tablets remained? He counted them. Enough to last him three days. And then what? Don't think about it, he said to himself, because there's nothing you can do about it. Nothing at all.

He glanced at Betony. She smiled, and put her fingers to her lips. On the far side of the clearing a creature had emerged from the trees. It was pure white, with the delicate muscular build of an Arab stallion. But there was a spiral horn in the middle of its forehead, the colour of old ivory, and it had cloven hooves and blue eyes. Felix heard himself catch his breath; it was one of the most beautiful creatures he had ever seen. After a moment, another brittlehorn followed it out into the open, and then a foal. The foal's horn had only just started to grow, and its legs were long and gangly. It was just as skittish as a young horse, however, and it bucked and pirouetted and danced sideways across the grass until it bumped into a log. Before long the herd had grown to eleven. The first brittlehorn had noticed the hairs now, and it trotted over and sniffed them. The second did likewise. Then they both lifted their heads, and looked round. They seemed very nervous all of a sudden; their necks were held high, and their ears were flicking back and forth, trying to catch the faintest trace of any sound.

Betony leaned as far out of the tree as she dared and called, "Brittlehorn! My name is Betony, and I have a message for you."

Felix elbowed her in the ribs.

"Oh yes," said Betony. "And we want to ask your advice about something."

The first brittlehorn pinpointed her position immediately and turned to face her, looking up into the tree. "Tangle-child!" it called.

4

It took Betony two attempts to scramble up on to the brittlehorn's back, and it took Felix five. It was a great honour to be allowed to ride these beautiful creatures – in fact, she'd only ever heard of it happening once before, when the Queen of the tangle-folk had twisted her ankle while dancing and a brittlehorn had come to her rescue.

Felix was enjoying himself. The brittlehorn's coat was warm and soft, and every so often she turned her head to speak to him. Her voice did have a horsey quality to it, but it wasn't one that made you want to laugh.

"We're going to miss Silvershank," she said, stepping delicately across a fallen branch. "He'd been over to the Tiratattle province, looking for new strains of grass. Have you ever been there?"

"I'm not from round here at all," said Felix. "I come from another world entirely."

The brittlehorn snorted.

"I do," said Felix. "I'm a boy. A human being."

Another snort. "I'd expect a remark like that from a jape-grin, but not from a tangle-child."

"I'm not a tangle-child," said Felix. "My hair's the wrong colour, and I don't have pointed ears."

The brittlehorn twisted her head round to stare at him, and nearly collided with a tree. "You're right," she said. "You do look like a human being. I thought all that mythical stuff was just moonshine. Can you do science?"

So Felix showed her the biro and the compass and the torch, and she neighed to the rest of the herd, and they all gathered round to marvel. By the time they reached the brittlehorns' valley, Felix was a celebrity.

Betony felt a bit put out. She was pleased with herself for having found Felix in the first place, but she thought she deserved a bit more credit for delivering Silvershank's message to the right people. Not that she'd actually delivered it yet. She was dying to meet the leader of the herd, and tell it to him in person.

There was a waterfall at one end of the brittlehorn valley, tumbling down into a deep turquoise pool. A meadow, fruit trees, and a mud wallow, which wasn't very attractive to a human being, but was the height of luxury for a brittlehorn. They came to a halt beside a cave.

Betony messed up her hair to appear polite. Meeting the leader of the herd was no small matter. In the event, he was a kindly old brittlehorn with a soft voice, and she told him what Silvershank had said before he died. "What do you think he meant?" she asked. "Tell them not to take ... tell them not to take what?"

"Could be any number of things," said the leader vaguely. "The one thing you mustn't take up here is the brazzle's gold. Serious retribution for that sort of thing; plagues of creepy-biters, infestations of fleas, boils. Of course, if you really get their backs up you get your eyes pecked out. But Silvershank wouldn't be telling us something we knew already. No, it must be something he took when he was over Tiratattle way."

"Something he stole, you mean?"

"Unlikely," said the leader. "Brittlehorns aren't thieves. There's nothing much we want, you see. A nice bit of grass, a few oats when we have a party, a mud wallow. No, there has to be another answer. I'll need to meditate on it for a while."

Felix cleared his throat. Betony glared at him.

"*Betony*," said Felix, "remember there's something important I want to say as well."

"Then speak, tangle-child," said the leader.

"I'm not a tangle-child," said Felix. "I'm a boy. A human being." The words were beginning to sound stale and overused.

The leader peered at him. "Explain yourself," he said.

So Felix explained himself yet again, demonstrating the biro, the compass, and the torch. He wondered what would happen when the batteries ran out.

"Remarkable," said the leader. "Quite remarkable."

"I don't know how I got here," said Felix, "but I do know that I want to be able to go back. I *have* to get back. My parents will be really worried about me."

"I'm sure they will," said the brittlehorn. "We'd be quite distraught if one of our own foals disappeared like that. Hmm. I'll need to meditate on that as well, you realise. Help yourself to some fruit, and have a swim in the pool. Then come back this evening, and I'll see if I've been enlightened about anything."

"Thank you," said Felix. It felt like progress of a sort.

Although the fruit was delicious, it didn't really fill him up. Betony produced some bread and cheese from her rucksack. Then she started to complain about her classmates, and the toadstool test she was due to have the following full moon.

"If that's all you've got to worry about you're well off," said Felix bitterly.

Betony looked as though she was going to give an equally sharp reply, then she must have seen something in his face because she said, "So what worries *you*, then?"

"Dying," said Felix.

"Everyone dies," said Betony.

"Most people have a reasonably long life first."

"And you don't think you're going to?"

"I *know* I'm not," said Felix. "I told you about the way I passed out; it's part of this illness I have. One day I simply won't come round again. I overheard them talking about it, in the hospital."

Betony looked thoughtful. "Why don't you ask the leader about it?"

"How could he help?"

"If anyone knows where to find a spell to make you better, he will."

Felix felt his whole body stiffen. "What do you mean, a spell to make me better?"

"Well," said Betony, "I can cure bruises – you know that. Maybe somewhere there's a cure for *your* illness."

The possibility that there might be a magical solution to Felix's condition was instantly terrifying. He had become so reconciled to his death that a glimmer of hope actually hurt, the way a sudden bright light could hurt his eyes after a long period of darkness. He tried to stop himself getting excited, because if nothing could be done the disappointment would be overwhelming, even worse than finding out about it the first time. But it was too late. The seed had been sown, and nothing on earth was going to stop it growing.

"I want to talk to him *now*," he said.

"You can't," said Betony. "He's meditating. You must never interrupt a brittlehorn when he's meditating."

"Not even for something as important as this?"

"It'll keep for a few hours, won't it?"

"If I drop dead in the next few minutes, you'll think differently," said Felix savagely.

"You look perfectly OK to me," said Betony defensively.

What do *you* know about it, thought Felix. How dare you

assume that because I look all right there's nothing seriously wrong with me? He felt really annoyed, so he got up and
walked over to the brittlehorn who'd brought him, and told
her everything. Her name was Snowdrift.

"You poor foal," she said.

"I'll run out of my tablets soon," said Felix, feeling sorry
for himself. And then he felt angry with himself as well,
because this was what always happened when he fantasised
about getting better.

"Tablets?" said the brittlehorn. "What are tablets?"

"Medicine." Felix showed her.

She sniffed them, and put out her long blue tongue and
tasted one. "Oh," she said. "Fertle, peribott and vamolin.
Easy. I'll get old Milklegs to mix you a gourd-full. It'll have
to be an infusion, we can't make them all solid and pink and
sugary like those."

Two hours later, Felix was sipping the new medicine and
feeling on top of the world. He had an extension, and it felt
wonderful. Maybe a long enough extension to sort things out
once and for all. No, no, he mustn't think like that. This was
a remission, nothing more. A good patch that teased you
into believing you were getting better – until you got worse
again. But he did feel better, right at that moment, and for
now, that was enough.

That evening, they presented themselves in front of the
leader and waited. The old brittlehorn had his eyes shut, and
his head was nodding gently as though he were asleep.

Suddenly he opened his eyes, and gave a little start.

"Ah," he said.

"Silvershank's message?" queried Betony.

"Ah," said the brittlehorn, as though he hadn't the faintest idea what she was talking about. Then, "Oh, the message. Yes. Dear, oh dear. What is the world coming to." He closed his eyes again.

After a minute or two of silence, Betony cleared her throat.

"Ah yes," said the leader, opening his eyes again and giving another little start. "I think I'll deal with the boy's problem first."

Felix stepped forwards.

"I think you died for a moment," he said, "and then something jolted you back to life. You were standing across the Divide, were you not?"

Felix nodded.

"Magic works in mysterious ways," said the brittlehorn. "You know, of course, that had you been reduced to liquid you would have flowed off in two directions. The Divide is a magical place, whatever world it's in. At least, I think it is. Anyway, if you stand – or lie – across it, with your ittybitties absolutely equally distributed for the length of your heartbeat, you will cross the Divide in another direction entirely."

Ittybitties? thought Felix. Atoms, maybe.

"It never actually happens, of course," the brittlehorn continued. "If there was no time delay everyone who stepped across the Divide would reappear in another dimension, because for the tiniest fraction of a second they would be half on one side and half on the other. But if you have to remain there for the length of a heartbeat, your ittybitty distribution would never remain stable – the blood is coursing through your body, and changing the balance all the time. If, however, you just happened to fall in the right place and if – for the length of a heartbeat – your bodily functions ceased, it would, I think, just be possible. Are you following me?"

"Almost," said Felix. "But look, if my heart wasn't beating how *could* I have lain there for the length of a heartbeat?"

"Your heart doesn't have to beat," said the brittlehorn. "In fact, in this instance it was most certainly not beating. It's just an expression of a period of time, relative to the creature concerned."

"Do you mean that I'll have to die again to get back to my own world?"

"Ah," said the brittlehorn, "if only it were that simple."

It didn't sound simple at all. "Why isn't it that simple?" Felix asked.

Betony kicked him on the ankle, and he realised that in brittlehorn terms he was being rude by persisting. But he couldn't stop now.

"Because it was sheer chance that you fell across the Divide the way you did. We could never get you back to that position, precisely half on one side and half on the other. Quite apart from the ticklish little problem of killing and then resurrecting you." He whisked a fly off his rump with his long white tail. "Balance. It's a remarkably difficult thing to achieve."

"You mean I'll *never* get back?" said Felix, appalled. "That I'll have to stay here for the rest of my life?"

"Looks that way at the moment," said the brittlehorn. "But nothing's fixed. Keep an open mind, that's what I say." He closed his eyes.

Milklegs wandered into the cave, and scratched himself against the wall. Betony cleared her throat again.

The leader opened one eye. "Yes?"

"The other question. The thing you mustn't take," she said. "What do you think it is?"

"No idea," said the brittlehorn.

"Supposing he meant a potion?" she persisted. "You can take a potion."

"You can take fright," said the leader. "Take a stroll, take sides, take the plunge ... Could be a potion, though. Tell them not to take the potion. Yes. That's perfectly possible."

Snowdrift came into the cave, and scratched herself on the same bit of rock as Milklegs.

"I've heard talk about a lot of new potions in Tiratattle," said Milklegs. "Maybe Silvershank caught something relatively minor, and bought the wrong potion. Maybe he was telling us not to make the same mistake."

"There you are, tangle-child," said the leader to Betony. "Satisfied?"

Betony wanted to say *not really*, but she held her tongue and just nodded.

But Felix wasn't finished, not by a long way. "Where's Tiratattle?" he demanded. "I need to go there. I'm sick, *really* sick; ask Milklegs, ask Snowdrift. I don't expect to live much longer. Supposing there's a cure for me in this world? If Tiratattle's the place where potions are being invented, then that's where I need to be."

"It's over a hundred miles away, Felix," whispered Betony. "We'd never be able to walk that far."

"Well, how do other people get there?"

"They go by fire-breather."

"Isn't there any other way? What about by brittlehorn?"

Betony gasped, and Milklegs snorted.

"You don't ride brittlehorns like you do fire-breathers," Betony hissed at him.

"He's not to know that," said Snowdrift. "No, I think it's a good idea, actually. If one of these new potions *can* cure him, it would be a very worthwhile expedition. I'd be prepared to take him, poor little foal."

"I want to go with him," said Betony. *Blazing feathers*, trying to help Felix had to be more worthwhile than sitting a toadstool test.

"I'll ask Chalky if he'll take you," said Snowdrift. "We'll leave in the morning."

Felix wanted to laugh because the name Chalky was so ordinary. Or maybe he just wanted to laugh because they really were going off to search for a miracle, and miracles might just be possible here.

He found it very difficult to get to sleep. The journey would take several days, and his parents would have to give up waiting and go back to England. He felt dreadful, although none of it was his fault. But when he *really* thought about it he realised what he actually felt was guilt. A horrible, gnawing guilt – because, most of the time, he was enjoying himself. He tossed and turned and tried to stop worrying. Then he thought – supposing I really *did* find a cure? And after that, supposing I *did* find a way to get back? They'd think it was worth the wait, wouldn't they? And that thought was so comforting that Felix fell asleep within two minutes.

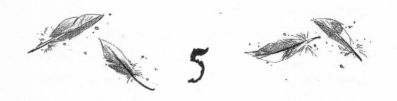

5

The crystal ball parlours were situated in a very run-down part of Tiratattle. Tansy had been really impressed by the town centre, with its rows of shops and tubs of flowers. This area was altogether more unpleasant. There were lots of canals criss-crossed with little bridges, and a smell of stagnant water and greasy cooking. The roads weren't paved any more; they were lined with deep wheel-ruts and caked with yellowy-green cuddyak droppings. Tansy heard her shoe squelch on something every so often, but she decided not to look down. The paths were littered with candle-stubs and dirty leaf-wrappings and broken pottery, and weeds sprang up everywhere. Some of them had thorns, which caught at her clothing as she passed by. The treehouses had missing struts and weatherworn nameplates, and the stalls below them weren't much better. Tansy chose the only door which wasn't rotting from the bottom up, and knocked.

A wizened little ragamucky appeared, wearing a brown

shawl over her head. "Two silver pieces," she said, holding out a wrinkled brown palm.

Ramson paid, and they went inside.

"We want to know what our sister Betony's up to," said Tansy.

"Who? You'll have to speak up, I'm a bit deaf."

"*Betony*."

The ragamucky ran her hands over the crystal ball and peered into it. Then she looked closer. Then, without a word she stood up, walked across the room and fetched a rather grubby cloth. She sat down again, spat on the ball, and rubbed it vigorously with the cloth.

"What's the matter?" asked Tansy.

The ragamucky simply shook her head, and peered into the ball again. Then she glanced up and said, "Is your sister some sort of celebrity or something?"

"No," said Tansy, "she's a perfectly ordinary tangle-child. Why?"

"She's sitting astride a brittlehorn," said the ragamucky. "And the brittlehorn seems perfectly happy about it."

"What?" shrieked Tansy.

The ragamucky peered into the ball once more. Then she picked it up, shook it, put it down, and tried again. Then she rubbed her eyes and had another go.

"You're not going to believe this," she said. "I'm not even sure I do. Maybe the ball needs a service. She's with a boy. A human child."

Ramson burst out laughing. "You're a fake," he said. "We want our money back."

The ragamucky looked upset. "I'm telling you the truth. I saw her call to him; his name seems to be Felix. That's not a tangle name, now is it?"

"*Moonshine*," said Ramson rudely. "I want a second opinion."

"You want a what?"

"A second opinion!" yelled Ramson, making sure he was facing the ragamucky so that she could lip-read.

"Very well. Go and get Woodsmoke, from next door. I won't say anything about this to her; she can just look into my ball, and tell you what she sees."

Woodsmoke reacted even more violently than the first ragamucky. "*Fangs and talons!*" she shrieked. "There are people who ought to hear about this. A real live mythical being ... a boy ... a human being ... how extraordinary." Then a secretive look crossed her face, as though she'd just had a very good idea that she certainly wasn't going to share with anyone present. "His name seems to be Felix," said the first ragamucky.

"Priceless," said Woodsmoke. "Are you sure it wasn't Helix?"

"You can't mistake the lip-shape of an F," said the first ragamucky.

"Well, sister," she said to the first ragamucky, "thank you for that. It's made my day." And then she left.

"Satisfied?" asked the first ragamucky.

"Yes, thank you," said Tansy, and she gave Ramson a shove. The two of them left the crystal ball parlour and walked away.

"Did you believe any of that?" asked Ramson. "I didn't believe any of it."

"I did," said Tansy. "The second ragamucky – the expression on her face. I suspect she's worked out some way she could make money out of that human child, if she ever got hold of him."

"Look," said Ramson, "Betony's OK, wherever she is. She isn't going to come to any harm whilst she's with a brittle-horn. Let's go back and find out a bit more about Global Panaceas."

Tansy made a face, but she didn't argue. They retraced their steps to the conference centre, and this time the magic carpet went down so fast she felt as though she'd left her stomach behind.

"I made my first crock of gold last year," someone called Helvella told them, "and I'm well on my way to the second. Global Panaceas was the best thing that ever happened to me."

"Are these new potions on general sale?" asked Ramson.

"Oh yes," replied Helvella. "You can get them just about anywhere."

"Hang on," said Tansy. "How have they managed to test them so quickly?"

Helvella gave her a sharp look. "Surely you're not suggesting that GP would put untested remedies in the shops?"

"Of course not," said Ramson. The idea was preposterous.

"I'd like to know a bit more about the safety procedures," said Tansy, obstinately.

"Look," said Helvella, "I must dash. I'm going to a wailing concert. The tickets cost a small fortune, but I can afford just about anything these days. Bye."

"Hmm," said Tansy, watching her go. "There's something about all this that doesn't feel right."

Woodsmoke chuckled to herself as she scuttled through the city. This information was worth a small fortune. She'd have to try and see Snakeweed in person, although it wasn't going to be easy. She was far too insignificant for him to be interested in her – but a human child. Oh yes. He'd pay well for that. Her feelings were slightly mixed, however. When she'd first seen Felix in the crystal ball, the strangest sensation had come over her. She'd wanted to find out where he lived, and pay him a visit in the middle of the night. She didn't want to meet him – no, she longed to clean his home for him, from top to bottom. It didn't make sense. She only cleaned her own home when there was no more usable crockery, and the dust made her sneeze. Why on earth should she want to break the habit of a lifetime for a human child?

She had to wait before Snakeweed would grant her an audience. Eventually she was ushered into his office, and she saw him close-to for the first time. You're a nasty piece of work, she thought, even for a japegrin. Your squinty little eyes are just a bit *too* squinty, your hair looks like a forest fire, and you've got more freckles than a brazzle's got feathers. And your clothes ... you think you look mighty fine in all those clashing purples, don't you? But she smiled her toothless smile, and he looked at her with distaste.

"A human child," he said. "Why should that be of interest to me? If it's true, of course, and I don't think for one moment that it is."

"Science, Snakeweed. Science."

"Go on."

"Well, all our legends tell of strange and wonderful cures for things. Tablets to relieve headaches."

"We can do that with magic. It's a powder you dissolve in water, and a ten-second spell."

"All right. What about transplants?"

"Moonshine. When a heart's worn out, it's worn out. Nobody can do anything about heart complaints. And I hardly think a mere boy is going to be able to tell us very much."

"No, but if we can find out how he got here, we might be able to go *there*. To his world. Just think of it."

Snakeweed thought about it. "Yes," he said, "I see. And not only could we market *their* cures over here, we could sell *our* magic over *there*. Where is this child?"

Woodsmoke looked evasive.

Snakeweed smiled. Then he went over to his safe, and muttered a quick opening spell. Woodsmoke could see the crocks of gold in there, lined up one behind the other like cheeses. Snakeweed lifted one out, and handed it to her. It was exquisitely heavy.

"Geddon," said Woodsmoke. "He's somewhere in the province of Geddon."

"His name?"

"Felix."

"*Felix*? Are you sure it wasn't Helix? I could imagine a brazzle being called Helix; powerfully magical mathematical shape, that, the corkscrew."

"You can't mistake the lip-shape of an F," said Woodsmoke smugly. "But there's one little snag."

Snakeweed looked as though he were about to snatch the crock of gold back again. But he simply said, "And what's that?"

"He's riding a brittlehorn," said Woodsmoke. "And there's a tangle-child called Betony with him, riding another one."

"Oh," said Snakeweed, "I don't think that will be a problem at all."

Felix and Betony had been travelling for several days now.

Felix was beginning to feel a bit like a knight on a quest –
he was looking for a Holy Grail, but one that would give
him a normal lifespan, not immortality. It was a curious
exercise in double-think. He mustn't get too hopeful, in case
he was disappointed – but without hope, the journey was
pointless. He tried *not* to think about it – but each night, as
he lay down to sleep, the possibility of a cure would return
to haunt him, tantalising and terrifying.

They always circled around the villages they came across
– but as they journeyed they collected edible toadstools, and
Betony would go into a village on foot and exchange them
for bread and cheese and eggs and fruit. They made camp
every evening, when Betony would light a fire with that
curious little wave of her hand and cook mushroom
omelettes. The brittlehorns would stand nose to tail under a
tree, dozing. After dinner Felix and Betony would talk, and
one night Felix decided to make a proper note of all the new
vocabulary he was learning. His bag had fallen apart the previous day, and he'd given his notebook to Betony to keep in
her rucksack. He'd given her the reading book as well – he
had far more interesting things to do these days than read a
story about a group of boys starting up a newspaper – but
she hadn't shown much interest in it. Reading stories obviously wasn't her thing.

"Right," he said, taking back the notebook, "I know a
brazzle's a griffin, a brittlehorn is a unicorn, and a tangle-child
is an elf. A fire-breather is almost certainly a dragon. But I've

heard you talk about other things. What's a ragamucky?"

Betony poked the fire with a stick. "We don't get many ragamuckies round here," she said, "they're city folk, they like their houses clustered together. They're very fond of their homes. No one knows why, exactly, because they don't look after them. They're really untidy."

"What do they look like?"

"Brown. Brown hair – straight, not tangled. Brown skins, brown clothes."

"They sound like brownies to me, apart from one thing – our brownies were supposed to clean people's homes in the middle of the night."

Betony laughed. "Ragamuckies can't be brownies then, they're the messiest creatures ever."

"What's a japegrin?"

"There's loads of them in Tiratattle. They like practical jokes, and they've got red hair and green eyes."

"Pixies, maybe," said Felix, writing it down in his notebook. "It's really strange, this language business. You speak English, and a lot of your words are the same as ours – grass, trees, toadstools. It's just the animal life that's different – and some of the plants. Actually, that makes a kind of sense. You only have different words for the things that crop up in our myths, and those things are nearly always animals – and the occasional bit from the plant kingdom, like the golden apples of perpetual youth. Do you have a fruit that gives eternal life?"

Betony laughed. "No."

Pity, thought Felix. I could do with something like that. "What other animals are there?"

"The flame-bird is pretty spectacular – mostly scarlet, though its wings are an iridescent blue, and it has the most beautiful song. When it's ready to die it collects some spices, makes a nest, and waits for sunrise. The sun sets fire to the nest, and it burns to death. Nine days later a chick hatches from the ashes."

"That's a phoenix," said Felix, writing it down.

"Tell me about some of *your* animals," said Betony. "I used to read about them in story books, but I'm sure most of them can't be true. I mean, the humungally can't be a real creature. Bigger than a brazzle, with great flapping ears and a nose as long as its legs?"

"That's an elephant," said Felix. "I've ridden one in a zoo."

Betony's mouth dropped open. "And the river-fatty? Big grey thing, with tiny little ears?"

"A hippopotamus."

Betony laughed. "Maybe your world does have some fun things. I wouldn't mind visiting it."

Felix felt a tug inside him. Roast dinners, ice-cream, Christmas trees, football matches; his parents. He bit his lip.

"Sorry," said Betony. "I keep forgetting you can't get back."

Snakeweed sat behind his desk, twiddling his thumbs and sipping a glass of fertle-juice. He needed to handle this carefully. A human child would attract enormous attention, and if he was going to use Felix for his own ends it would be much better if the boy's existence remained a secret. Taking advantage of grown tangle-folk was one thing; exploiting a child who was a phenomenon was something else entirely. The publicity would be a disaster. No, this needed to be kept very quiet indeed.

He got up, went over to the safe and removed a wooden box. He opened it, and took out the two shiny black pebbles within. Then he rubbed the first one. The pebble started to glow, and a putrid stench filled the room.

The sinistrom slowly materialised, gradually losing its transparency until it was a solid being. Snakeweed rubbed the second pebble, and another sinistrom took shape. He put both the pebbles back in the box, returned it to the safe and

recited the closing spell. Then he went and sat down again, and surveyed the two shadow-beasts in front of him. They were so oddly proportioned – as though the front half had been made from a powerful carnivore, and the back half from a smaller one. Their heads seemed too big for their bodies, and their backs sloped down at an angle, finishing with a small tail. Their jaws could snap limbs as easily as twigs; they had large ears that picked up the faintest of sounds, and eyes that could see in the dark. The downside was that they smelt disgusting; they stank of rotten eggs, with a whiff of unwashed armpits and decaying toadstools thrown in for good measure.

"What is your pleasure, master?" asked the first sinistrom.

"I want you to find something for me, Architrex," said Snakeweed. "A human child."

Architrex glanced at the second sinistrom. Then he said, "But master, humans are mythical beings."

"It appears not," said Snakeweed. "One has been seen near Geddon. Riding a brittlehorn."

Architrex lifted his lip and smiled, although it looked more like a snarl. "Very funny, master," he said. "Always the jester." Then he laughed, and the sound echoed round and round the cave in a series of cackles.

"Oh yes," replied Snakeweed dangerously, "I'm renowned for my sense of humour. I've often thought how amusing it would be to put your pebble into a glass of fertle-juice, and watch it turn to treacle." He glanced at the glass of fertle-juice on his desk.

Architrex stiffened.

"*That* was a joke, Architrex," said Snakeweed. "The boy on the brittlehorn isn't."

Architrex looked worried. "I can't deal with a brittlehorn," he said. "You know that."

"Ah," said Snakeweed. "I've got a little something that will take care of that. And talking of taking care of things … I think it would be a good idea to get rid of the tangle-child that's with him – Betony – as well as the raga-mucky who brought the child to my attention. Her name's Woodsmoke."

"Certainly, master," said Architrex. "Do you want her to suffer?"

Snakeweed made a couldn't-care-less gesture. Then he said, "Oh, you'd better ask her if there's anyone else who knows of the boy's existence before you finish her off. And you can relieve her of the crock of gold I gave her, too."

Architrex bowed his head. "Anything else?"

"No. But I want the boy unharmed."

"Can I frighten him a little?"

"Excellent idea," said Snakeweed. "Then I can do the paternal bit, and gain his confidence."

The sinistroms padded to the door, and Architrex opened it with his forepaw. When they left, the stench went with them.

* * *

"Who is it?" asked Woodsmoke, kicking a couple of bones under the rancid settee she called her chaise longue.

"Woodworm patrol," said Architrex, from the other side of the front door. He could have wrenched it off its hinges with his jaws, but he liked to do things properly. "You've got a couple of very dodgy struts. We need to do an inspection."

Fangs and talons, thought Woodsmoke, just as I was about to count my gold. Never mind.

She kicked the crock under the settee as well, got up, and opened the door. As soon as she saw the sinistroms she tried to shut it again, but they simply pushed their way in.

"I'm Architrex," said Architrex, "and this is Vomidor." He liked to observe the formalities; it was sheer bad manners to kill someone if you hadn't been introduced to them first.

"What do you really want?" asked Woodsmoke.

"Information," said Architrex. "Who else knows about the human child?"

"No one," said Woodsmoke.

"So how did you find out?"

"Saw him in the crystal ball."

"You don't have a crystal ball, Woodsmoke," said Architrex, gently taking her arm in his jaws. Then he got a bit less gentle.

Woodsmoke told him everything.

"Four targets," said Architrex to Vomidor, as Woodsmoke writhed on the floor. "The other ragamucky, the tangle-child, and her brother and sister. The ragamucky and the siblings we can deal with before we leave; the tangle-child we'll kill when we capture the boy. Oh, Woodsmoke – one last thing. Where's that crock of gold?"

Woodsmoke told him.

Architrex looked at the settee in distaste. "I think feeling around under there is your job, Vomidor," he said.

Vomidor gave him a filthy look, but he complied. Architrex was the higher-ranking of the two.

Just before Woodsmoke died, she thought – what a pity. I never got the chance to clean Felix's house for him.

6

"We're taking the next fire-breather back," said Tansy.

"No way," said Ramson, clearing some herbs off the quilt. There was hardly room to swing a sickle in here; he'd pushed a lot of things under the bed to make room, but there still didn't seem to be a clear surface anywhere.

Tansy glared at her brother. She was the eldest, but he always behaved as though *he* were. "You stay, then," she snapped. "I'm going back."

"Suit yourself," said Ramson.

Tansy packed her things, and made her way to the fire-breather terminal on her own. She had to queue, and she stood there seething. It would be getting dark soon; flights stopped at sunset. There was only one fire-breather left in the embarkation area at that time in the evening, but fortunately it was one of the *Whopper* range. Tansy preferred the big ones; the take-off would be smoother, and there was more leg-room as the seats on the saddle were arranged in two rows, either side of the creature's spine. There would be in-flight catering as well – a little table flipped down from the seat in front, beneath the windshield, and there would be packets of nuts and miniature gourds of fertle-juice. She watched the passengers climbing up the rope ladder, settling themselves into position and fastening their seat-belts, and her heart sank as one by one the seats filled up.

Then there was a cancellation, and she got the last place. As she climbed into the saddle she saw a shadow lurking in the trees at the edge of the runway. She looked harder. The shadow stepped out of the trees, and Tansy put her hand to her mouth. Nothing else was that peculiar front-heavy shape. It was a sinistrom. It started to lope towards the fire-breather with long easy strides, and she went cold. Nobody else seemed to have noticed it. The baggage handlers had packed up and gone home, and the terminal was deserted apart from the fire-breather and its twenty passengers. She glanced at the other travellers. It was clear that *someone* on the fire-breather was the sinistrom's target. Who could it be? She nudged the lickit in front of her, and pointed.

"What?" said the lickit.

Tansy pointed again.

The lickit turned, looked, and yelled, "Get a move on, will you! There's a sinistrom heading this way!"

The fire-breather didn't need telling twice. It got to its feet and sprinted off down the runway. Tansy was in the back seat, and she could see the sinistrom gaining all the time.

Another few seconds and it would reach the fire-breather's tail. She could see its eyes fixed on her, and she thought – it's after *me*. Why, for goodness' sake? I haven't upset anyone important. I don't understand. It came level with the tail, and gathered itself to spring. The fire-breather put on a final spurt, reached take-off speed, spread its wings and lifted into the air. Its tail flicked sideways and caught the sinistrom on the snout; the beast lost its footing and somersaulted across the runway. The fire-breather applied maximum thrust, and Tansy felt herself rammed into her seat as they soared upwards. Then they were high above the city, and she was on her way home.

Ramson polished his sickle. Then he polished it again. After that he sat on the bed, twiddling his thumbs and feeling guilty. Then he thought – why don't I go and see another ragamucky, and get a different reading? He polished his sickle for a third time. Then he put it away, climbed down the ladder, and headed off downtown.

The first crystal ball parlour he found was closed. The second had a long queue. The third looked so repulsive that he rejected it out of hand. The fourth one he came to was the one he'd been to with Tansy. He stood outside, wondering whether to go in and ask the ragamucky to admit she'd been winding them up. The house next door to *that* had a rusty sign on the door, with *Woodsmoke* scrawled across it in brown paint. It was ajar. Curious, Ramson walked over and stuck his head round the doorjamb.

It was very dark inside, and there was an unpleasant smell ... Ramson took a candle out of his pocket, and waved his hand over it. The sight that greeted his eyes made him feel quite faint. Woodsmoke was sprawled on the floor with two deep gashes in the shape of a large X across her body.

Ramson just stood there for a moment, paralysed by shock – then he knew he was going to be sick. He stumbled outside and took a gulp of fresh air, just managing to keep the contents of his stomach inside his stomach. He had to tell someone. He went back to the parlour he'd visited with Tansy, and was about to knock when he realised that this door was ajar as well. With his heart in his mouth, he stepped inside. The ragamucky's crystal ball lay smashed on the floor, next to her body. Ramson just stood there, feeling too numb to move.

"Most considerate of you to hang around like this," said a voice. "Saves all that tedious detection business."

Ramson turned round. A japegrin was standing there, dressed in black and wearing the insignia of the militia. The black only accentuated the fiery colour of his hair, so that it almost looked as though it were burning.

"I suppose I'd better arrest you," said the japegrin, regarding Ramson steadily with his squinty green eyes.

"I didn't do it," said Ramson.

"That's what they all say," said the japegrin.

"Why would I want to?"

"Ah," said the japegrin. "We'll find all that out in due course. Come along."

And by the next day Ramson was duly accused of the murder of both ragamuckies. The wounds could well have been inflicted by a sickle, and Ramson's sickle had been so scrupulously cleaned that it seemed a clear indication of his guilt. That, and the fact that he'd visited the crystal ball parlour the previous day, and been most dissatisfied with the service. So dissatisfied that he'd had an argument with his sister about it, and she'd gone off in a huff.

Architrex stood outside the jail and swore quietly to himself. There was no way he was going to be able to break in and accomplish the third killing. But it was doubtful that Ramson would say anything about the human child. It would sound like the ravings of lunatic, desperate to prove that his victim had provoked him beyond endurance. No, Ramson wouldn't talk.

Felix was still trying to add things to his vocabulary book. "I'm having trouble with the worrit," he said. "There doesn't seem to be a parallel."

"The worrit's a shadow-beast," said Betony. "It's not the only one, either. They're ... well ..." She shivered. "They're not very nice. Brazzles aren't shadow-beasts. They can be dangerous, of course, but they can also be very helpful – as long as they don't think you're after their gold. Shadow-beasts are malevolent things, and they only do harm. The worrit's the only one we get in Geddon. Oh, and vampreys – leathery winged things that suck your blood, and drain you of hope. We often see them flying, but they don't land in our area."

"Vampires," said Felix.

"And then there's the sinistrom."

"What does that look like?"

Betony shuddered. "A bit like a worrit, but out of proportion – the front half is bigger than the back. It can change shape to look like a lickit, although it can't keep it up for all that long. Then it turns back into this horrible thing with massive jaws, and it has this weird laugh."

"Aha," said Felix. "A sort of devil-hyena. Nasty."

"They stay in their pebbles most of the time."

Felix looked confused. "Are they tiny, then?"

Betony laughed. "No. You rub the pebble to summon them. I've never actually *seen* it done, of course, but everyone knows about it. The pebble starts to glow with the friction. Then the glow kind of flickers out like a flame, collects itself together until it's the right size, wiggles about until it's the right shape, turns brown, and solidifies into a sinistrom."

"It takes quite a while, then?"

"Not really. About as long as it takes to light a candle."

"So what do the sinistroms do *inside* their pebbles?"

"Nothing. They shrink to a pinpoint of energy – it must be like going to sleep. When you kill any shadow-beast the energy is snuffed out, and it just disappears. For ever."

"How do you kill them?"

"The same way you kill anything else. But you can also destroy them by dunking their pebbles in fertle-juice."

"Do they reproduce themselves – have puppies, kittens, whatever?"

"Of course not, silly. They were all created when a spell went wrong, thousands of years ago. One hundred and sixty-nine of them. No one knows how many are still around."

"You get a lot of spells going wrong here, don't you?"

"Doesn't science make mistakes, then?"

Felix remembered the hole in the ozone layer, the Chernobyl disaster, drugs with unexpected side-effects. "Yes," he said, "you're right. Science does make mistakes too." His mind moved on to cloning. "These sinistroms – are they all identical?"

"No. Their age depends on the amount of time they've spent out of their pebble. Some of them are hundreds of years old, and others are just youngsters. They're *meant* to obey whoever has rubbed their stone and summoned them. But there are stories of sinistroms who have ... um ... interpreted this rather loosely. The clever ones." Betony felt pleased with herself. It was a very grown-up way of expressing it.

"You said they can change themselves into lickits. What's a lickit?"

"They're not shadow-beasts, they're like us, but they always wear white and they specialise in cooking. Magical cooking, you know? Sweets that turn your hair green for as long as you suck them."

Felix couldn't find a parallel here either. "And a diggeluck?"

"They wear grey, and they dig for gold. They like being underground."

"Gnomes," Felix decided. "Tell me a bit more about vampreys."

"Will you please change the subject?" said Snowdrift. "You're raising the hairs on my mane."

"Ssh," said Chalky. "Look. What's that, over there?"

Felix peered into the gloom of the surrounding vegetation, and then he saw it – a flash of red. The red moved a little way to the left, and he caught a glimpse of a beautiful iridescent blue.

"I think it's a flame-bird," said Chalky. "How odd. They don't usually settle on low branches – they live right up near the top of the canopy, because they like the sun. It's not singing, either."

"Even a flame-bird doesn't sing *all* the time," said Betony.

They left the path, and moved closer. When they were just a few yards away Felix could see that the bird was holding something in its beak and its head was nodding, as though it were finding it difficult to stay awake. Suddenly it lost its grip on the branch altogether, and tumbled to the ground.

Betony slid off Chalky's back, ran over and crouched down beside it. "It *is* a flame-bird," she whispered. "I think it's ill. Oh, the poor thing. It's been collecting spices to build its funeral pyre." She picked it up, and cradled it in her arms.

I'm looking at a phoenix, thought Felix. How incredible.

Snowdrift trotted over and sniffed it. The flame-bird opened its eyes and croaked, "Greetings, brittlehorn." Its beak was cracked, and the inside of its mouth was red and raw.

"I can see you're in deep trouble, sister," said Snowdrift. "Unless you can collect all your spices and build your nest, you will not be reborn. Can we help?"

"Please," whispered the flame-bird.

"I know the ingredients," said Snowdrift. "Rest, little sister, and we will have your nest ready by dawn. Lay her down on the ground, Betony, in the shade."

Betony did as she was told, but she was looking very thoughtful. "Have you taken something for your cracked beak?" she asked.

Snowdrift kicked her. "She's too weak to undergo an interrogation, Betony."

The flame-bird's head lolled to one side, and Betony stiffened.

"She's gone to sleep, that's all," said Snowdrift. "She'll get a little of her strength back when the sun rises. Meanwhile, we've got a job to do."

She recited a list of spices, and Felix and Betony went looking for them together.

"We mustn't get lost," said Betony, glancing round for a landmark.

Felix waved his compass at her.

Betony grinned. "Hey," she said. "Science. Useful stuff, Felix."

The first thing they collected was a bunch of poppies. The next item on the list was the gum from a tree, which Betony had to climb, though this was no hardship – she was brilliant at it. By the evening, they had all but one of the ingredients.

Chalky had selected a fork in a tree for the nest, which would get the first shaft of sunlight the next morning. Snowdrift went off to look for the last item – the bark of some plant or other, and Betony and Felix started to construct the nest by torchlight. The phoenix was still asleep, its red breast rising and falling in a slow, gentle rhythm.

By moonrise the nest was completed, and Snowdrift had returned with the missing spice, which smelt remarkably like cinnamon. They all snatched a few hours sleep – and then Chalky was nuzzling Felix's ear and saying, "Wake up, human-child – the sun will be up shortly. It's time."

Betony had placed the phoenix in its nest. Then they all retired to a respectful distance, and watched. As the first beam of sunlight hit the nest the bird got to its feet, and turned to face the sun. Then it opened its beak, and started to sing.

It was the most exquisite birdsong Felix had ever heard. Trill after trill, pure and liquid; patterns repeated, re-arranged, elaborated; changes of key, major to minor and back again. As the sun grew hotter the bird's song became more powerful. And then Felix began to think he could hear words in it. He listened – yes, something about life coming out of death. It wasn't a concept he was comfortable with. Then he thought he heard his name. He listened even harder. Something about brazzle feathers. Then he heard Snowdrift's name, and a line about the Water of Life. It sounded more like a warning ... Don't *something something something*. Snowdrift had her ears pricked, and she was concentrating hard. The words almost had a neigh in them, and they were hard to make out. After that came Betony's name, and something about her sister ...

And then, quite suddenly, there was a lick of flame at the edge of the nest. The bird spread its wings, and stood on tiptoe. Its song became even more powerful, and now it was singing about itself ... fire ... feathers ... ashes ... potions ... The nest became an inferno; the flames were everywhere, and the twigs were glowing red. Sparks were shooting up into the sky, and falling to the ground. The flame-bird's song faltered for the first time. Then its feathers caught fire, and the song ceased altogether. The bird collapsed into the funeral pyre, and after a while the flames died away. All that was left was a pile of silver ash. They stood in silence for a while.

"I bet Agrimony's never seen *that*," said Betony.

"Flippant child," admonished Snowdrift. "The flame-bird had messages for all of us, if we had ears to hear them."

"Hmm," said Betony. "I'm not sure mine was based on much evidence, to be honest."

Snowdrift looked really angry. "The flame-bird told you

that your sister loves you, but you can't expect her to replace your mother," she said.

Betony made a face. Then she said, "What message did she have for *you*?"

"Something rather more worrying," said Snowdrift. "She told me that Silvershank took a new remedy for an eye infection, called the Water of Life, and that was what killed him."

"And what's even more worrying," said Chalky, "is that the flame-bird took something itself, for that cracked beak."

"My message was about brazzle feathers," said Felix.

Chalky snorted. "You're about as likely to find one of those as you are to find an unattended crock of gold in Tiratattle."

"Talking of which," said Snowdrift, "we ought to be there tomorrow."

Betony's eyes lit up, and she started to count the coins she had in her purse. "Shopping," she said. "I'm going to have a spending spree."

Felix felt in his own pocket. What use were Costa Rican notes going to be here? How was he going to be able to buy his potion, assuming there was a suitable one? He looked at Betony.

She bit her lip. Then she said, "I'll only have my spending spree after we've bought your medicine."

Felix felt like hugging her.

Tansy dismounted, and dodged out of the way as the fire-breather exhaled a great puff of smoke. She made her way to Grisette's, and banged on the door.

"Is Betony here?" she asked.

"Betony? No. Should she be?"

"I told her to come here."

"Did you?" Grisette looked faintly annoyed. "She's probably staying with one of her friends." She walked to the foot of the elegant rope ladder and shouted, "Agrimony! Was Betony at school today?"

A pert little face appeared over the smooth bevelled edge of the platform. "Betony?" queried Agrimony. "I haven't seen Betony for days."

"Come down here, child."

Agrimony climbed down the ladder, and joined them. "No one's seen Betony since the day you left," she said. "We all thought she'd gone with you."

Tansy took a deep breath, and told Grisette and Agrimony everything that had happened.

Agrimony's face darkened. "It *can't* be true," she said. "Not *Betony*, of all people. It wouldn't be fair."

"What do you mean?"

"She doesn't *deserve* to meet a real live mythical being. She doesn't do her homework, she plays truant, and when she *does* go to school she mucks around."

"Agrimony!" said Grisette, shocked. "Tansy is really upset, and saying things like that doesn't help."

"I don't care," said Agrimony, and she stormed off.

"If I were you," said Grisette to Tansy, "I'd pay the brittlehorns a visit. It's a long shot, but they might know something."

Ramson sat in his cell, twiddling his thumbs. Everything was grey in there; the stone walls, the stone floor, the stone ceiling. The only other occupant was even dressed in grey – a diggeluck, who was snoring louder than a fire-breather. He didn't look terribly well, either. His face was purple and blotchy, and he had some sort of rash on his arms. Ramson hoped whatever it was wasn't catching. He didn't have any of his herbs with him, and the sickle had been confiscated as evidence. If only he hadn't polished it like that the previous day. He knew the punishment for murder. The guild representative would order that he be burned at the stake, and his ashes would be used as fertiliser. The jail had a thriving kitchen garden.

The diggeluck rolled over on his bench, and fell on to the floor. He opened his eyes, and stared at Ramson. "Who are you, youngster?" he asked.

"Ramson," said Ramson irritably. "You?"

"Progg. Why are you here?"

"They think I murdered a couple of ragamuckies, but I didn't."

"Wouldn't blame you if you had," said Progg. "You can't trust ragamuckies."

"Why are you here, then?"

Progg looked suddenly evasive. Then he said, "Ever met a japegrin called Snakeweed?"

"Yes," said Ramson. "Why?"

"He's bad news," said the diggeluck. "He's got a couple of sinistrom pebbles."

Ramson's eyes widened. "You're kidding."

Progg shook his head. "And he's doing seriously unethical stuff with potions."

Ramson leaned forward. "Tell me more," he said.

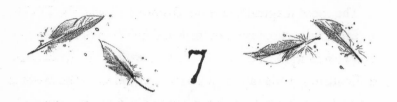

7

Ironclaw sat on the peak of Tromm Fell, in a thoughtful mood. He'd just spent a few happy hours playing with imaginary numbers, and then he'd noticed a little sprig of bloodwort on the ground. He had a vague recollection that he'd picked it for someone, but he couldn't quite remember who. He let his mind wander on to transcendental numbers. He liked trifles, and he remembered reciting one of them to someone. Now who could that have been? He looked at the sprig of bloodwort again. Oh yes; he'd been about to demonstrate his ability to detect poisons, so that he could check whether he was awake or not. He was quite certain he was awake now, and the bloodwort was real enough.

Then he remembered the torch. The torch had been really interesting; it hadn't been magic at all, it had been *science*. He'd met a mythical being, a human child. And he'd asked the boy to wait for him, but had forgotten to go back. How stupid was that? He'd missed the most wonderful chance to find out about another world's mathematics. Mind you, the boy must have got here somehow.

The most magical place on Tromm Fell was the Divide, and that was where the boy had said he'd appeared. He flew over to it, and landed with his feet on either side. It was a bit difficult to get his tail to lie in the right place – the tassel at the end of it seemed to have a mind of its own, but finally he managed it. What did you have to do, mutter a spell or something? He couldn't think of one that was appropriate. Something to do with dimensions would be along the right lines, but he didn't know of any. Then he had an idea. Supposing he could *calculate* the right spell? Supposing it didn't consist of words at all, but numbers? Numbers could be real, rational, irrational, complex, imaginary, transcendental ... He fluffed out his feathers, feeling really excited. This could take him months; it would be the most enormous fun. He needed to clear a really big piece of ground, so that he could scratch his theories in the dust. He flew a little way down the hill, selected a hollow that wouldn't get too much interference from the wind, and started to smooth it over with his wings. He hadn't had a really good project like this for ages.

Betony walked into Drokking, the last village they would encounter before Tiratattle. There were japegrins all over the place; this was a residential village for those who worked in the town. Nobody seemed very interested in her toadstools, even though the ones in the shops were selling at quite ridiculous prices. After an hour she'd only sold a quarter of her stock, and her customers had been strangely furtive. She was feeling fed up.

"I'll have *that* one," said a voice. She turned to see a japegrin standing in front of her.

"Just *one?*" said Betony miserably.

"Only kidding," said the japegrin. "I'll take the lot."

They haggled for a while, and finally arrived at a price that both would accept.

"I haven't seen you around here before," said the japegrin, handing over some unfamiliar coins. "Your accent is pure Geddon, and your hair's ... well, a bit straight, isn't it?"

The coins were very cold. Too cold ... and wet. She looked at them. They were melting away.

The japegrin burst out laughing.

"Give me back my toadstools," demanded Betony.

"It was a joke," said the japegrin, handing over some proper coins. "Lighten up. How did you get here, anyway? Geddon's a long way away." Then he noticed a long white hair on Betony's sleeve, and picked it off. "That came from a brittlehorn's mane, if I'm not mistaken," he said. "You get more interesting by the minute."

Betony picked up her rucksack. "Time I was off," she said.

"Not so fast," said the japegrin. "If you've been riding a brittlehorn you're not just any old tangle-child, are you?"

"I don't know where that hair came from," lied Betony.

"Perhaps it stuck to me when I was having a nap in the woods."

"There aren't any brittlehorns in the woods round here," said the japegrin, his green eyes narrowing slightly. "I'd like to get to know you a bit better."

Not if I can help it, thought Betony. She took a deep breath, and then she turned and ran. When she was certain she'd got away she went into a shop, bought some bread and cheese for supper, and headed back to the woods as fast as she could.

"Excuse me," said a lickit with an unsavoury smile. "You haven't seen an unfamiliar tangle-child here in Drokking, have you? I'm a truant officer, and I'm tracking down a young female from Geddon."

The stallholder shook his head. There was something a bit odd about this lickit. Its white gown was clean for one thing; lickits were usually spattered with splashes of rainbow-icing or stained with peribott, and there was something almost carnivorous about its smile. Predatory.

"*I* have," said a japegrin who was in the process of selling the stallholder some toadstools. "She ran off when I started asking her questions. Makes sense now, if she was cutting school. But do you know – I could have sworn she had a brittlehorn hair on her sleeve."

"How extraordinary," said the lickit, unexpectedly licking its lips. "Thanks, anyway."

The stallholder looked at the japegrin. "Was it my

imagination, or did that lickit have a powerfully unpleasant smell?"

"I don't think you imagined it," said the japegrin, holding his nose. "And it wasn't burnt sugar, either. Now then, how much are you going to give me for these toadstools?"

The stallholder named a price, which was twice what the japegrin had given Betony.

"Daylight robbery," said the japegrin.

"You're all the same, you japegrins," said the stallholder, who was a ragamucky. "Profit, profit, profit. And you know you're not allowed to sell things on the sly – there's a distribution arrangement for toadstools."

"Do you want them or not?" asked the japegrin.

"Oh, go on then," said the ragamucky.

Betony lit the campfire; they toasted the bread, stuck the cheese on sticks and melted it over the top.

"Where do you think we ought to start looking for medical spells?" asked Felix. He was trying very hard not to get excited, now that they were so close to Tiratattle. But the *maybe … just maybe* thought wouldn't leave him alone.

"I don't know," said Betony, her mouth full of bread and cheese.

"You do realise we're not coming into Tiratattle with you, don't you?" said Snowdrift.

Betony nodded.

"We don't feel very comfortable in towns. We'll drop you

a mile or so from the walls, and then we'll head off back to Geddon."

"We're really grateful," said Felix. "We'd never have got this far without you."

Snowdrift lifted her head and sniffed, and a dreamy expression crossed her face. Chalky glanced at her, and then he did the same. After that he licked his lips, and looked thoughtful.

"What is it?" asked Felix nervously.

"Oats," said Chalky. "I can smell oats."

"What, growing?"

"No," said Snowdrift. "Oats in an oatcake. Somewhere in the direction of the road."

"I'll go and take a look," said Betony, knowing how much brittlehorns loved oatcakes. Perhaps it was a travelling salesman – a lickit was the most likely candidate – and she could buy the brittlehorns some as a thank-you present.

When she got to the road, there was no one in sight. But there was a pile of oatcakes on the verge, just sitting on a leaf-wrapping, completely unattended. She picked them up, and after a moment's hesitation she left a couple of silver coins in their place.

"Hey, party-time!" neighed Chalky, when she returned with them.

"There's only four of us," Felix pointed out.

"There'll be eight by the time we've finished those," said Chalky.

"He'll be seeing double," Betony explained. "Then he'll sing a few brittlehorn songs, and fall asleep."

"Oh," said Felix. "A bit like getting drunk, then."

Betony looked perplexed.

"Never mind," said Felix.

The brittlehorns tucked in straight away, and before long they'd finished the lot. Chalky had been greedier than Snowdrift, and eaten twice the amount she had. He was very cheerful to begin with, and sang them a song about mud wallows, and then another one about grass – then he seemed to get a bit wobbly on his legs, and started to slur his words. Snowdrift went and lay down under a tree.

Chalky lay down as well. "Don't feel too good," he said.

Felix laughed.

Betony glared at him. "What's so funny?"

"That's exactly what happens in my world, when people get drunk."

"It's not what happens here," said Betony. She was looking worried.

Snowdrift lifted her head. "Something odd about those oatcakes," she said. She laid her head down again, and sighed heavily. "My horn aches."

Betony went cold. She could hear Silvershank's voice in her head, saying exactly the same thing. She didn't know what to do. She hadn't been able to do anything to help Silvershank, except give him a drink of water. Panic was rising like bile inside her, and she couldn't stop it.

"What's the matter?" asked Felix, suddenly realising her fear was real.

"They're going to die," whispered Betony. "There was something in the oatcakes. Oh, who would do such a thing? And *why*?"

"Do you think it's that Water of Life stuff the flame-bird sang about?"

Betony shook her head. "I don't know. I don't know what to do. I feel so helpless. If they hadn't offered to bring us here, this would never have happened to them."

Felix went over to Chalky, knelt down beside him and stroked his head.

Chalky opened one eye. "It's not your fault, human child," he said. And then the eye glazed over and fixed in one position, and Felix realised that Chalky was dead. He was stunned. It was so sudden, so shocking, so utterly dreadful. He'd seen dead animals before, but this was different, so different. Chalky had been his *friend*. It was his first real experience of absolute loss. He would never hear that comical whinnying voice again – and the knowledge actually *hurt*, deep inside.

Betony was crouched beside Snowdrift, the tears running down her face. Snowdrift was breathing with difficulty but she managed to say, "It can't be us they want, it must be the human child. Whilst we lived, we protected him. Run, both of you, run for your lives. *Now*."

"We can't just leave you here," said Betony.

"You must. I am not going to survive. Please go." She closed her eyes.

"Snowdrift," cried Betony, "*Snowdrift.*" She put her arms round the brittlehorn's neck, and tried to lift her head. There was no response, although Felix could see that Snowdrift was still breathing – just.

Betony stood up, and wiped her nose with her sleeve. "I think we'd better do as she says."

It was getting dark. "Here," said Betony, taking off her cap and allowing the blonde hair to tumble over her shoulders. "You wear it. It'll hide your ears, and most of your hair; you'll look like a tangle-child from a distance."

"Where are we going?"

"Tiratattle. My brother and sister will be there somewhere, we'll find them and then everything will be all right." But she'd said it with more confidence than she felt, for she couldn't imagine explaining all this to Ramson, and her brother coming up with a remotely sensible solution.

Felix suddenly had the sensation that something was watching him. He peered into the gloom. Were there worrits round here? He squinted harder, and then he saw something move. Something a bit like a dog, but not quite. Something front-heavy, with ears that looked a little too big for it. Something with spots.

"So," said Architrex, emerging from the shadows in his hyena-shape, "this is a human child, is it?"

A faint smell wafted across the glade; not a very pleasant one.

"You're a sinistrom," said Felix, feeling rather pleased with himself at the snap identification. But when he looked at Betony, she'd gone as white as a sheet and her hands were gripping the rucksack as though she wanted to squeeze the life out of it.

"Very good, human," said Architrex.

Vomidor stepped out of the shadows next to him. "Do you want me to dispose of the tangle-child straight away?" he asked Architrex.

"What do you mean?" said Felix.

"We don't need Betony," said Architrex. "We only need you."

Betony was standing as still as a stone, her eyes wide with terror. There seemed to be no colour left in her face at all.

"Well?" asked Vomidor.

"Might as well," said Architrex. "But you can take your time about it, if you like. I'm not in any hurry. Oh, and don't forget to introduce yourself properly." He lay down on the grass, his paws stretched out in front of him like a sphinx.

Vomidor grinned and said, "Vomidor, junior sinistrom grade four, seventy-three disembowelments, twelve cut throats and a beheading, at your service." He went over to a stone, and started to sharpen his claws. "Life has some lovely little touches sometimes, doesn't it, Architrex?" he said. "Fancy *paying* me for poisoned oatcakes. Two silver coins.

You've got to laugh, haven't you?" And he did laugh, long and horribly.

It seemed to have become very dark all of a sudden, and the campfire was dying away. Felix could see the pale shapes of the brittlehorns' bodies lying under the tree. And then Snowdrift raised her head one last time and whispered, "Stone you were, and to stone you will return, for as long as I have breath in my body."

Architrex froze, really sphinx-like now.

Vomidor stopped what he was doing and simply stood there, one leg raised, as still as a statue. He looked odd, unbalanced; it was a position that would be hard to maintain in the normal course of events. His eyes were wide and unblinking – and although there was a slight breeze, not a hair on his coat was moved by it.

"*Run*," said Betony, and she grabbed her rucksack and sprinted off into the woods.

Felix followed her and they blundered through the under-growth, thorns catching at their clothing. He had to watch his footing – there were dead branches and rainwater gullies everywhere, hidden by dead leaves. Eventually they found the road.

"We passed a river earlier," panted Betony, "if we can cross it, they won't be able to track us."

She led the way, her pale hair streaming out behind her. The road was just earth, but it was much easier to run on. The trees on either side were very dense now, and sometimes they met overhead. It was like racing down a tunnel.

Felix kept pace with her for a while, but it was such an effort. He found himself slowing down, there was a pounding in his ears that didn't synchronise with the pounding of his feet, and his chest was beginning to hurt. He wasn't meant to do things like this. Betony reached the river first, and he saw her scramble down the bank and into the water.

"Hurry!" she called. "As soon as Snowdrift dies, they'll be able to move again. Then they'll be after us; they never give up."

He saw her wade out into the middle of the river, and felt a momentary sense of relief that it was just shallow enough to ford. But when he got to the bank himself, he knew he wasn't going to make it. He was so tired, his legs felt like rubber, he could hardly get his breath at all now. He had to stop and put his head between his knees, because he knew that if he didn't, he would pass out. When he lifted his head again Betony was nowhere to be seen, and one of the sinistroms was standing in front of him.

"Good try," said Architrex. "Are you going to come quietly?"

"Go to hell," said Felix.

"Never heard of the place," said Architrex. "Anyway, we're going to Tiratattle."

"*Murderer,*" said Felix.

"Why, thank you," said Architrex. "Now then. I'm sure you don't want me to have to use force, do you?" and he yawned. He wanted to give Felix the impression that this was all a bit of a bore, but he also wanted to give him a really good view of his jaws.

Felix glanced across the river. The other sinistrom had swum to the far side, and was casting around like a hound that had lost the scent.

"He'll find her," said Architrex. "And then he'll disembowel her." He was quite pleased at the horrified expression that passed over Felix's face. "I could always break a few of *your* bones if you like," he said. "That has a wonderfully persuasive effect."

Progg leaned back against the grimy wall of the militia cell, and looked at Ramson. "It's a long story," he said.

"I've nothing better to do," said Ramson.

"I'm a diggeluck," he said, "and diggelucks likes working underground. There's something comforting about a nice muddy tunnel. I were a miner; used to dig for crock-gold. Made a living, but nothing fancy. Anyway, this japegrin offers me a regular wage to work for him, and hand over all the gold I find. Not a bad deal, thinks I, so I says yes. And he takes me to this mine where he's got hundreds of diggelucks working for him, and because there's hundreds they can go really deep, see? And there's more gold down deep. Much more. But it's dusty work because we're using drilling spells, and after a while I realises I'm getting a nasty cough. And then I starts hearing about diggelucks what can't work any more, they're so sick. And I thinks – time to get out, Progg. So I gets out. But the cough don't go away – it gets worse." He coughed violently to demonstrate.

Ramson moved away slightly.

"Well," Progg continued, when he'd got his voice back, "I starts hearing about diggelucks who've died because of this cough, and I gets windy. And then this japegrin looks me up, and he says he's got this new potion that's going to make all the difference. Won't cost you anything, he says – it's on trial. You just got to answer lots of questions, and keep taking it. Fine, says I."

"It all sounds above-board to me," said Ramson.

"So far," said the diggeluck. "Well, I starts taking it like he says, and I answers his questions, and he fills in his forms. Then I gets this itch, and I starts scratching, like. And when I tells him about it he says, 'Nah, that's caused by something else,' and he doesn't write it on his form. And then I gets these blisters – see?"

He rolled up his grubby sleeve a bit further, and Ramson could see red-raw patches of flesh, with scabs in between. "Nasty," said Ramson, moving to the far end of the bench.

"And what's more, the cough don't get any better, but I can see he's putting ticks in little boxes that says I'm improving. I points this out, and he gets cross. Then I tells him I'm not going to take his potion any more, and he just shrugs, and goes. And two moons after that his potion's on sale in the shops. Snakeweed's Cough Mixture, it's called.

Two moons! A potion trial ought to take years."

Ramson nodded. The pair of stone statues in the yard at home were pretty strong evidence that thorough testing was a good idea.

"So I goes to this Snakeweed, and I asks to see the trial documentation. And when he shows it to me, it's all been filled in as though I'd been taking the stuff for years, and there's no side-effects, none whatsoever. So I tells him what I thinks of his researchers, and he says he'll investigate it."

Progg had another good cough, and scratched his arm until it bled. Ramson felt queasy.

"Well, two days later I goes out for a fertle-juice, and when I gets back there's this militia-being standing in my parlour, and he arrests me for stealing gold when I was working in the deep mine. So where is this gold, I asks, and he points to this crock I've never seen before in my life. It's a plant, I says, but he just laughs and carts me off here."

"And you're sure Snakeweed knew about all this, and set you up?"

Progg laughed. "I weren't born yesterday. And then this ragamucky gets shoved in the same cell as me, and she tells me all about this potion for cracked beaks, and how Snakeweed's been selling it to just about anything with wings — apart from fire-breathers, of course, because they don't *have* beaks. But birds is all different, and what works on a triple-head don't work on a flame-bird. The ragamucky gets burnt at the stake, for killing one of Snakeweed's researchers. And after that this lickit gets put in with me, and he's telling me all about this Water of Life stuff that Snakeweed's selling, and how it kills brittlehorns."

"But surely," said Ramson, "if this is the way Snakeweed works, sooner or later everyone's going to know about it. And then they won't buy his stuff any more."

"He's got big plans, has Snakeweed," said Progg. "And like I said earlier, he's got two sinistrom pebbles; he'll use anything to get what he wants. And what he wants to do is sell his rubbish all over the world, and it'll take ages for everyone to cotton on. He'll be a very rich japegrin long before that."

Ramson scratched himself absently on his arm as he mulled it all over. Then he realised what he was doing, and looked at his skin in alarm.

"What I've got isn't catching," said Progg. "What you've got's fleas."

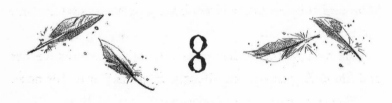

"Surprise!" said Grisette. "A brilliant brainwave for breezing off to the brittlehorns!"

Tansy followed Grisette outside, and her mouth dropped open in astonishment. A small fire-breather was lying curled up on the ground, asleep. He had the deep green colouring of a young male, but he was big enough to wear a saddle that would take four people. "Is he *yours*?" asked Tansy, amazed. She'd never known anyone who could afford the wages of a *personal* fire-breather before.

"Agrimony's father made two crocks of gold last year," said Grisette, "and Agrimony kept pestering him. His name's Sulphur, and we only got him a couple of days ago. I've taken him for a spin round the village, and he's quite nippy."

The fire-breather opened his blood-red eyes, looked at Tansy and yawned. Tansy saw a long row of white teeth. Then he sneezed, and a little puff of smoke left his nostrils.

"You're going to *lend* him to me?" she asked, astonished.

"Your mother was an old friend of mine," said Grisette. "You probably haven't noticed, but I give her a good dusting every time I pass by."

The next morning they went out into the yard together and found Agrimony, stroking the fire-breather on his nose.

"You're up early," said Grisette, surprised.

"I want to go too," said Agrimony. "I've never seen a brittlehorn."

That's not what Betony told *me*, thought Tansy.

"You've got your toadstools to learn," said Grisette.

"I know them all," said Agrimony.

"I think she does, too," said Grisette, with a fond smile.

"I really do want to go, more than anything in the whole world."

"Oh, all right," said Grisette. She turned to Tansy. "You don't mind, do you? She won't be any trouble, she's such a lovely child."

Tansy *did* mind, but she couldn't really say so. "Fine," she said.

They both climbed on to the fire-breather, who got to his feet, made his way out of the yard and trotted down the path. He had to use the main road as a runway, but Agrimony ordered him to toot his warning snort, and everyone got out of the way. As Sulphur made his run and took off, Tansy could see that Agrimony was looking as smug as a lickit with a new oven.

They soared up into the air, and then Sulphur banked so sharply that if Tansy hadn't been wearing her seat-belt she'd have fallen off. They shot off in the direction of Tromm Fell at a ridiculous speed, with Agrimony urging the fire-breather on. With a sinking heart, Tansy realised that Sulphur hadn't completed his training, and it was going to be a very bumpy ride indeed.

When Felix and Architrex reached Tiratattle, Architrex assumed his lickit form. It only took a couple of seconds, and for a moment Felix had no idea what was happening. The sinistrom seemed to collapse into itself, and then re-emerge from the amorphous mess into something resembling a large elf – but an elf dressed from head to toe in white. He then escorted Felix to the conference centre. His grip on Felix's arm was almost brutal, and Felix was sure there would be deep red marks once he let go. He tried to look round once they were inside the town walls, but it was difficult to take everything in with that nagging pain in his elbow. Supposing he shouted for help? He glanced at Architrex's lickit face, and Architrex smiled unpleasantly at him. There was still something of the hyena about him. Felix decided against it, and started trying to identify the people instead. The one carrying a pickaxe and looking miserable had to be a diggeluck. Definitely a gnome – he could imagine it sitting in a suburban garden, fishing. And a ragamucky *was* a brownie – its skin was a deep mahogany, and its clothes were almost the same colour. There were japegrins everywhere, red-haired and pointy-eared. Their green eyes really did squint, and their movements were quick and decisive; pixies. He saw a cart in the distance, but it was being pulled by something completely unfamiliar.

The conference centre appeared to be a cave, but once they were inside it opened out like a vast shopping complex. They walked to something that resembled a lift shaft, and waited. A magic carpet arrived, a little wonky, like something out of a pantomime. They flew down to the sixth level in a series of jerks, with the carpet wittering non-stop about special offers on cures for motion-sickness. When they arrived at Snakeweed's door, Architrex went back to his hyena-shape, nudged Felix with his nose and gave him a shove. Felix opened the door, and went into Snakeweed's office.

A japegrin with brighter red hair than most and a lot of

freckles was sitting behind a desk, reading through some papers. He was wearing a tight-fitting violet suit, and a pointed hat with magenta stars on it. After a moment or two he looked up.

"I've brought the human child, master," said Architrex.

"Where's Vomidor?" The japegrin's silky-smooth voice had an unpleasant after-taste, like cod-liver oil.

Architrex looked evasive.

The japegrin glanced pointedly at a glass of juice on his desk.

Architrex stiffened, and the hairs on the back of his neck stood up. "The tangle-child escaped," he said, his voice developing an ingratiating whine. "Vomidor is tracking her. He'll find her, and —"

Snakeweed looked daggers at him.

Slashes and gashes, thought Architrex, I'd forgotten. I'm meant to be the nasty one, so that Snakeweed can play kindly uncle to the boy. I mustn't let on that Snakeweed was perfectly happy to let us rip Betony to pieces.

"And the brittlehorns are well?"

"Ah," said Architrex, remembering to play his part properly this time. "There was a bit of an accident. The brittlehorns are dead, I'm afraid."

The japegrin tut-tutted, as though this were sad news indeed. "I think you'd better get back out there and help Vomidor, Architrex, before anything nasty happens to the little tangle-child."

"Yes, master," said Architrex, and he went.

"Well, Felix," said the japegrin, "my name is Snakeweed."

"A bit of an accident?" said Felix, holding on to his temper with great difficulty. "Two of the nicest, kindest, noblest creatures I've ever met are dead, and you call it *a bit of an accident*?"

"I believe it was Architrex said that, not me."

"And that's another thing," said Felix, his voice still rising despite his attempts to keep it under control. "How come you're friendly with shadow-beasts?"

"What do you know of them?"

"I've met a worrit."

"Really," said Snakeweed. "Look, I wouldn't say I was *friendly* with Architrex exactly, he's just another employee. Did he give you any bother? Apart from the brittlehorn business, that is."

"He told Vomidor to take his time about killing Betony."

"He wasn't meant to harm her," said Snakeweed, shaking his head. "He exceeded his authority. I shall discipline him."

"What do you want with me?"

"I want to help you, Felix. I help you, you help me. What do you want? I'm very wealthy. Last week I wouldn't have believed in your existence – you're a mythical being. But here you are, large as life, from a world which uses science, not magic. And science interests me a great deal."

"I don't know all that much about it."

"You know a lot more than we do. And if you can tell me

how you got here – well, perhaps we could go to your world together, and I could learn more."

"I don't *know* how I got here," said Felix. "And I certainly don't know how to get back again. If I could, believe me, I would."

"You don't like our world, then?"

"I *do* like your world, actually. Apart from the worrits and the sinistroms. What's bothering me is my parents. They'll be worried sick about me. And there's something else, as well."

"Something else?"

"I'm very ill," said Felix. "I'm not going to live for much longer."

Snakeweed looked sceptical. "You look all right to me."

Felix gritted his teeth. "The brittlehorns made me a potion to keep me going, but it hasn't *cured* me. When I was running away from Architrex the old tiredness came back, and if I hadn't stopped running I'd have passed out again. I used to do that all the time."

"We have hundreds of potions. Perhaps we have one that will do the trick."

"That's why we were coming to Tiratattle in the first place," said Felix, trying really hard not to let the agony of hope overwhelm him again. "You asked me what I wanted, earlier. *That's* what I want. To get better."

"What is the nature of your illness?"

"It's my heart," said Felix.

Snakeweed hesitated. Then he said, "I'll make some enquiries."

But Felix hadn't missed that fleeting reaction. There's nothing he can do, he thought. It was a wasted journey, and the brittlehorns died for nothing.

"You can stay here, in the complex," said Snakeweed. "Have a bath, and put on some clean clothes. Then we'll meet for dinner, and you can tell me all you know about science. And I'll get our best people working on the problem of finding a bridge between your world and ours. There must be one. You must tell them everything that happened to you when you crossed over – every tiny detail. I'm sure we'll find an answer. Sooner or later."

"If it's later it'll be too late for *me*," said Felix.

Betony watched from the top of the tree as Vomidor ran up and down the bank, trying to raise a scent. She felt really pleased with herself – she'd waded downstream a little way until she found a branch that hung over the water, and then she'd hauled herself out and wriggled her way along it. After that she'd climbed as high as she could and spent the night there, knowing the sinistrom would come back.

Vomidor was getting desperate. Now and again he gave a little whine, and once in a while he stopped and stood very still with his ears pricked, listening. Then he'd start the sweep again, up and down, up and down, sniffing at everything. He's so ugly, thought Betony. That out-of-proportion body and that spotty fawn coat. Silly little tail, for such a big creature. His ears are too big, and his eyes are too small, and he smells disgusting. Eventually Vomidor gave up, swam back to the other side of the river, and trotted away.

Betony waited for several hours, but Vomidor didn't return again. So, with much trepidation, she climbed down the tree. Where should she go? Tiratattle wasn't a sensible option; they'd be looking for her, expecting her to try and find Felix. On the other hand, it would take weeks for her to get back to Geddon on foot. She thought wistfully of the brittlehorns, and the hopeful start to the journey. Hope was so important, if you wanted to keep going.

All of a sudden, she wondered how Felix coped. What must it be like, to wake up every morning and think, is this going to be the last sunrise I see, the last breakfast I eat, the last ... the last what? What did he do every day, in his world? She'd asked him a bit about science, and a bit about mythical beasts, but she didn't really know what his life was *like*. He'd mentioned hospitals – what was a hospital? What was a drip? She realised that she'd done most of the talking because he'd been so interested in *her* world. It suddenly occurred to her that this was an escape. There weren't any hospitals and drips over here, he could forget about them. And she'd forgotten about his illness, at the very moment when it had mattered most. She started to walk back in the direction of Tiratattle.

* * *

Ironclaw studied his calculations, and rubbed out a couple of lines. Oh, this was such fun. He'd been at it for several days now, and he'd forgotten to eat for two of them. Then one of his friends, Granitelegs, had come by with a haunch or two, and they'd talked about the Divide and thrashed out a few things over a bucket of fertle-juice. It had been a blinder of an evening.

He added another line, then stepped back and surveyed it. He'd cracked the central question, he was sure of it. It was something to do with balance; if you divided yourself into two, which bit of you did the *me* go into? It couldn't go into both, he was sure about that now. He'd tried to think himself into it, but it just wasn't possible. One consciousness could not become two. The thing about being yourself was that you were one; that was what being an entity *meant*. So if some thing – some set of circumstances – tried to divide your essential self right down the middle, what did it do? It escaped, that's what it did. When the pressure got too much, it escaped right into another dimension entirely. It was like trying to crack a really shiny pebble into two with your beak; the slippery surface would only take so much before it shot out of your grasp with the velocity of a seed exploding out of a pod. That was the why of it – the how of it was going to be rather more tricky.

Presumably, the setting had to remain the same if you wanted to get back to the same place. Within certain parameters, maybe. Standard deviation of particle distribution, perhaps. He thought about the pebble again, and imagined it perched on the Divide. So what other requirements were there? An absolutely equal distribution of the ittybitties that made up the organism, obviously. Ittybitties were the smallest particles you could get – so therefore they were *in*divisible. Plus what? A time-lapse, presumably. Otherwise everyone who crossed the Divide would shoot off into another dimension the second they reached the critical division.

He ruffled his feathers, and scratched his neck with one of his hind feet. What he needed was a spell that did an on-going calculation of the ittybitties with sufficient precision for his purposes. Then he'd need to add that to one that froze the subject for the right amount of time when it was in exactly the right place. It would be a bit like dying, he thought. Everything would have to stop for a moment. So how did you go about calculating someone's ittybitties? Weight would be a factor, and age. Oh yes, he could see a way to solve that one … He wrote a few more lines in the sand, and muttered the spell to himself under his breath. It sounded rather good. Classy, even. Now he needed a freezing mechanism – he'd have to muck around with the odd equation to do that properly.

He was singing raptorial songs to himself when Granitelegs landed on the rock above him, wiping out the last few digits with a flurry of air.

"Whoops," said Granitelegs. "Was it crucial?"

"No," said Ironclaw, writing them in again.

"How's it going?"

"Rather well," said Ironclaw. "Come and have a look."

Granitelegs had a look. "Oh," he said, "it's a balance thing, then."

"It's all about the indivisible self," said Ironclaw.

"A number that can't be divided?" said the other brazzle. "Not possible, surely? Apart from zero."

"Dividing zero by any number is a legitimate operation," said Ironclaw, "although the answer's always zero, naturally. That's by the by, however. I think I can best demonstrate what I'm talking about with a pebble." He looked round, and after a few trials and errors selected a particularly smooth black pebble with a faint sheen to it that seemed to say, *choose me*. "If I place this in my beak and try to crack it," he said, placing it in his beak, "wenner pwesha gesh too muth it thoots ..."

"Take it out," said Granitelegs, "you sound like a worrit."

Ironclaw removed the pebble and completed his proposition. Then he put the pebble back in his beak and crunched down on it, hard.

Three things happened simultaneously.

The shiny black pebble, as predicted, shot out of his beak and landed several yards away.

A crack appeared in Ironclaw's beak, and he put his head under his wing and yowled with pain.

A sinistrom began to materialise.

*   *   *

Betony reached Tiratattle the next morning. She'd given Felix her cap and she was aware that she was attracting glances, so the first thing she did when she got inside the walls was to buy another. This meant that she had very little money left, and the prices of everything were sky-high. Tiratattle wasn't quite what she'd expected. It seemed to be divided into different bits; diggelucks were more numerous in one area, lickits in another. The lickit district smelt delicious, spicy and sugary and fruity, mixed with the scent of burning charcoal. Little puffs of steam came out of windows and doors, and lickits bustled past with trays of sweets on their heads. She'd assumed that everyone was wealthy in Tiratattle, but it slowly became obvious that this wasn't the case. Some areas were really run-down, particularly the raga-mucky quarter; others were a lot more affluent, the japegrin precinct especially. The streets there were wide and clean, and there were some hideously expensive purple ensembles in the shops. After several attempts she finally found a cheap tree hotel that had a vacancy. It was called Dozover, and it was on the border of the ragamucky and japegrin areas. She paid her deposit, and wondered how she was going to get the balance.

"You're lucky to get this," said the innkeeper. "There's one of those conference things going on, and everywhere's booked up. Mind you, there's a story to this room. The being who had it before you was arrested for murder."

Betony's eyes widened.

"Killed two ragamuckies, he did. Went along to a crystal ball parlour, and accused them of cheating him. Disembowelled them with his sickle. The very same sickle I saw him cleaning afterwards. In fact ..." She crossed the room, and picked something up from the floor. "Look at that," she said. "It's the sheath."

Betony looked. It was just like Ramson's, made of polished woods of two different colours. She looked closer – and there was that little nick in it, when she'd tried to draw the sickle out herself, when she'd been a lot younger. It had been too heavy for her, and she'd dropped it on the sheath. Her brother a murderer? Ridiculous. He was the most squeamish person she knew. She remembered him practising for a spelling test, when he'd been trying to turn a toadstool into a bar of soap. What he got was a creepy-biter, which made a bee-line for Tansy's big toe. Tansy had screamed like a vamprey as the creepy-biter bit her, and their father had come running. He stamped on it immediately, and then went off to get a healing salve. Ramson took one look at Tansy's toe, and went very pale. Then his eyes drifted across to the green and red jelly-mess spread on the ground, and he fainted.

"Left all his stuff here," said the innkeeper, "apart from the sickle, of course. That's evidence. I'll have to chuck the rest out – those crucibles aren't any use to anyone, and the herbs are, quite frankly, second-rate."

Betony picked up the bag of herbs and looked at it. It

held the ingredients for the dental reconstruction remedy. "Did he stay here on his own?" she asked.

"No – but his sister left after an argument, and went home."

"Home?"

"Geddon. You may not have heard of it – tiny place, right out in the back of beyond."

"So where is he now?"

"In jail. They'll burn him at the stake tomorrow, I expect. They usually do burnings on a Tuesday."

Just when you think life can't get any worse, thought Betony, it does. I wonder if the jail allows visitors? Well, there's only one way to find out. She climbed down the rope ladder, and headed for the town centre.

9

Although the jail was a grim stone building it had a lovely garden, full of luscious fruits and vegetables and bright flowers.

Betony had to wait for a few minutes in the guardroom. There was a brazier burning in the corner, although what was being cooked over it was anybody's guess. The walls were splashed with something that looked disturbingly like dried blood, and there was a dark stain on the floor. Eventually the guard came back, and she was taken to Ramson's cell.

Ramson was so shocked to see her that his legs gave way and he sat down heavily on the bench, next to the most disgusting-looking diggeluck Betony had ever seen. "How on earth did you get here?" he asked.

"On a brittlehorn," said Betony.

Ramson put his head in his hands. "It was all true, then," he said. "All true."

"What was all true?"

"What the ragamucky told me. I didn't believe her. Tansy did, though, and she's gone back to Geddon. She doesn't know I've been arrested."

"What happened?"

"I discovered the bodies and the militia discovered *me*, standing there. And I'd cleaned my sickle." He looked at her. "The rest of it's true as well, I suppose? The human child?"

"His name's Felix," said Betony, and she told him the whole story.

"I bet I knows who's behind it all," said a voice.

Betony had forgotten all about the diggeluck.

"I told you Snakeweed had some sinistrom stones, didn't I?" said Progg, sitting up. "Is this human child for real?"

Betony nodded.

"And can he do science, like?"

Betony nodded again. She opened her rucksack to take out the torch for a demonstration, then she remembered that Felix had kept it in his pocket. She looked for something else to show them, and came across Felix's reading book. It didn't look quite like a tangle-book, so she gave it to her brother whilst she searched for the biro. When she found the biro, she scribbled in the margin to show him how it worked.

Progg was seriously impressed. "Well, there you are then. Snakeweed would see your Felix as the best money-making idea he'd come across for a long time. Scientific cures. I can see it on the labels, nice red lettering, picture of a human being next to it. That's where you go looking for him. In the conference centre."

There was a loud knock at the door, and Betony's visit was at an end.

Felix lay on his back in warm frothy water. The bath was as big as a small swimming pool, and bore more of a resemblance to a Roman bath than anything else. There were statues of mythical creatures in the alcoves – except they weren't mythical creatures, were they? They were historical figures. He carried on floating on his back, reading the inscriptions on the statues. There was a marble brazzle, large as life, perched on a rock. Underneath it was a brass plaque, which read:

Flintfeather, mathematician and apothecary to the king,
407–413.
In our feathers lies our strength.

On the matching plinth on the other side was a bird he didn't recognise at all; it had three heads. The plaque there read:

Trigon, most terrible scourge in the province of Tiratattle,
670–684.
Killed by Gean the Great.

Felix turned over, and tried to doggie-paddle through the azure water to the steps at the side. He managed a couple of metres – the furthest he'd ever swum – and he felt elated. Neatly folded on a bench was the creamiest, fluffiest towel he had ever seen. When he climbed out of the water the towel lifted itself immediately, flew through the air like a plastic bag caught in a gust of wind, and wrapped its soft warmth around him.

One of the things Felix had missed about his own world was the creature comforts. He'd assumed they just didn't exist over here, but he was obviously wrong. Camping with Betony had been tremendous fun, but it wasn't exactly luxurious. Felix knew that when he was feeling low – tired, the whole illness thing – that was the time when he really appreciated being pampered. And this was pampering beyond belief.

The towel dried him, gently and thoroughly – then it flew over to a laundry basket, lifted the lid, and popped itself inside. Felix smiled. When he turned round there was a pile of clean clothes waiting for him, and his old clothes were nowhere to be seen. This wouldn't have bothered him too much, apart from one thing – the compass and the torch had been in his trouser pocket. Betony, presumably, still had the other things in her rucksack.

They were tangle-folk clothes, and, naturally, they were all emerald green. As Felix put them on, each item adjusted itself to his size. The sleeves of the tunic shrank as soon as he put it on, stopping at his wrists. The cap cuddled his head until it was just the right shape, and the shoes did something similar. He glanced at himself in one of the mirrors on the wall. "Very nice," said the mirror. "The hair's wrong though. Would you like it bleached?"

Felix thought about it. Although he was quite happy with his hair the colour it was – a nondescript mid-brown – over here it stood out like a sore thumb. If he wanted to escape – although, right at this moment, it wasn't the thought that was uppermost in his mind – blending in with the other tangle-folk wouldn't be such a bad idea. His eyes were the wrong colour as well, of course – but they weren't so noticeable, and his ears were now covered by the cap. "OK," he said.

"Take off the cap, then."

He took off the cap, and watched the procedure in the mirror. First of all the tips got lighter – the brown just seemed to leach away. Then the blondness worked its way up each hair towards the root, until his hair was the same colour as Betony's. He blinked at himself. It was going to take some getting used to.

A ragamucky appeared in the doorway. "If you're ready to eat, Felix, your meal is waiting."

Felix followed her into another room. Snakeweed was sitting at the far end of a long table, which was covered with silver dishes, crystal glasses, and fine white porcelain.

Just before the ragamucky left, she sidled up to Felix and whispered, "You can be as messy as you like in your room, because there's nothing I'd like better than to clean it for you."

So brownies really do like doing housework for humans, thought Felix. He sat down.

"Welcome," said Snakeweed, pouring him a glass of something amber-coloured and sweet.

The meal was just as magical as the bath. All his favourite dishes – how did they *know*? Things he thought he'd never eat again – a prawn starter, then roast beef and Yorkshire pudding; and then, miraculously, strawberries and cream.

Snakeweed laughed. "We found the recipes in a book of myths and legends," he said. "The prawns were easy – they're the larvae of creepy-biters."

Now don't be silly, said Felix to himself. There's nothing wrong with eating insects – witchetty grubs are considered to be a delicacy among Australian aboriginals.

"What do you reckon on the strawberries?" asked Snakeweed.

"Perfect," said Felix.

"Magic, of course," said Snakeweed. "Each one was originally a lickit toe. We always cut off their toes before we execute them."

Felix blanched.

Snakeweed laughed. "Only joking." Then he placed the torch and the compass on the table and said, "Tell me the purpose of these scientific instruments, and show me how they work."

Although Felix didn't exactly *like* Snakeweed, co-operation might be the only way he had of getting back to his own world. He picked up the torch. "It's operated by batteries," he explained, unscrewing the end and emptying them on to the table. "They store something called electricity, which powers the light. The bulb ..." He unscrewed the other end, and showed it to Snakeweed. "It has something called a filament, which glows when electrical energy passes through it. The only other important thing is the switch – this thing – which breaks the current in this position, and re-connects it in the other position." Then he put the torch back together, and switched it on. Nothing happened. He closed his eyes, hoping he simply hadn't tightened everything up sufficiently. Then he tried again. Still nothing. "I think the batteries have run out," he said.

Snakeweed didn't say anything.

Felix picked up the compass. "This is a direction-finder," he said. "This arrow always points north – to the pole." But the needle was swinging around all over the place, refusing to settle into any one position. "Maybe it's because we're underground," said Felix. "Or perhaps there's some other magnetic force that's preventing it doing its job properly. We ought to try it outside."

"I see," said Snakeweed. Then he stood up, walked over to Felix and wrenched off the green cap. He seized Felix's head in his hands, turning it this way and that, and peering at his ears. "A very neat job," he said. "No scars at all."

He let go, and Felix just stared at him.

"You're not a human being at all, are you?" said Snakeweed. "I don't know how you've managed to change your eye colour, but your hair's back to normal now, isn't it? Someone's been playing a joke on me. Japegrins are very fond of practical jokes. Well, I'm even better at them. I think burning you at the stake would be most diverting."

"I *am* a human being," said Felix desperately.

"Prove it," said Snakeweed.

Felix's mind went blank. What on earth could he do that was scientific? He couldn't think of a single thing.

"You've got until tomorrow," said Snakeweed. "I'm a busy being." He clicked his fingers, and a lickit entered. "Take this creature to the jail," he said. "And if he can't show me any science by the morning, burn him with the others. And while you're there, pick up the fruit I ordered." He glanced at the objects on the table; then, with a sweep of his arm, he knocked them to the floor. "And take your rubbish with you," he sneered.

Felix picked up the torch and the compass, and the lickit escorted him to the magic carpet, holding his arm in a vice-like grip. Was it a lickit – or a sinistrom? Its smell was different though, it reminded him of marzipan. As they waited for the carpet to descend, Felix noticed that his compass was going really berserk now. The carpet shaft wasn't as well-finished as the rest of the complex, and there were a number of stones lying at the bottom. Felix bent down on the pretext of adjusting the buckle of his new shoes, and picked one up. The compass-needle swung round and pointed to it immediately. It's magnetic rock, thought Felix, no wonder the instrument wasn't working properly. He tried to explain this to the lickit, so that they could go back and tell Snakeweed, but the lickit simply laughed. Felix was going to have his night in jail, it seemed, but at least he now had hopes of convincing Snakeweed of his humanity the following day.

Granitelegs stared as the sinistrom solidified into its four-legged shape. Ironclaw still had his head under his wing, although his yowls had subsided to whimpers.

"Ironclaw," whispered Granitelegs, "stop being such a wimp for a moment and look at this."

Ironclaw's head emerged from an untidy mess of fluffed-out feathers. His beak was badly cracked, and the end of it was loose and wobbled. Granitelegs reflected that maybe his friend wasn't over-reacting after all.

"What is your pleasure, master?" inquired the sinistrom.

Ironclaw glanced round. Then he realised that the sinistrom was talking to *him*. Well, *peck me where it hurts*, he thought, I don't want to be in charge of one of these.

"Get rid of it," hissed Granitelegs.

Ironclaw wasn't at all sure how this could be accomplished. His beak was hurting too much for him to think as logically as he would have liked. He needed the pebble, but where was it? There were lots of pebbles up here on the Divide. His eye fell on the sprig of bloodwort. It was very effective on worrits – how would it cope with a sinistrom? There was only one way to find out. He picked it up in one of his talons – he really didn't feel his beak could cope with it at the moment – and took off. The sinistrom backed away. But Ironclaw could manoeuvre far more easily in the air, and he dropped the little piece of bloodwort right on top of the sinistrom. The shadow-beast froze, one paw slightly raised.

Well, thought Ironclaw, I didn't expect *that*. He landed next to Granitelegs, feeling pleased with himself. The pain was subsiding slightly, but only slightly.

Granitelegs said, "If you wanted an opportunity to try out your dividing spell, I think you've just found the perfect subject."

Ironclaw looked at Granitelegs. "Good thinking," he said. "Help me move him onto the Divide, then."

Neither of the brazzles particularly wanted to touch the sinistrom, even as a statue. After a lot of, "After you," and "No, after *you*," they finally picked it up between them, and placed it over the Divide. Ironclaw took a deep breath and recited his spell, the numbers tumbling out like tiny gems. It still sounded classy. The sinistrom moved a fraction to the right, and then froze again. There was a pause of about a second, which seemed to take for ever, and then – the shadow-beast simply wasn't there any more.

"Two birds with one stone," said Granitelegs. "Though to be honest, I loathe that phrase. Congratulations, Ironclaw. A very neat piece of work."

Ironclaw felt a sudden need to preen himself. The trouble was, his beak was still hurting far too much to even attempt it.

"You ought to get that seen to," said Granitelegs. "Apparently there's a new potion they've invented, somewhere over Tiratattle way. Works really quickly."

"Expensive?"

"Don't be such a skinflint," said Granitelegs. "We've got enough gold up here to buy Tiratattle itself."

The pain in Ironclaw's beak had dulled to an ache that he knew was going to interfere with his concentration. "It's a long flight," he said grumpily.

"The sooner you're off, the sooner you'll be back," said Granitelegs.

Somewhat reluctantly, Ironclaw raided one of his crocks and filled a leg-bag with gold coins. Then he flew off into the sunset.

The sinistrom shook himself, and glanced round. Weird. This didn't look like Tromm Fell at all. And what exactly had happened to him? It had been a bit like going in and out of your pebble at a hundred and sixty-nine times the normal speed – there one minute, gone the next, and then *here*. He felt as though something had tried to cut him in two with a blunt blade; but instead of being cut, he'd been *squeezed*,

squeezed beyond endurance. He sniffed himself all over, but there was no evidence of any physical damage. He thought about it. Perhaps it was more in the nature of a mental squeezing, so he checked himself over there, too. Name: Grimspite. Age: One hundred and eleven. Rank: Junior sinistrom, grade seven. That all seemed to be in order. He licked himself, but he still tasted the same.

Where was his master? He listened, but all he could hear was the drone of insects. He sniffed the air. The odours were strange and unnerving, and there was no smell of brazzle at all. He had another good look round, but he couldn't see Ironclaw anywhere. What was a sinistrom to do without a master? The prospect was most alarming. He'd have to make his own decisions. He'd never done that; he'd always done precisely as he'd been told. That was what sinistroms did.

He sat down and scratched himself behind the ear. How did you go about making a decision? Did you have to do a lot of thinking – or did it happen quite quickly, like a bolt of lightning? Was it difficult, or was it easy? What happened when two things were equally balanced, how did you opt for one rather than the other?

He couldn't stay here indefinitely. It was much hotter than it had been on Tromm Fell, and he would get thirsty before long. He couldn't see a stream anywhere, so he'd have to go and look for one. But which way? How did you decide, if you didn't have a mission? His missions in the past had always been of a violent nature. Threatening things, torturing things, burning things, killing things. That was how you decided which way you were going to go – in the direction of your victim. But he didn't have a victim.

Then he noticed a strange piece of wood, fixed to a post. He went over to it. There was some sort of diagram on it, and a red arrow with some gobbledegook printed on it. Underneath were some rather more sensible words, which said: *You Are Here*. To begin with, he didn't see the point. He *knew* he was here, he didn't need a sign to tell him. Then he realised that the little black line represented the Divide, although it wasn't the same Divide as the one on Tromm Fell. After that he identified two paths leading away in opposite directions. It *would* have to be two, wouldn't it? How was he to decide between them? Then he noticed a little blue squiggle – a stream, maybe? He wanted a drink, and a stream was just the job. The concept of pleasing himself was a new one on him, sort of scary and exciting at the same time. Hey, he thought, I just made a decision. I. Me. Grimspite.

It suddenly occurred to him to wonder which world this might actually be. He'd heard of other dimensions, but like most people, he hadn't really believed in them. Divides were strongly magical places, though. Maybe that *was* the answer. He'd crossed over into another world, and been changed somehow in the process.

He trotted off down the path, feeling on top of the world.

The last time he'd felt as good as this was when he'd just disembowelled something.

Granitelegs sat on the rock, looking at Ironclaw's calculations. He understood most of them, but some bits of it were quite beyond him. Ironclaw always had been cleverer than him, much as it pained him to admit it. His own work with the volume of eggs and the moving of rocks paled into insignificance beside this. He wondered what sort of world the sinistrom had ended up in. Did they use thirteen as a number base? Thirteen was such an important number in spells that it would make sense, despite Ironclaw's assertion that numbers like eleventy-three lacked elegance. The sinistrom wouldn't be interested; all they cared about was ripping things apart. What a waste.

A breeze ruffled his feathers, and he glanced up at the sky. There were clouds on the horizon. This was unusual at this time of year, and he felt vaguely uneasy. Then he started to think about the square root of minus one having two solutions, and he forgot all about the weather. A clap of thunder made him jump. The sky had gone very dark all of a sudden, and then he felt the first raindrop. Within seconds the rain was pouring down, and Ironclaw's calculations had turned to mud.

Felix walked along the dim corridors of the jail, escorted by the lickit. Faces peered at him through iron bars; there were some creatures he recognised, like tangle-folk and even a few japegrins, but there were others that were totally unfamiliar. Eventually, they came to a cell at the end of a long passageway; the lickit muttered a few words, and the door opened. He pushed Felix inside, slammed the door shut again, and recited what was presumably a closing spell as the words were followed by a metallic click.

The cell was already occupied. A creature covered with revolting sores and scabs and dressed in grey was lying on a bench. Sitting next to him was someone who reminded Felix of a gangly male version of Betony.

"Hello," he said. "My name's Ramson. What's yours?"

"*Ramson?*" said Felix. "Is that a common name?"

"Fairly," said Ramson, looking slightly perplexed.

"Do you have a sister called Betony?"

"Yes."

"I'm Felix," said Felix.

The creature that had been lying down suddenly sat up. "I'm Progg," he said. "So what have you done to upset the high and mighty Snakeweed?"

"It's a long story," said Felix.

"I'm all ears," said Progg.

And he is, Felix thought; his ears are the biggest I've ever seen on something with a vaguely human form. Wow, I've never spoken to a gnome before. He sat down on the floor and filled them in on everything, from his illness to the things that had happened since he'd lost touch with Betony.

Then Ramson explained what had happened to *him*, and for good measure Progg added his own tale afterwards.

"We really need to get out of here, don't we?" said Felix.

"Been saying that for months," said Progg. "There's a closing spell on the door, though. Moves the lock across."

Felix went and looked at it. Then he noticed that the compass needle had gone crazy again. It's magnetic, he thought. A magnetic lock. The spell must reverse the poles somehow. And then he remembered the piece of rock he'd picked up in the carpet-shaft. It was worth a try. He took it out of his pocket, and held it up to the door. Nothing happened. So he turned it the other way round, and suddenly there was that metallic click again. He pushed the door very gently, and it opened an inch or two. Then he heard footsteps outside, so he shut it again. The footsteps passed by.

"Did I just see what I thought I saw?" said Progg.

Felix grinned. "It's a magnetic lock. We can leave any time we like."

"Science," said Progg, in an awe-struck voice. "To think I'd live to see that."

"We'd better wait for night-time," said Ramson. "Less chance of being spotted. We'll head for where Betony's staying, and then decide what to do. Once they know you've got away, they'll be watching the fire-breather terminal. But there's hope now." He patted Felix on the shoulder.

Hope. Felix swallowed. There didn't seem to be much hope for *him*, not in the long term.

"I knows what you ought to be doing about your illness," said Progg suddenly. "Forget all these new-fangled remedies of Snakeweed's. You ought to go to the library in Andria, and see if there's anything of any use there. Come to think of it, so should I."

"How are we going to get to Andria without a fire-breather?" said Ramson.

"We'll face that one when we comes to it," said Progg.

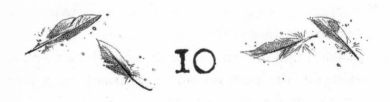

10

Sulphur executed a knife-like turn that left Tansy's stomach behind, and dropped like a stone into the brittlehorns' valley. He braked at the last moment, landed awkwardly, and only just kept his footing.

"Wow," said Agrimony, "that was really exciting."

No it wasn't, thought Tansy, it was totally irresponsible. The fire-breather let out a puff of smoke and lay down to let them dismount.

The valley was very quiet. A group of brittlehorns were standing by a cave, heads down, looking thoroughly dejected. One of them raised his head and looked at her. "What do you want?" he asked.

Tansy was a little taken aback; brittlehorns had impeccable manners. She explained about being Betony's sister, and was even more taken aback when this was not well-received.

"I'm Milklegs," said the brittlehorn. "I knew it was a bad idea; told the leader as much."

"What was a bad idea?"

"Using a brittlehorn as a beast of burden, and going to Tiratattle."

"Betony's in *Tiratattle*?"

Milklegs snorted. "And Snowdrift and Chalky are dead as a result of it. The leader saw it all in the pool."

"You can use the pool like a crystal ball?"

"Only when the weather's right," said Milklegs.

"Could you try it for me now?"

The brittlehorn shook his head. "There's a thunderstorm on the way. And anyhow, we're all in mourning, and it wouldn't be right."

"Can I speak to the leader, then?"

Milklegs shrugged.

Tansy took this as a yes, and went over to the leader. He was standing there with his eyes shut. Tansy cleared her throat.

The leader opened one eye. "Yes?"

Tansy explained everything all over again.

The leader sighed and said, "What is the world coming to."

Tansy waited.

Eventually he sighed heavily again and said, "They were poisoned by sinistroms."

"Who were?"

"Snowdrift and Chalky."

Sinistroms. An image of the one on the runway at Tiratattle flashed through Tansy's mind. It was too much of a coincidence. "What about Betony?"

"Betony?" said the leader.

Tansy wanted to scream. "Betony. My sister."

"Ah. The tangle-child. She got away. But the boy didn't."

"He was killed too?"

"No idea."

Tansy could see that she wasn't going to learn anything further. She would either have to find a way of contacting Ramson, or go back to Tiratattle herself. She stood there, twiddling her tangles between her fingers, wondering what to do.

"My mother won't mind if you keep Sulphur a bit longer," said Agrimony. "She'd say go, I know she would."

If I go straight to Tiratattle, thought Tansy, I'll have to take Agrimony with me.

"I won't be any bother," said Agrimony. "I can help look for Betony."

Agrimony just wants a trip to Tiratattle, thought Tansy. She isn't worried about Betony in the slightest. But I don't have any choice; I'll have to take her. I can't leave her here – the brittlehorns are all in mourning, and I've intruded too much already.

"All right," she said. "But I'm driving this time."

"Do you know how?" asked Agrimony.

"I can give instructions as well as anyone else," said Tansy acidly, "and better than some."

Midnight. Felix unlocked the door of the cell, and he,

Ramson and Progg tiptoed out and made their way down the corridor. Felix could hear creatures snoring as they passed; the deep rumble of diggelucks, and the squeaky snuffles of lickits. Now and again someone cried out in a dream, and once they heard a thump as someone presumably fell off their bench.

"There's a guardroom at the entrance," whispered Progg. "We'll have to be very careful."

The guardroom was lit with a brazier. The lickit in charge was roasting some nuts and shaking them about in a battered metal container, his shadow large and black against the wall. This was good, as the noise masked the sound of their footsteps. They crept past, hoping that the lickit wouldn't suddenly decide to look up. He didn't, but a few seconds later Progg made a sort of strangled sound in his throat. Felix glanced at him in alarm, and realised that Progg was trying to stifle a coughing fit. Progg shook his head; it was clear that he couldn't contain the cough for much longer. He waved a hand at them, telling them to run, and then he doubled over. The coughs came out one after the other like machine-gun fire, and the lickit was on his feet and out of the door and running towards them. As they hesitated the lickit raised a crossbow, and fired.

Progg went down like a sack of potatoes, dead before he hit the floor, and the lickit stopped to reload. Poor old Progg, thought Felix. I've encountered more death here than I ever did in my own world. The only corpse I ever saw before was a boy who died in the bed next to me, in hospital. He shivered.

Ramson seized Felix by the arm, and the two of them raced across the entrance lobby, and out into the night. A few seconds later, an unearthly wail filled the air. "It's the alarm," panted Ramson. "The guard won't leave the jail, but there will be others looking for us within minutes."

They sprinted down the road, and turned off into a side-street. Felix knew he couldn't keep this sort of speed up for very long.

They came to a canal, but there was no bridge over it. The ground was littered with gnawed bones and candle stubs. "Oh *bites and stings*," said Ramson, "I could have sworn this was the right direction."

Felix suddenly remembered his compass. Although he didn't know where they were going, at least he could make sure they didn't travel in a circle. "This way," he said, and they jogged, a little more slowly, along the bank of the canal. They weren't going directly away from the jail any more, but it was better than doubling back without realising it. The piles of rubbish increased the further they went, and the water began to smell stagnant and horrible. Felix noticed something white floating in the scummy water, but he didn't look too closely. Then some sort of creature raised its snout above the surface, and the floating object disappeared. A series of bubbles popped up, lingering a moment before they burst. The smells got worse.

Eventually, they did come to a bridge, and Ramson said, "The crystal ball parlour was *that* way, so Dozover – can you *believe* it, she's staying in the same tree hotel? Anyhow, Dozover must be in *this* direction."

The bridge was so rickety that Felix was worried it would collapse beneath them. A plank of wood fell out when they were halfway across, and if Ramson hadn't grabbed hold of him Felix would have fallen right through. When they made the other side Ramson said, "Thank goodness for that. You don't know what's lurking down there, you really don't."

After a few hundred metres they came to a road. It was lined with trees, and afforded quite good cover. They were walking now, and Felix was slowly getting his breath back. He suddenly realised that he hadn't passed out once since he'd been taking the brittlehorn's potion – but he didn't have it any longer, it had been in Betony's rucksack. The area gradually improved. He could see houses in the trees now, a few of them with lights still in the windows. There was nobody about, which was fortunate.

They came to a dwelling that called itself Dozover, and Ramson stopped. "I don't want to wake the innkeeper," he said. "She'd recognise me." He picked up a stone and threw it through one of the windows. After a moment or two Betony's blonde head appeared. Her face lit up in the most enormous smile; then she put her finger to her lips, waved the rucksack at them and indicated that she was going to pack up her belongings, and meet them at the foot of the tree.

It seemed to take for ever. At last Betony's legs appeared, and after that the rest of her. She ran over to Felix and gave him a big hug. Felix was so surprised at this unexpected demonstration of affection that he felt himself blush.

Ramson looked just as surprised, so Betony kicked him. Then she pulled the brittlehorn potion out of the rucksack, and handed it to Felix.

"That's not one of Snakeweed's remedies, is it?" asked Ramson.

"No," said Felix, taking a swig. The potion worked its magic immediately, refreshing him from the top of his head to the tips of his toes.

"I think I preferred your hair brown," said Betony, looking critically at Felix. "But it's a good disguise. I think we should leave Tiratattle as quickly as possible. They'll be searching for all of us."

"Progg's dead," said Ramson, and he explained what had happened. He'd seen three dead bodies in a very short space of time; it wasn't what he was used to, and he felt faint whenever he thought about it. Then he told her what Progg had said about the library at Andria.

"That's where we'll go, then," said Betony.

"Don't be ridiculous," said Ramson. "It's even further away than Geddon."

Betony turned to him, her green eyes flashing with undisguised fury. "You're such a rubbish brother, you never cared where I was or what I was doing. All you ever asked me was

whether I'd learned my lichens or my tree-barks or my rhi-
zomes, so that I'd become a herbalist like you and you
wouldn't have to support me. Well, I've found something *else*
I want to do. I want to help Felix get better. What do *you*
care about, apart from yourself?"

Ramson looked blank.

"Don't you care about what Snakeweed is doing? Selling
all these untested spells, and causing untold misery?"

"Yes, of course I do."

"Well, do something about it, then."

Ramson stared at her. It was rather a tall order.

"You come to Tiratattle," fumed Betony, "and you get
yourself into no end of trouble – which Felix, I might add,
got you out of. I think you should stay here, disguise yourself, find a way to stop people buying his potions."

"All right," said Ramson, hardly believing he was saying
this, "I'll try."

"The way we'd do it in my world," said Felix, "is to use
publicity. But I don't know how you'd go about it here; you
don't have television, or radio, or newspapers."

"Come *on,* Felix," said Betony, "let's get going before it
gets light."

Ramson ruffled her hair. "You're quite something Betony,
d'you know that? I'm proud of you."

Betony felt an unexpected lump rise in her throat. Her
brother had never said anything like that to her before.

*   *   *

149

Ironclaw needed a rest. Tiratattle was further than he remembered – he'd been flying for some time now, but it was obvious that the beak injury had taken it out of him. He landed by a pool, and slaked his thirst. Then he noticed a japegrin, sitting on a rock, watching him. Ironclaw nodded his head in acknowledgement, and the figure stood up and walked over.

"Nasty injury you've got there," he said. "My name's Squill. I might have a little something that could help you."

Nice one, thought Ironclaw, I needn't fly any further. "Got one of those new potions, have you?" he said.

"At a very competitive price," said Squill, taking something out of his rucksack.

Ironclaw looked at the gourd. It said, *Snakeweed's Beak Remedy* in large blue letters. "Just the job," he said.

"Five gold coins," said Squill.

"*Five?*" squawked Ironclaw. "Ridiculous."

They haggled for a bit, but the japegrin wouldn't back down. Eventually Ironclaw took the gourd, but he did feel he'd handed over rather too much of his precious gold. The japegrin said goodbye, and hurried away.

Ironclaw opened the gourd, and tasted a tiny little bit of the potion on the tip of his tongue. Then he started to think about prime numbers, and his mind drifted. After a few minutes he became aware that there was a rather nasty taste in his mouth. Had the japegrin played a practical joke on him? Then he remembered the gourd, and decided to see what was in it. The list of ingredients looked okay, but the label had something called a *quaff-by* date on it, which had passed two moons previously. Would it still be all right to drink, or not? Then he noticed that one of his talons had changed colour. The stuff was pure poison. Ironclaw felt really angry – in fact, he thought, if he met Squill again he'd peck his eyes out. He'd have to go all the way to Tiratattle after all; he'd start out again at first light.

The next morning, he could see Tiratattle in the distance almost as soon as he took off. He'd been closer than he'd thought. The roads leading to the town radiated out like the spokes of a wheel, and he could see travellers on them, some alone, some in little groups. He had very good eyesight, like all brazzles, and he could focus on something with one bit of his eye and see it magnified to many times its actual size. He started doing it for fun – a solitary diggeluck here, a party of lickits there. Two tangle-children. One of them looked strangely familiar. He waited until he was a bit closer, and then he homed in on them again.

The one he'd partially recognised wasn't a tangle-child at all; it was the human boy. He'd disguised himself quite well, the green clothes and the bleached hair looked totally authentic, and his ears were hidden beneath his cap. But the blue eyes were unmistakable, and so was the science thing he had hung round his neck. Ironclaw hadn't asked what that was, he'd only seen the torch operating. There were symbols on it, as well. Numbers. It was definitely time to renew his acquaintance – and he could tell the boy how he'd solved the spell for sending things across the Divide. Well, nearly solved it. There was always the risk that the sinistrom had ended up dead on the other side. He went into a dive, and landed on the ground in front of them.

The female tangle-child went rigid with fright. She'd obviously never seen one of his kind at close quarters before, and though he said it himself, he was a fine figure of a brazzle.

The boy smiled and said, "Ironclaw. What a lovely surprise. This is my friend, Betony."

"Pleased to meet you," said Ironclaw, eyeing the science-thing round Felix's neck.

The tangle-child found her voice and said to the human, "Do you two *know* each other?"

"Certainly," said Felix, "although he didn't have that horrible injury to his beak last time I saw him. What happened, Ironclaw?"

Ironclaw told him. Felix got very excited when Ironclaw explained how he'd invented a spell for getting back across the Divide, and Ironclaw felt he had to point out that there were still a few little bits to iron out.

"But you're on the right lines, aren't you?" said Felix.

"Oh yes," said Ironclaw. "It's only a matter of time."

Then he told him about how he'd been diddled by Squill, and Betony said, "Thank goodness you didn't drink it; it would have poisoned you."

"I know," said Ironclaw, "I tested it with my talon." The claw had dipped into it by accident, of course, but it sounded good. "I'll have to get a fresh supply in Tiratattle," he said.

"No, don't," said Betony. "It hasn't been properly tested. We met a flame-bird who nearly died because it took some of that stuff."

"Oh," said Ironclaw. His beak started to ache again.

"Hang on," said Betony, "I think I might have something that will do the trick."

She opened her rucksack, and took out the herbs that Ramson had left behind in his room at Dozover. There was a little piece of paper in with the herbs, and it gave the recipe for the dental reconstruction potion, as well as the spell you had to recite.

"I'll need to light a candle," said Betony. "And I'll want some water, and somewhere where there isn't any wind." She glanced down the road. In the distance, people were approaching. A brazzle so far from its home territory was going to attract a lot of attention. She could see a rocky outcrop a couple of miles away.

Ironclaw followed her eyes. "Do you need the shelter of those boulders?"

Betony nodded. It was still a long walk.

"Hop on, then," said Ironclaw.

Betony's mouth dropped open.

Felix walked round behind the brazzle, and climbed on to his back; Betony scrambled up behind him. "This is even more of an honour than riding a brittlehorn," she whispered. She was gripping him very tightly round the waist – too tightly. Felix tried to loosen her hands a little. "Sorry," said Betony in a small voice. "I've only flown once before. A three-minute taster session on a fire-breather; it was a long time ago, and I don't remember much about it."

Ironclaw took a bit of a run, and launched himself into the air. It wasn't the most elegant of take-offs, and he felt Felix dig his knees in, and take a firm grip of the feathers in front of him. Then he found a thermal, and they soared upwards.

II

Grimspite drank and drank. The water in this hot jungly place was really good; cold and clear. But when he'd finished drinking, the same problem still confronted him: what should he do next? He sat down and thought about it. Then he remembered – decisions were all about what *he* wanted to do. What *did* he want to do? Kill something? There didn't seem to be much point, without a master to congratulate him. He had a good scratch, and that was fun. Then he rolled in the mud at the side of the stream, and that was fun too. After that he lay down in the shade and panted for a bit, which was OK. Then he heard voices.

Oh good, he thought. They sound a bit like tangle-folk, or japegrins. He slunk into the shadows, because that was what sinistroms did, and watched.

Two mythical beings came walking along the path. Grimspite stared. Then he screwed his eyes tight shut, and opened them again. No, he wasn't imagining it – they were definitely humans – one male, and one female. How extraordinary. Perhaps he really was in another dimension. The female was carrying a bunch of flowers, and crying. He heard her say, "I don't want to go home, David, it seems like giving up."

The man said, "We can't stay here indefinitely, Alison. We'll do what we said we would – say a last goodbye to Felix exactly where he disappeared, on the ridge, and go back to England."

Grimspite felt that this could be interesting, for some reason he couldn't quite put his paw on, so he followed them. When they got to the Divide the woman knelt down, laid the bunch of flowers across it, and said a few words so quietly that even Grimspite's ears couldn't catch them. The man just stood very still, staring into the distance.

Obviously, they were performing some sort of spell. He waited to see what would happen. After a while, the man sighed deeply, and the woman stood up. The incantation must have failed – probably because they'd forgotten the candles. Grimspite thought he should point this out, so he stepped out of the undergrowth and said, "I think you should have lit a couple of candles."

The humans turned to look, and froze.

The man said, "Don't move, Alison."

She isn't moving anyway, thought Grimspite, why is he telling her not to do something she isn't doing?

"I'm going mad," said the woman. "It's a hyena, and it just told me to light some candles for Felix. I've lost my mind completely."

"You don't get hyenas in Costa Rica," said the man.

"I can see it, David, large as life."

The man swallowed, and blinked a few times.

"You must be able to see it as well, or you wouldn't have told me not to move."

The man hesitated. "Perhaps it's escaped from a zoo," he said eventually.

"But it spoke to me. Did you hear it speak to me?"

"Yes."

Grimspite looked at the flowers. He didn't recognise any of them. He glanced back at the man. "Don't you have any candles?" he asked.

"We're not Catholic," said the man.

"Oh God," said the woman, "we've *both* gone totally insane."

"I can go and look for some, if you like," said Grimspite. It suddenly occurred to him that he was offering to help these humans as though they were his masters. It was just like a mission. Yes, it solved his problem rather neatly because he still hadn't made any other decisions. He could see that scratching himself and rolling in the mud weren't long-term solutions, and it was clear that he couldn't go back into his pebble because his pebble wasn't here any more. It was in another world.

"That's very kind of you," said the man in a strange, choked sort of voice.

"Right," said Grimspite, "I'll be as quick as I can."

As he trotted off back down the track he heard the woman say, "Maybe we've had a touch of sunstroke."

The man replied, "I sincerely hope so."

They're a bit odd, thought Grimspite, but if their spell is something to do with squeezing things from one world to another, they're the right masters for me. I wonder where I can find some candles in this place? And will I need to dis-embowel anyone to get them?

He pricked up his ears. In the far distance, he could just hear a bell beginning to toll. Bells meant beings, where there were beings there might be candles. He headed towards it.

Betony took a deep breath, and looked down. She could see Tiratattle spread out below her; the wide boulevards in the town centre, the tree-lined avenues of the suburbs where Dozover was perched, the tiny little streets in the slum quar-ter, all crammed together. The pattern of the canals, the strip of green that must be the runway at the fire-breather terminal – and beyond the walls the edge of the forest they'd travelled through. Ironclaw hardly seemed to beat his wings at all – and when he did, it was with a slow, smooth, lazy action. There weren't any of the sudden jerks and heart-stopping swoops she'd imagined at all, and she began to relax.

Felix had flown many times before – but there had always been the hum of the aircraft engines, and the curious lack of smell that occurs on aeroplanes. This was so different. The fresh air against his face, the silence. He knew about thermals, the way hot air rose and created an updraught, and he was fascinated at the way Ironclaw used it, circling up and up until he reached sufficient height to glide to his destination.

All too soon they were losing height and the rocky outcrop was appearing before them, getting larger by the second. Ironclaw managed a very creditable landing, and they slipped off his back and on to the ground.

Betony found a protected overhang with a tiny waterfall trickling down the rockface. She measured out some water in one of Ramson's crucibles and crumbled the herbs into it, making a paste. Felix watched, fascinated. The mixture gradually turned to the most beautiful pale lilac-blue, and gave off a fragrant scent that whispered, *try me, try me.* Felix almost wished he had a broken beak himself.

Betony let the paste cool; then she applied it, filling in the little chip that was missing and carefully manipulating the loose bit back into the right position. She smoothed the mixture over the mend the way Felix had seen his father fill cracks in a wall with filler, and then she stood back to survey her work. After that she waved her hand over it, and sang a little song about teeth. The lilac paste gradually turned transparent, like PVA glue, and within a couple of minutes Ironclaw's beak was solid again.

Ironclaw tapped the tip of it on the ground. "Hard as a sinistrom's heart," he said. "How much?"

"How much what?"

"How much should I pay you?"

"Nothing," said Felix. "You're a friend."

Betony glared at him. Didn't he understand anything about how people made a living? There weren't going to be any toadstools in this bare rocky terrain – and it didn't look as though there were going to be many settlements, either. Andria was a long way off; they had to cross the mountains, and they still had to *eat*.

"You could return the favour another way, though," said Felix.

Ironclaw put his head on one side. "How?" They didn't want his gold? How very bizarre.

"You could fly us to Andria," said Felix.

Betony gulped. Even she wouldn't have had the nerve to suggest *that*.

Hmm, thought Ironclaw, there's a library in Andria. I wonder if there's a section on mathematics? "It's a deal," he said. "But I need to hunt first. I could always bring you back a leg of something, if you like."

That night they camped beneath the overhang, eating roast something-or-other, and drinking the water from the little waterfall. Felix showed Ironclaw how to use the compass, and explained about magnetism. Ironclaw found the whole subject quite riveting, especially the concept of dividing direction into degrees.

Tansy looked down at Tiratattle as the fire-breather circled above it, waiting for permission to land. Eventually the little puff of smoke that gave the OK appeared, and Sulphur went into his descent. It had been a rough ride. There had been a thunderstorm, and Agrimony had suddenly lost her nerve and screamed for what seemed like hours.

The landing was perfectly normal, if a little shaky, and there weren't any sinistroms anywhere. Tansy and Agrimony took Sulphur to the stables, and left him there with all the other fire-breathers. Then they made their way to Dozover. Agrimony wanted to stop and look through shop windows all the time, and Tansy had to keep dragging her away.

The innkeeper's mouth dropped open as soon as she laid eyes on Tansy. "I never expected to see *you* again," she said. "Your brother's on the run."

Tansy's eyes widened. "What for?"

"Murdering two ragamuckies," said the innkeeper, with relish.

"*What?*"

"He should have been burnt at the stake today," said the innkeeper, thoroughly enjoying being the bearer of bad news, "but he escaped. So if you haven't got anywhere to stay, that room's vacant again – the last tenant did a moonlight flit."

Agrimony looked appalled. "It's a dump," she said. "Can't we go somewhere else?"

"We'll take it," said Tansy, wanting to slap Agrimony very hard.

They put their things in the room, and Agrimony said, "Can we go shopping now?"

"I can't believe I'm hearing this," said Tansy. "Don't you have any feelings? Honestly. I've lost my sister, my brother's on the run for murder, and you want to go *shopping*?"

"What are we going to do instead, then?"

"We're going to look for Betony," said Tansy, between clenched teeth. "We're going to make enquiries."

Agrimony gave her a look that said, *as if that's going to get us anywhere.*

They left their belongings at Dozover, and walked back into the centre of town. Agrimony trailed around behind Tansy, making no secret of the fact that she was sulking. There were a lot of posters of Tansy's dopey brother Ramson nailed to tree-trunks, although they weren't particularly good likenesses; the drawings were hurried and poorly executed. She kept stopping to look in shop windows, and sneaking inside when Tansy wasn't looking. Tansy would go in, haul her out again, and shout at her.

And then a japegrin came over to them. "My name's Squill," he said, staring hard at Agrimony. "Such a pretty face ..."

"Agrimony," said Agrimony. "My name's Agrimony."

"Agrimony," said Squill. "What a lovely name."

"Where's this leading?" asked Tansy shortly. No one ever told *her* she had a pretty face – her nose was too long, and her chin was too pointed.

"Well," said Squill, "I came to Tiratattle for an interview, and I'm delighted to say that I am now in charge of an advertising department. I've been looking for a face to launch our latest products, and Agrimony fits admirably. She'll be famous, and she'll earn a lot of money."

Agrimony had gone quite dewy-eyed.

"She'll need to be kitted out differently, of course – jade is the green of the moment in Tiratattle, and I can just see her – jade tunic, jade trousers – maybe even a touch of lime here and there."

Tansy scowled. "Is this some sort of practical joke?"

"No," said Squill. "I never mix business with practical jokes."

"What do I need to do?" asked Agrimony.

"Simply come with me," said Squill. He glanced at Tansy. "Don't worry," he said, "I'll return her this evening. Where are you staying?"

"Dozover," said Agrimony, making a face.

Squill smiled. "Here," he said to Tansy, "take my business card. Give her to me for the day, and we'll talk again this evening."

Tansy scrutinised the card. It was a state-of-the-art magical one, and showed where the owner was at any given moment. Squill was based at the conference centre, she'd be able to find him with no difficulty. And dragging a reluctant Agrimony round Tiratattle was slowing her down. "All right," she said.

Agrimony squealed with delight. Squill hailed a cuddyak

cart, and he and Agrimony climbed into it. It was uphol-
stered in purple leather, and adorned with violet feathers.
This was travelling in real style; Agrimony looked thrilled.
The cart pulled away, and Tansy watched them recede into
the distance.

She went into a fertle-juice bar. No, the owner hadn't seen
a tangle-child with straighter than average hair. Tansy
ordered a drink; she wanted to sit down for a bit.

A lickit came over and sat down beside her. He was
dressed in white, the way all lickits were, his head covered
with a hood, and his face in shadow. He smelt as though he
hadn't had a bath for a while. Tansy moved away slightly.
Then he said, in a gruff sort of voice that sounded as though
it were disguised, "I know where Betony's gone."

Tansy froze. Sinistoms could take lickit form; the
smell didn't bode well. Lickits *could* smell of burnt toffee,
or mouldy flour, or even rotten eggs – but they did
wash.

The lickit glanced round. "We can't talk here," he said,
"let's go outside."

Tansy shook her head.

"Come outside, and let me talk to you properly."

Tansy looked around in desperation. Who could she turn
to? The bartender? He wouldn't want it to be common
knowledge that sinistroms frequented his establishment. If
the lickit returned to its four-legged form, there would be
total panic.

"*Fangs and talons*," hissed the lickit, "don't you recognise me?"

"Yes," said Tansy. "I do. You tried to drag me off the fire-breather. I don't know why you want to kill me, but I'm not going outside with a sinistrom, not for all the gold on Tromm Fell."

"Is this lickit bothering you?" enquired the bartender. Then he sniffed, and a wary expression crossed his face.

"On my way," said the lickit, and he got up and left.

When Tansy finally did pluck up the courage to leave the bar, she looked up and down the road for a long time before she ventured on to the street. There weren't any lickits in sight, so she walked away as briskly as she could, but with no clear idea of where she was going. When she found herself in the slum area again, she decided to try a crystal ball parlour. It was the only thing left she could think of to do.

As she was hesitating outside one of the shacks, something leaped out of a doorway, seized her by the arm and put a hand over her mouth. She found herself spun round on the spot, and she was face to face with the same lickit again.

"Idiot," said the lickit, "it's *me*. Ramson." He shook off the hood, and took his hand away from her mouth. "It's a pretty neat disguise, isn't it?"

"Only if you take a bath," said Tansy, really annoyed. "I thought you were a sinistrom."

"Oh," said Ramson. He sniffed underneath one arm, and

wrinkled his nose. Then he said, "Betony's fine. She's on her way to Andria with Felix, the human child."

"*Andria?*" gasped Tansy. This got worse and worse.

"Listen," said Ramson, "they'll be looking for you as well. I've got a room over one of the crystal ball places. I think we ought to disguise you too, and then I'll fill you in on everything."

"I've got Agrimony with me," said Tansy.

Ramson looked horrified. "Agrimony? That simpering little idiot? Why?"

"Grisette's lent me her new fire-breather, and the condition was that Agrimony came too. But would you believe it, this japegrin's offered her a job – advertising, or something."

"I bet she'll be promoting Snakeweed's potions."

Tansy looked indignant. "Well, I'll put a stop to that *right* away. I don't approve of Snakeweed any more."

"You'll approve of him even less when I tell you the whole story," said Ramson. "If we want to stop him, Agrimony might be the way to do it."

"So," said Snakeweed, toying with a pebble as he spoke to Architrex, "it looks as though you've fouled up."

Architrex could feel his tail creeping further and further between his legs. Surely it was Snakeweed who'd decided the boy wasn't a boy after all, and sent him to the place from which he'd escaped?

"*Is* he a human being then, master?"

"So it would appear," said Snakeweed. "He used science to open the cell door." He held the pebble up to the light, just above his glass of fertle-juice.

Architrex watched, transfixed, with whatever passed for his heart in his mouth.

Snakeweed smiled, and dropped the pebble dead-centre into the glass. It landed with a loud plop, and Architrex raised his nose to the ceiling and howled. After a moment or two he realised that he hadn't turned to treacle, the way he should have.

"That wasn't your pebble, Architrex," said Snakeweed. "But next time, it *will* be. The human must be found, and found quickly – and Ramson must be eliminated too."

"There are posters all over the town."

"You failed with the sister as well, didn't you?"

"She'll be back in Geddon by now," said Architrex uncomfortably.

"She can wait, then. And the tangle-child got away too, didn't she?"

Architrex felt sick. He'd never had so many failures in all his two hundred and fifty-three years before.

Snakeweed suddenly changed the subject. "I have my researchers working on the dimension business," he said. "They're making good progress, but not good enough. What we really need is a brazzle, to do the calculations."

"I've never heard of a brazzle co-operating with anyone except a brazzle before," said Architrex.

"One was seen on the road out of Tiratattle yesterday," said Snakeweed, picking up another pebble. "Find out what it was up to, Architrex."

"On my way," said Architrex, and he left as quickly as he possibly could.

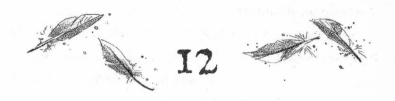

12

On the second night, Ironclaw, Betony and Felix camped in the foothills of the mountains. They had flown over a vast ochre-coloured plain with very little vegetation – just the occasional tree, and scrubby little bushes. Once in a while they had seen herds of some strange striped creatures with long legs and lyre-shaped horns.

"They look a bit like zebras," said Felix. "Only zebras don't have horns."

"Are zebras for real, then?" asked Betony.

Felix told her about a few more of the animals in his world – but she hadn't heard of anything that resembled a giraffe, or a leopard. Felix supposed there were a lot of animals that hadn't found their way into Betony's mythology, same as there would be beasts over here that hadn't turned up in any of *his* world's legends. It was a bit like evolution: palaeontology showed that the fossil record had to be incomplete. There must be all sorts of creatures that hadn't made the transition from bone to stone, from unknown species of dinosaurs to missing links. There were exactly the same patches of ignorance here; *she'd* never heard of a whale; *he'd* never heard of a cuddyak.

Betony waved her hand, and set light to a little pile of twigs and dried moss. She started to feed the fire with dead leaves and sticks.

"How do you do that?" Felix asked her.

"How do I do what?"

"Set fire to things."

"I sort of concentrate very hard, and recite the spell in my head."

"Can anyone do it?"

"Of course."

"Could *I* do it?"

"I've no idea. You can try, if you want."

"Tell me the spell."

"Don't fight; flame, light; ignite; burn bright." She fumbled in her rucksack. "Here. Try the candle."

Felix concentrated as hard as he could on the candle, waved his hand across it, and recited the spell in his head. The candle didn't light; instead, the pale green wax seemed to melt and then reform itself, changing colour in the process. A small orange armour-plated creature materialised in front of him, raised its tiny segmented body up on its hind legs and hissed at him, full of miniature bravado.

Felix jumped back as though he'd been stung, and Betony burst out laughing.

"Good try," she giggled, "I'll give it seven out of thirteen." She waved her hand, and the creature turned back into a candle. Then she grew more serious and said, "I wonder if Ramson's thought of any way of dealing with Snakeweed yet."

"It wouldn't be a problem in my world," said Felix. He explained a bit more about newspapers, watching her face in the firelight, and thinking how pretty she was. The turned-up nose, the slanting green eyes, the white-blonde hair. She poked the fire with a stick, and frowned.

"The thing I don't understand," she said, "is how do they manage to write all those newspapers each day? It must take thousands and thousands of people to do it."

"But *you* have books."

"Books cost a lot of money; a scribe's time is expensive. That's why the only library is in Andria."

The penny suddenly dropped. "Your world hasn't invented printing yet, has it?" he said.

"What's printing?"

Felix explained. Ironclaw looked absolutely fascinated, and asked if there were books of logarithms. "We do all that on calculators and computers, these days," said Felix. And then he got side-tracked, and had to explain. Initially, Ironclaw looked a bit dubious at the idea of a machine doing the leg-work, and commented that it must make a lot of mistakes.

"No, that's the point," said Felix. "They don't make mistakes, they can't. It's the humans who program them who introduce the errors." He started to explain binary numbers, but found Ironclaw was way ahead of him.

The brazzle started to flick his lion-tail from side to side with excitement. "Do they print books on mathematical theory in your world?" he asked.

Felix nodded.

"Wouldn't that be something," said Ironclaw. "I'll have to return to my calculations as soon as we've completed our trip."

"Good," said Felix, smiling. "Because I want to get back to my world too."

"But only after we've ... you know," said Betony.

Felix's smile vanished, and for a moment his face looked pinched and almost old. Betony could have kicked herself. She was beginning to realise that Felix didn't like being reminded about his illness.

"I used to think you could do just about anything with magic," said Felix. "If you needed more books, you'd be able to conjure them up out of thin air. But you can't, can you?"

Betony burst out laughing. "No," she said. "Magic's got rules. There are things you can't ever do, like making gold, or changing the seasons, or bringing someone back from the dead."

"We can't do those things either," said Felix bitterly.

Betony realised she'd put her foot in it again. So she went on hurriedly, "I always thought science could do far more interesting things than magic, though."

"What *can* magic do?"

"It can make people better, and it can make them sick. It

lights fires, and puts them out. It locks doors, and unlocks them. I keep trying to turn a pond-hopper into a song-merchant, although I'm beginning to think Agrimony was having me on when she said it was possible. But science sounds more exciting. You can make thousands of books in no time at all; you've told me about something you call ice-cream, which is so cold it makes you shiver. I've never even *seen* something frozen. The weather doesn't change very much in Geddon. When we cross the mountains, it'll be the first time I've seen snow. You can travel enormous distances in a day. I've never even seen the sea, it's too far away. The king and queen live in Andria," she added, as an afterthought.

"That's something else I've been meaning to ask you," said Felix. "I don't really understand how your country works."

"What's a country?"

"An area of land, that includes lots of towns."

"Oh," said Betony, but the concept didn't seem to make sense to her.

Felix tried another tack. "Do the king and queen have unlimited power?"

Betony stared at him. "What do you mean?"

"Can they make laws, or levy taxes, or pass sentence of death?"

"Of course not. They dance in the moonlight, and lead the singing. Kings and queens are born to be kings and queens. You wouldn't expect somebody to be able to administer a whole country by an accident of birth, surely?"

"So who is in charge?"

"No one."

"But in Tiratattle – there was a militia, and a jail. Who organises that?"

"The guilds."

"Guilds of craftsmen?"

"Yes. Saddle-stitchers, treehouse builders, candle-makers, that sort of thing."

"And Global Panaceas."

"I suppose so."

"And what happens when one guild becomes much bigger than all the others, so that it controls everything?"

"I don't know," said Betony. "It's never happened."

Agrimony was having the time of her life. She'd got a whole new set of clothes – jade, she felt really daring – and her hair had been tangled by a professional tangler, and seeded with beads. She'd been sketched by fifteen different artists, and asked if she'd make various appearances at dance festivals, to say how wonderful Snakeweed's headache remedy was.

At first she didn't quite get it. "I don't have headaches," she said.

"Oh yes you do," said Squill. "You used to get the most terrible headaches in the world before you took the potion. And you've had peribott-rash, and snick-pox, and a broken ankle. And every single one of these things has been completely cured by one of Snakeweed's remedies."

"I *haven't* had snick-pox," protested Agrimony, really offended.

"You get paid a quarter-crock of gold for each appearance you make, with a bonus at the end of the year if sales have doubled."

"What else would you like me to have had?" asked Agrimony. "Candle-burns, scalds, ear-rot?"

Squill patted her on the shoulder. "I knew you were the right choice the moment I saw you," he said. "Another fertle-juice, my dear?"

Agrimony nodded. She was feeling very grown-up.

"We may have a slight problem with your sister," said Squill. "She didn't seem terribly keen on the idea."

"Oh," said Agrimony, "that wasn't my sister. That was Tansy, don't worry about her. She's come to Tiratattle to look for *her* sister, Betony. I just came along for the ride."

Grimspite trotted happily down the path, licking his lips. He'd flushed some sort of weird bird out of the undergrowth, and killed it with no trouble at all. Ripping something apart had made him feel more at home in the place, and the end-result had been unexpectedly delicious. There were a lot of very tiny birds flying about as well, with really bright colours, but they really weren't worth bothering about.

By the time he came to the first building it was late evening, and the place was shut up for the night. He carried on down the path, and began to see a lot more habitations. They were very strange – they weren't built in trees, they weren't part of a cave system, and they didn't have a *keep out* spell at the gate. You could just walk straight up to them. He stopped at one of them, and jumped up on to the little platform thing that ran around the outside. There were plants in pots, and great hanging curtains of some purple flower that grew against the wall. He walked along the platform, and decided to hop in through one of the windows. Only it wasn't like any window he'd ever come across before; he bumped his nose against something hard, and fell back on to the platform. Hmm, thought Grimspite, shaking himself, they do have spells then, but not like any spells I've ever come across. The windows were all the same, until he reached one that stretched right the way down to the floor – and this one was open. There was a miniature sun hanging from the ceiling, and a box full of flickering light against the far wall. A woman was sitting on a very strange chair, watching the light-box. Grimspite sniffed, but he couldn't smell any candles.

He moved on to the next house. This was no better – there was no scent of burning whatsoever, although there was a bowl of some sort of meat on the platform. He tried a mouthful, but it was quite disgusting. Then something hissed at him, and he spun round. A small black furry creature was glaring at him, its fur standing on end, and its back arched. If he hadn't been full of bird, Grimspite would have made short work of it. He gave it a quick snarl to show it who was boss, and went to the next house. No better.

The bell had stopped tolling a while back, but he could now see the building that housed it. A far more solid construction than the others, with great wooden doors that were barred shut. Grimspite wandered over, and did a circuit of it. And there was the smell; the faint but unmistakable odour of wax. *That* was where they kept their candles, inside that building. But there was no way Grimspite could open that door, he would have to wait until someone came along and did it for him. He found some nice rotten toadstools under a tree, and rolled in them. Then he had a really satisfying scratch.

"Honestly," said Tansy to Ramson, hating her new lickit clothes and feeling cross, "there are times when you really are the limit. We're in the most appalling mess, and you're just sitting there reading myths and legends."

Ramson looked up. "There's a reason for it."

"It'd better be a good reason," said Tansy.

"It's really interesting," said Ramson.

"Oh good," said Tansy sarcastically.

"No, listen. In this legend a group of boys start a newspaper. A sort of information sheet. And they make hundreds of copies."

"Must have taken them weeks."

"No, Tansy, they *printed* them. It explains the whole process in here, it's brilliant, it's science."

"So why hasn't anyone done it?"

"Because it's *Felix's* book," said Ramson. "Betony gave it to me when she visited me in prison, and I forgot to give it back. Look: it's been printed, not handwritten."

Tansy looked a bit closer. Then she seized hold of it, and flicked through it. The letters were so neat; all exactly the same size. It was the most perfect book she'd ever seen.

"This is astonishing," she said. "How do they do it?"

"It's so simple," said Ramson, "I don't know why no one's thought of it. You make lots of tiny back-to-front letters – a woodcarver could do it – and you arrange them in a tray, so that they're fixed into place. Then you cover them with ink, put your sheet of paper on top, and press it against it. When you lift the sheet up, the letters are all the right way round. Then you cover the letters with ink again, and carry on until you have as many copies as you need. When you've finished you can re-arrange the letters and print something else."

"That *is* amazing," conceded Tansy. "But how does it benefit us?"

"I'll tell you," said Ramson. "It's obvious that the ragamuckies must have been murdered by Snakeweed's sinistroms. Discredit Snakeweed, show the whole of Tiratattle that he's using sinistroms, and my name will be cleared. Global Panaceas will go out of business. We're going to start up a newspaper, Tansy, and we're going to tell everyone just what's been going on."

"Paper is terribly expensive."

"I'll think of something," said Ramson.

"I'm going to have to go back to Dozover to meet Agrimony," said Tansy. "What on earth am I going to say to her?"

"Nothing, just yet," said Ramson. "Let her have her fun. You see, she's my secret weapon."

Oh dear, thought Tansy. Agrimony is about as reliable as a ragamucky's personal hygiene. She walked back to Dozover, hoping to slip up to her room without the innkeeper spotting her – but she was out of luck.

"Oy!" shouted the innkeeper. "Where do you think you're going, lickit? I told you to get lost half an hour ago. Coming round here, harassing my residents ..." She stopped, and peered at Tansy. "*Bites and stings*," she said, "what *do* you look like?"

"I'm going to a fancy-dress party," said Tansy, saying the first thing that came into her head.

"Surely you could have chosen something a bit more ... well, *seemly*," said the innkeeper.

"What did you mean, you told me to get lost half an hour ago?"

"Oh, that was a genuine lickit," said the innkeeper.

A genuine lickit, or a sinistrom? Tansy's heart started to beat faster. "Is Agrimony back yet?" she asked.

"Yes," said the innkeeper shortly. "She wants to watch her tongue, that one."

Tansy climbed the rope ladder, and made her way to her room. Agrimony was sitting there, wearing the very latest fashions of absolutely everything. Tansy thought she looked a sight.

Agrimony stared at Tansy, and then she said, "What *do* you look like?"

Having exactly the same thing said to her in the space of two minutes didn't improve Tansy's mood in the slightest. "I might say the same thing to you," she retorted.

"I'm going to get paid a fortune for making appearances at dance festivals," said Agrimony. "What's your excuse?"

Tansy had to fight the urge to slap Agrimony quite hard this time.

"Anyway," said Agrimony, "Squill says I can have a room at the conference centre. I thought I'd better come and tell you. This place is just so *squalid*."

"Fine," said Tansy. It would solve a lot of problems. She could vacate this room altogether, and go and stay with Ramson. And if a sinistrom *had* been sniffing around, the sooner the better.

Architrex watched Tansy climb down the rope ladder. He'd made enquiries about Ramson at the terminal. In the process he'd met Squill, booking a flight to Andria whilst Agrimony had her hair tangled, and he'd heard about Tansy's return. It hadn't been easy tracking her, but he'd managed it. How very considerate of her to disguise herself as a lickit – they would look like a couple. He sauntered over, and took her arm.

Tansy smelt him a split second before she felt his hand on her sleeve, but it was too late.

"Let's go for a little walk," said Architrex, "down by the canal. I think there are a few things you can tell me."

She could feel his nails digging into her; she could imagine what they'd be like if he transformed into his other shape, longer, sharper, the sort of claws that shred flesh like paper. Although his arm lay lightly against hers his grip was incredibly powerful, propelling her along as though she were a child, with no effort whatsoever.

"You belong to Snakeweed, don't you?" she said.

"I'm not sure that *belong* is exactly the right word," said Architrex. "My name is Architrex, and I'm a very senior sinistrom. I *serve* Snakeweed – that would be a better way of putting it. And your family has caused him no end of trouble."

They'd turned off the main road, and were walking down a side-street.

"Now then," said Architrex, "let's start with Felix."

"I've never met Felix."

"But you know about him. Where is he?"

"I've no idea," said Tansy.

The grip tightened. It was beginning to hurt. "Let's try Betony."

"Betony's not in Tiratattle any longer."

"I'd realised that," said Architrex. "So where is she?"

"I don't know."

"You're not making this very easy for yourself," said Architrex. "How about Ramson?"

"He's left Tiratattle as well."

"You're lying," said Architrex.

They'd reached the canal now. It was absolutely deserted, not a japegrin or a diggeluck or a lickit anywhere. The stagnant smell of the water was mingling with Architrex's shadow-reek, and Tansy wanted to throw up.

Suddenly Architrex let go of her arm. She had her back to the canal, and there was nowhere to run. She knew what he was about to do – change into his four-legged form, so that he could use both his jaws *and* his claws. There wasn't going to be any escape. He was going to torture her until she gave him the information he wanted, and then he was going to kill her. Better to die now, and keep her information to herself. She took two steps backwards, and flung herself into the canal.

Architrex howled with rage. She'd done it mid-change, caught him when he couldn't do anything about it, outthought him. He looked at the surface of the water, green with slime, and waited. A little while later, a few bubbles appeared. And a little while after that a white shoe floated to the surface, and there was a sudden swirl; something was stirring down there, something big. The water suddenly erupted, and Architrex caught a glimpse of a leathery tail.

Oh well. He may not have got the information he wanted, but at least he could tell Snakeweed he'd eliminated one of the problems. He trotted off back down the path in the direction of the conference centre.

13

"It's going to be very cold up there," said Ironclaw, looking at the mountains in front of him. "I'm aiming for the pass, so that we don't have to go too high. *I'll* be all right, of course – I've got feathers." A thought suddenly struck him. "When we camp," he said, "you two can snuggle up against me."

The idea was a bit revolutionary. Brazzles didn't do snuggling. Male and female brazzles had totally different interests, and they only met up every century or so, to mate. It was a brief courtship, because they didn't have anything to talk about. Hens didn't seem to like mathematics at all; they were historians on the whole. They were the ones who brought up the chicks, and although the males provided the food they weren't terribly reliable. Ironclaw remembered an incident forty years previously, when he'd gone off to hunt and got involved in knot theory instead. He'd tried to explain this to his female, but she'd become extremely angry and pecked two of his wing feathers out. The chick had been a male, however, and he'd become rather more engaging as he got older. Ironclaw remembered with pride the first time his offspring had solved a quadratic equation. Then, it seemed, in no time at all he'd grown up and flown off.

Felix and Betony climbed on to his back, and Ironclaw launched himself into the air. Betony wasn't nervous any more. The view was spectacular; she could see snow up ahead, impossibly white and glistening in the sunshine. They flew for a while in silence, and she wondered how the toadstool test had gone. Agrimony usually came top, but that was because Grisette spent hours going over it with her. Well, Agrimony was going to be emerald with envy when Betony got back. Betony was going to have more stories than anyone else her age, and she was going to make the most of them. She pictured the weekly story-telling sessions the village had, when the elders talked of distant lands and sailing ships and sea monsters. Then she would stand up – she, Betony – and tell them about her flight on a brazzle with a mythical being. *That* would make them all sit up and take notice.

They stopped for lunch. It wasn't terribly exciting – some dried fruit, a lump of cheese and a few biscuits that Betony produced from her rucksack. Then they flew onwards again.

It *was* getting colder. The trees were different now, all the same colour, dark green and spiky, and she could see patches of snow in the gaps between them. And then the trees had snow on their branches, becoming fewer and further between until there was just jagged grey rock, and snow. The sun sank lower in the sky, turning the snow an amazing pinky-orange colour, and the shadows deep turquoise. And then, quite suddenly, everything disappeared. She could hardly see Felix in front of her, let alone Ironclaw's head. The world below had vanished behind a pale grey veil. She held on to Felix a lot tighter, the way she always did when she was frightened.

"It's all right," said Felix reassuringly, "it's only a cloud. We'll come out the other side in a moment."

But they didn't come out the other side, and it got colder and colder. Her hands were going numb, and it hurt to breathe. If she were finding it difficult, what must Felix be going through? He was only replying to her questions in monosyllables now. She had her arms round his waist, and his body felt colder than hers. She suddenly realised how thin he was – she'd never noticed that before. Supposing he passed out up here – would she be able to keep him on Ironclaw's back? Did she have the strength? At last she felt Ironclaw begin to lose height, and soon there were bits of cold white stuff everywhere, in her eyes, in her mouth, up her nose.

"It's a blizzard!" she heard Ironclaw call out. "I can't fly in this, I'm going down!"

They weren't very far from the ground when the cloud dispersed, and they landed in a heap in a snowdrift. Betony sat up and looked round. She couldn't see very much at all, the snow was falling so thick and fast it blotted out everything. It was just as soft as it looked, but it was colder than she would have believed possible. Within moments her fingers had turned blue, and she couldn't feel them properly. Ironclaw shook his feathers, and blinked. Felix was digging, for some reason, but he seemed to be making hard work of it. "What are you doing?" she asked him.

"Constructing a shelter. Then we'll all curl up in it until the storm's passed." He stopped for a moment, breathing hard. Then he said, "The air's thin up here. I don't think it's very good for me."

"Well, let me do it, then," said Betony. She could see that he didn't like having to admit defeat, but it wasn't the right time to get wound up about pride. She started to dig, following his instructions, and eventually they had a hole with an overhang that was big enough for all of them. They climbed in, and buried themselves in Ironclaw's feathers. The feathers on the outside were damp, but the ones underneath weren't; they smelt slightly dusty and oily at the same time, musky and nice. The hole heated up with surprising speed, and the warmth was so comforting that she fell asleep.

When she woke up it was morning, and the storm had passed. Ironclaw was snoring gently, but Felix was nowhere to be seen. Betony stood up, and climbed out of the hole. The sun was shining, and the sky was blue. Then something hit her on the side of the head, and exploded in her face. She heard Felix laughing. She wiped the snow out of her eyes and said, "What did you do that for?"

"It's a snowball," said Felix. "You pick up a handful of

snow and scrunch it into a ball, like this, then you throw it at someone. It doesn't hurt."

Right, thought Betony, and for the next ten minutes they piled up stores of missiles. Then they let them loose, one after the other. Every time Betony scored a hit, Felix clapped his hands dramatically to the spot, as though he'd been shot with an arrow, and then dissolved into giggles. He was such good company when he was feeling OK. Betony was a much better shot than Felix, however, and in the end he held up his hands and said, "Enough. I surrender to your superior fire-power, oh empress of the ice-mountain."

"What else can you do with snow?" asked Betony.

"You can slide around on it," Felix said, and he told her about skiing and snow-boarding. But it was all theory; his parents hadn't let him do any of it.

"Snow's really good fun," said Betony. "I just wish it wasn't so cold!"

"We should have collected some wood," said Felix. "Then you could have lit a fire for us." He was shivering now, and his nose as well as his hands were turning blue. Suddenly, Betony didn't like the look of him at all. She opened her rucksack, and got out the potion. But to her astonishment, it wouldn't pour out of the gourd. The gourd wasn't squashy any more; it was as hard as stone.

"It's frozen," said Felix. His lips were the most alarming colour, a pale blue.

"I think you'd better warm yourself up against Ironclaw

for a bit," said Betony.

Felix didn't argue, he just climbed back into the hole again. Ironclaw muttered "If the square root of two is ..." in his sleep, and started snoring again. And once more those feathers did the trick – they warmed him up faster than he would have believed possible, and he felt almost reborn.

They had breakfast – more dried fruit, cheese and biscuits. Ironclaw shook the snow from his feathers, and they climbed aboard once more. As they flew into the pass, Felix could see that it was a sort of road. And a little while later, he could see a small group of two-legged figures, and what appeared to be a couple of pack-animals.

"Ironclaw!" shouted Betony. "Let's go down and see if we can buy some warmer clothes from those people!"

When the figures saw the brazzle swooping down towards them they scattered, leaving the pack-animals behind, and ran for the shelter of the rocks. Ironclaw landed in the middle of the road, and as Felix slid off his back he heard something whizz past him.

"*Blazing feathers*," squawked the brazzle, his head turning from side to side as he scanned their surroundings, "they're trying to kill us!"

Another whizz, and this time Felix could see that it was an arrow, for it buried itself in the snow a few yards in front of him. A third, a fourth – sooner or later one of them was going to find a target.

"Stop! Stop!" yelled Betony, jumping down off Ironclaw's back and waving her arms in the air.

The attack ceased, and there was silence. It was such a complete silence, in that high icy place, that Felix felt he could almost touch it. He shivered. He couldn't see anyone – whoever owned the curious beasts a little way off had concealed themselves extremely well. The creatures seemed to be some sort of cross between a yak and rhinoceros, and they were covered in coarse brown hair. There were horns on their noses, and their hooves had been painted in different colours, presumably to denote ownership. They were wearing harnesses, and carried wickerwork panniers that were filled to the brim with packages wrapped in hide and tied up with thongs. He had a feeling they were the same species as the animal he'd seen in Tiratattle, pulling a cart.

"We want to trade!" shouted Betony. "Look, we're unarmed!" She spread her arms wide, and after a moment Felix did the same.

"You don't *need* to be armed if you have a brazzle with you," called a voice.

"He's not hunting," said Betony. "He's taking us to Andria."

Ironclaw tried to look sweet and harmless, but it wasn't frightfully successful.

"Tell him to lie on his back with his legs in the air!"

"No chance," said Ironclaw.

"Please," said Betony.

"It's undignified," said Ironclaw.

"Dead dignified," snapped Betony, "or a live laughing-stock? Your choice."

Ironclaw lay down rather gingerly in the snow, and raised his talons above his head.

A japegrin emerged from behind a rock, an arrow notched on his bow.

"We want to buy a couple of cloaks, if you have any," said Betony. "We're not dressed for this weather – you can see we're not."

Two more japegrins came out, and the three of them walked over. "We're not carrying clothing," said one.

"We're carrying potions," said another.

"Don't you have a spare blanket or something?" asked Betony. "We can pay." She'd have to ask Ironclaw for a loan, but Felix was looking fragile again, and keeping him warm was more important than worrying about debt.

"*I've* got a spare cloak," said the second japegrin. "I'll sell it you for two gold pieces."

Ironclaw made a strangled sort of sound in his throat.

"I've got a spare as well," said the third.

"OK," said Betony.

"Can I get up yet?" asked Ironclaw.

The first japegrin raised his bow immediately.

"Oh for goodness' sake," said Betony, "he's not going to hurt you. And he's the one with the gold."

The japegrin lowered his weapon.

"Two gold pieces was a joke, wasn't it," said Ironclaw, struggling to his feet.

"No," said the japegrin, raising his bow a fraction.

Ironclaw bad-temperedly took four gold pieces out of the little leather pouch he kept strapped to his leg, and passed them over. The second japegrin went over to one of the pack-animals, and pulled a parcel out of the wickerwork basket.

The rhinoceros-yak shied to one side and snorted, and the japegrin hit it over the nose, swore at it and said, "Cuddyaks, more trouble than they're worth."

The cloak had been wrapped around a number of gourds, which fell into the snow and rolled a little way. Felix stiffened. He could see *Global Panaceas* written on them in large blue letters.

"You're a long way from home," said Ironclaw off-handedly. "Tiratattle folk, am I right?"

The japegrin nodded.

"On your way to Andria?"

The japegrin nodded again.

"You work for Snakeweed?"

"Yes. What's it to you?"

"Oh, nothing at all," said Ironclaw. "But Andria have their own potions, and I was just wondering how you were going to promote yours above theirs."

"There's a big sales initiative," said the second japegrin. "You know the dance festival they have each year? We're setting up a stall, and Snakeweed's flying over in person to give a talk. It's a golden opportunity; we get a really good percentage of everything that gets sold."

"Percentages can be funny things," said Ironclaw, "if you haven't agreed on the variables first."

"Look, brazzle," said the first japegrin. "We weren't born yesterday. You stick to your business, whatever *that* is, and we'll stick to ours."

Ironclaw shrugged. "Fair enough," he said.

Felix wrapped the cloak around him, and Betony put hers on as well. Then they said goodbye rather stiffly, climbed on to Ironclaw's back, and soared up into the sky. Felix watched the japegrins reload the potions on to the cuddyaks, and start off again in the direction of Andria. Gradually, the figures became tiny little dots, and disappeared from sight.

"Snakeweed in Andria," said Felix. "That's bad news."

"Andria's a big place," said Betony. "The chances of just bumping into him aren't very high."

They seemed to travel for hours, passing over one set of

peaks after another. But they were warmer this time, and it wasn't the ordeal it had been the day before. Then, quite suddenly, they were on the other side of the mountain range and they could see the foothills sloping down to a strip of flat countryside. And beyond that, the sea.

Betony gasped. Although she knew, in theory, that it was very big, she hadn't appreciated just how vast an ocean could be. It looked as though it went on for ever. She could see Andria, situated on the edge of it, just a blot of a different colour at the moment. The spiky trees appeared beneath them again, and the patches of snow became more infrequent until they disappeared altogether. After that the foothills began, with trees and bushes, and then they gave way to a gently undulating countryside with meandering rivers and grassland. It got warmer.

They landed for lunch, and took off the cloaks. The moment they laid them on the ground, the cloaks burst into flower. Felix blinked. Then, before his eyes, the magical mass of flowers wilted, died, and turned to dust. All that remained of the garments was a smudge of browny-beige on the grass.

"About the four gold pieces ..." said Betony to Ironclaw, feeling she had to apologise for her lack of funds, and let him know she'd pay him back. It didn't help that the cloaks had been a typical japegrin practical joke, and were now worthless.

"Forget it," said Ironclaw.

"What?" She couldn't believe her ears.

"Forget it. We're friends."

On the spur of the moment, Betony gave him a hug. Ironclaw looked embarrassed, and lashed his tail.

"This library," said Felix. "What do you know about it?"

"It's the biggest library there is anywhere," said Ironclaw. "The books have been collected for centuries, and they're irreplaceable. Books from all over the world, on every subject you can imagine. I've always intended to pay it a visit, just never got round to it. My female went there a couple of times. She was an historian, you know."

Felix was surprised at this mention of a partner; Ironclaw behaved like someone who very definitely preferred to live on his own. Then he wondered whether the tense was important. "Was?" he said, trying to sound sensitive, and prepared for a tragic tale.

"We didn't get on," said Ironclaw. "Haven't seen her for forty years. Told me I didn't live in the real world, and that relationships weren't things you could work out with addition and subtraction signs. Anyway, she was researching a brazzle called Flintfeather. Died a couple of hundred years ago, but he did a lot of important work on weights and measures. Not my sort of thing, you understand. I don't really like the practical applications, actually *doing* things with the results. Once I've solved a problem I lose interest in it."

"Flintfeather?" said Felix, suddenly remembering the

bath he'd had at the conference centre. "I saw a statue of him, in Tiratattle."

"Did you? He wrote a thesis about the relationship of body-mass to potion theory, very well received. But he trod on too many tangle-folk's toes – they're the ones who are meant to be the herbalists, japegrins have only got into that sort of thing relatively recently. After he died, his thesis disappeared, and all the work he'd done was lost. There was only one copy, you see. And it all hinged on something to do with brazzle feathers. What was it he said? Oh, that's right. 'When the scales are evenly weighted, a feather is all it takes to tip the balance.'"

"There was an inscription on the statue," said Felix. "*In our feathers lies our strength.*"

"No one knows what he meant," said Ironclaw. "My female did a great deal of work on him, but she hadn't got anywhere the last I heard."

"Was he a sort of doctor, then?"

"An apothecary," said Ironclaw. "Apothecary and mathematician to the king, I believe – not that I've ever heard of a king being interested in anything like that. But I think the thing that really shot him to prominence was a cure he effected on one of the princes. Something that had never been done before."

"What?" asked Felix.

"I've no idea," said Ironclaw. "I stopped listening at that point – she did go on, you know. I just used to nod."

The brittlehorn potion had melted again by now, so Felix had his swig, although he was wondering how much longer it would last. "Are there any brittlehorns in this area?" he asked Ironclaw.

"Couldn't tell you," said Ironclaw. "I found geography about as interesting as a cuddyak-pat."

They finished their lunch, and Felix went off into the bushes for a pee. As he was buttoning up his tangle-trousers he saw a candle-stub on the ground, so he decided to have another go at the ignition spell. Once again the candle failed to light. The wax turned purple, and rounded itself into a sort of plum. Felix picked it up – and as he did, the fruit shouted "Surprise!" and burst between his fingers, splattering him with a bright magenta juice. He tried to wipe it off, but the colour seemed to be indelible. He went back to Betony shame-faced, and she had hysterics. It wasn't until Ironclaw glared at her that she pulled herself together and recited the counter-charm that cleaned him up.

"You're not concentrating hard enough," she said. "You have to make a real effort to *think* it alight."

"Same old problem, then," said Felix bitterly. "Not enough energy."

They set off again. Betony could see things that could have been treehouses every so often now, surrounded by curious patterns – lines, on the landscape, that bordered areas that were different colours. Greens, browns, yellows. She pointed them out to Felix, wondering what they signified.

"They're hedges and fences," said Felix, surprised. "This is all farmland."

"What's farmland?"

He turned round to look at her. "Farms. Where you have fields for different crops."

She still looked blank.

"How do you get your food, in Geddon?" he asked her.

"We gather it. Some folk gather one thing, and other folk gather another. The fathers go hunting sometimes, as well, although we don't eat meat very often."

"You don't plant things, and harvest them?"

"Why would we want to? Everything's there."

Felix thought back to his geography lessons, at school. Perhaps there simply wasn't the population pressure in Geddon; there really was everything everyone needed right on hand. But what about Tiratattle? He hadn't seen any farms around there, but maybe it was just a question of time. "How long has Tiratattle been in existence?" he asked.

"Ages," said Betony. "But it's only become big recently. In my grandmother's time it was the same size as Geddon."

Betony's world is at one of the crucial moments in its history, thought Felix. It's just beginning to change over from hunting and gathering to farming. And that's when the trouble starts, isn't it? That's when the trees get cut down, the animals lose their habitat, villages turn into towns. And that's when diseases really get going, because they never had so many host creatures all together before. Snakeweed's selected the up-and-coming market, no doubt about that. He'd be a ruthless businessman in any world.

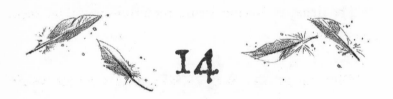

Agrimony looked round her room at the conference centre with undisguised delight. She was on the ground floor, but she was aware that there were several levels beneath her and the whole concept seemed terribly sophisticated.

"All mod cons," said Squill. "There's a mirror in the bathroom, that will advise you on your make-up, and the towels are all self-propelled, naturally. There's a mini-bar, where you can mix yourself a fertle-juice – or even a shreddermouth-lullaby, if you feel so inclined."

Agrimony had no idea what a shreddermouth-lullaby was, but she wasn't going to ask.

"The bed's a levitating one, if you miss the treehouse ambience, and the wardrobe will press your clothes for you if you ask it nicely. Now then. Tomorrow morning. How well up are you on the latest moonlight dances?"

"I can do the dusk hop."

"It's a bit dated. How about the midnight wriggle,

and the star squirm?"

Agrimony shook her head. She'd never heard of them.

"You'll get a dancing lesson tomorrow morning, then. Can you sing?"

"Yes."

"Give me the first verse of *When I went out one moonlit night*."

Agrimony looked blank.

"Singing lesson after the dancing, then. You're going to have to work quite hard, you realise that, don't you?"

"I don't mind," said Agrimony. "I always come top in toadstool tests."

Squill laughed. "Toadstools are collected by toadstool collectors these days; they don't do anything else except collect toadstools, so there's no need for anyone else to mug up on them."

Agrimony looked at the pale green walls, painted to look like a faded forest glade, the milky green carpet on the floor. The pile was thick and soft, and it felt very luxurious.

Squill followed her gaze. "I bet you don't have one like that at home."

Agrimony shook her head. "Does it have to be cut regularly?"

"I'm sorry?"

"How fast does it grow?"

Squill burst out laughing. "It isn't a living plant,

Agrimony. It's made of fibres. Dead plants. It stays like that."

Agrimony vowed to keep her mouth shut from now on.

"If there's anything you want, just tell the mirror. I'll see you in the morning. OK?"

"Yes," said Agrimony in a small voice. She was trying very hard not to feel out of her depth.

After Squill left she played with the bed for a bit, making it go right up to the ceiling and down again. Then she tried to mix herself a shreddermouth-lullaby, but it tasted revolting. After that she sat on the carpet and felt bored. Eventually, she went into the bathroom, and talked to the mirror.

Ramson was experimenting with bits of wood. He'd managed a very creditable A, and was well on the way to completing his B. However, it was a slow process, and he could see that it was going to take him a long time to get sufficient letters for his purpose. He finished the B, and decided to go out for a drink.

The fertle-juice bar was packed, which was good, as Ramson felt he was less conspicuous in a crowd. It was a walk-in shack at the side of the road, with cheap wooden benches crammed together, and badly drawn pictures of dancers in faded colours on the walls. The noise was indescribable, the floor was wet with spilt drinks, and the place was full of ragamuckies and diggelucks. There were a few lickits, and no japegrins at all. People sat on window-ledges and tables, sliding the empty chalices to one end to make more room.

After a while the diggeluck sitting next to Ramson turned to him and said, "Twenty years."

Ramson didn't really want to strike up a conversation, but he felt he had no alternative other than to say, "Twenty years of what?"

"Friends for twenty years," said the diggeluck, "him and me. Dug for gold together, we did. Loved him like a brother. And now this."

And once again, Ramson felt obliged to say, "And now what?"

"Dead," said the diggeluck. His wrinkled face was wet with tears.

"I'm sorry," said Ramson.

"Me too," said the diggeluck, and they sat in silence for a while. "The thing is," said the diggeluck, "he was sick, see? And they goes and arrests him – for something he never done – and then he dies in prison. Poor old Progg."

"Progg?" said Ramson.

"Yeah."

Ramson took a deep breath. "My name's Ramson," he said. "There are posters of me all over Tiratattle. I'm not a lickit, I'm a tangle-person. I was in the prison too; Progg was killed when we were trying to escape together."

The diggeluck gave him a sharp look. "You the one who

killed those ragamuckies?"

"No. I was set up as well," said Ramson. "It was a sinistrom who really killed them."

The diggeluck drew his breath in sharply.

Ramson threw caution to the winds and told him everything, even the newspaper printing project.

When he'd finished, the diggeluck held out his hand and said, "The name's Dibber. How can I help?"

"Can you carve wood, to a very precise finish?"

"Like a professional," said Dibber. "And what's more, I knows a spell what makes replicas once we got the prototype sorted."

Better and better.

"And do you have anywhere we could turn into a printer's, just for a little while?"

The diggeluck thought for a while. Then he said, "There's a shed at the back of the treehouse I'm staying in. We could rent it."

"I don't have much money," said Ramson.

"I do," said Dibber.

It was the first time Ramson had seen a smile on the diggeluck's craggy face.

"Shortly after I split with Progg," he said, scratching his hairy arm, "I found a very rich seam. I'd come to Tiratattle to split the proceeds with him. Only fair. And it's only fair that I uses his share to try and nail that villain Snakeweed. When do we start?"

"Right now," said Ramson, and they went back to his little room and started on the C and the D.

"One out of four," said Snakeweed, his green eyes flashing malice. "Not a very impressive record, is it Architrex? Tansy was the least important target. And aren't you rather losing your touch, drowning her in the canal instead of tearing her to shreds?"

Architrex looked at his paws and said nothing.

"Did you find out anything about the brazzle?"

This was slightly better, though not much. Architrex had made some enquiries. "Yes," he said. "Some lickits saw it land on the road out of Tiratattle. They were too far away to see what happened, exactly ..." He looked at his paws again. This was going to sound as unlikely as a ragamucky having a spring-clean.

"Yes?"

"Well, the brazzle landed next to two tangle-children." And as he said the words, he thought, *that's it*. That's why I can't find any trace of Felix and Betony. Because the two tangle-children *were* Felix and Betony. "But when it took off again," he said, "the children weren't there any more."

"Are you suggesting that a brazzle killed and ate two tangle-children, in the space of a few minutes, in broad daylight, on a main highway?"

"It's possible," said Architrex, feeling very fortunate all of a sudden. "And it's also possible they were Felix and Betony."

"That would be very convenient, wouldn't it Architrex? Apart from one small consideration – the fact that we wanted Felix *alive*."

Forgot about that, thought Architrex. Should I tell him what really seemed to have happened – that they climbed on to the brazzle's back, and flew off towards the mountains as though they'd just rented a fire-breather? The idea of making a decision of his own like this was alien to Architrex's nature, but Architrex wasn't just any old sinistrom. He was a lot brighter than most, and from time to time he'd felt that it was just possible that reason could overcome instinct. If there had ever been a time to try putting it into practice it was now, so he decided against telling his master the rest of the story.

Snakeweed was looking thoughtful rather than angry. "In which direction was the brazzle headed?"

"Andria."

Snakeweed smiled. "I'm going to Andria myself in a few days' time. You can come with me, Architrex. You're to find that brazzle, and ask it what it had for dinner on the road out of Tiratattle. Then you can offer it a contract to research into the dimension question."

Architrex really didn't fancy dealing with a brazzle at all. "What on earth can you offer it that it would ever want?"

"If this brazzle has developed a taste for tangle-child flesh," said Snakeweed, "which would be a first, I grant you, but not impossible – then I can make it an offer it can't refuse. As many tangle-children as it wishes."

Architrex had to admire that one. It was so delightfully cold-blooded.

"It's a shame we seem to have lost Felix," said Snakeweed. "But if a brazzle can solve the last bit of the dimension problem, the maths part that my employees don't seem to be able to crack, well – we don't *need* the human child any more. We can just go straight into his world, and start finding out about science." He leaned back in his chair, and fiddled with a lock of his ginger hair. "I suppose that makes looking for Ramson a waste of time now, if the brazzle really did eat the boy. If there's no Felix, we don't need to shut Ramson up any more. Although if someone *does* turn him in, let me know. I can always spare an hour or so to watch someone who's given us so much trouble burning at the stake."

"So what would you like me to do now, master?"

"Go out to the Andria road, and sniff around where the brazzle landed. You ought to be able to pick up the scent of the two children; it hasn't rained recently. Let me know if it *was* them – although, at the moment, brazzle-food does look like the most plausible explanation for their disappearance."

"On my way," said Architrex. He wasn't sure how he felt about lying to a master. Then he thought, I didn't really lie, did I? I simply didn't tell him everything I knew.

* * *

Tiratattle had seemed huge to Betony, but it was nothing compared to Andria. As they circled above it, she could see that many of the buildings weren't made of wood at all – they were constructed from stone, and they were standing flat on the ground like stalls. The roofs were made of overlapping slabs of slate, shaped like giant fish-scales, and they were a dull blue-grey. There were a few exceptions, however. One building, which stood on its own in the middle of an expanse of grass, seemed to consist of different sections, each of which had its own dome-shaped roof. These roofs were pale green, but they didn't look as if they'd been skim-coated with moss or lichen.

"I think that's the palace," said Ironclaw over his shoulder. "The dance festivals take place on the lawn surrounding it."

To someone who was used to living in London, Andria was simply an average-sized town. Felix found the architecture very interesting, though. The overlapping slate roofs looked like the backs of prehistoric creatures, and the domes reminded him of university towns like Oxford or Cambridge. A wide sandy beach lay between the sea and the town, and there was a little harbour. A few boats lay at anchor. Beyond the harbour wall, one boat had raised a red triangular sail and was heading off out to sea. Andria was far more like a town in Felix's world than Tiratattle had been.

They flew over another building. They were lower now,

and Felix could see it more clearly. This one was made of wood, with asymmetrical window-frames and doorways. Pear-shaped windows, kidney-shaped windows, twisted beams, sloping walls, an undulating roof. It was almost as though the place had grown there, like a tree. The wood went from cream to chocolate, with every shade of coffee and caramel and butterscotch between. Each piece of timber was as smooth as a polished pebble, though whether it had become like that through craftsmanship or weathering was difficult to say. The structure was very big, although it was only one storey tall. Statues stood in the grounds, which were set to lawn and latticed with little paths.

"That's the library," said Ironclaw. "It's older than all the other buildings, even older than the palace. That's why it's made of wood."

He circled round one more time, and landed near the entrance. The children climbed off, and stared. The library seemed as old as time in some ways, and almost a living creature the way it sprawled there, long and low, with a ground-plan that must have resembled a jig-saw puzzle piece. Then they let their eyes travel round the grounds, taking in the paths that snaked through the grass, the huge old trees that grew here and there, and the stone figures.

"Oh look," said Felix. "There's another statue of Flintfeather." This statue had a book under one wing, and held a pair of scales in its beak. The same words as before were carved beneath: *In our feathers lies our strength*.

To Betony's surprise, nobody gave Ironclaw a second glance. People came and went, in ones and twos usually, and she overheard earnest conversations about the structure of closing spells, and the properties of wax. There were a lot of tangle-folk here, as well as creatures that even Betony couldn't identify.

Ironclaw was having a quick preen, prior to entering the building. He didn't usually bother about his appearance – he kept his wings clean enough to fly, and oiled his breast feathers occasionally, but that was about it. After the preen he raked out the dirt between his toes, and polished his talons on the grass. Then he wiped his beak in a similar fashion, and spoiled the whole effect by scratching his stomach with his back leg, and making the hair stand up on end.

Felix was asking Betony the names of the creatures that passed by, and jotting them down in his notebook. "That's a centaur," he said, as a very dignified beast trotted by, carrying a pile of books.

"Wise-hoof," said Betony.

"And that's a faun," said Felix, as a self-important little thing strutted by, half goat and half elf – although he had horns that curled out of his hair like unfurling ammonites.

"Small-tail," said Betony. "They're the scribes. You can

place an order with them for a book to be copied out, but it takes ages."

"Ready?" asked Ironclaw.

They walked up to the curved wooden door, which was open, and entered the library. It was cool and dark in there after the bright light outside, and Felix thought it smelt of old bibles. There was a desk in the lobby, shaped like a kidney-bean, and beyond it he could see shelves and shelves of books, all different colours, all different thicknesses. The titles were handwritten on the spines in gold.

"You need the medical section," said Ironclaw. "It's that way. I'm going to the mathematics room, and I'll meet you in the lobby at sunset." He hurried off, his neck feathers bristling with excitement.

They walked in the direction he'd indicated, passing through archway after archway, each one curved in a slightly different way, each one leading to a new subject area. Felix saw categories such as: *Candle-craft before 450*, and *Triple-head maintenance manuals*.

"What on earth do you use a triple-head for?" asked Felix, suddenly remembering the giant three-headed bird he'd once seen in a film. The roc, that was it.

"No idea," said Betony, so they pulled out one of the manuals and flicked through it.

Felix laughed. "They use them as cranes! We have a piece of machinery that does the same thing – lifts heavy objects. Though our cranes can only cope with one load at a time – your triple-head can manage three things at once."

"Oh look," said Betony. "There's another brazzle."

This one was a little smaller than Ironclaw, and its plumage was different – a sort of tawny-gold colour. Every feather was in place, and every claw shone.

"It's a female," Betony whispered. The brazzle was leafing through a book on the history of Andria; her eyes were a striking yellow, and she looked very severe.

Felix and Betony moved on, and eventually they found the right room. The books weren't very logically arranged, to Felix's mind. One side dealt with diseases that were best tackled with potion-based remedies; the other side favoured ones that responded more readily to the spoken spell, with only a small amount of herbal enhancement. Dividing things into parts of the body didn't seem to have occurred to anyone. Felix sighed, and started at one end, and Betony started at the other.

The books reminded Felix of mediaeval manuscripts. The lettering was exquisitely illuminated, and the pages were thick and creamy and parchment-like. The drawings were beautiful too – even if they did show fractures and swellings and rashes. He tried to identify the different diseases he saw, but it was difficult. He would come to a conclusion about something – measles, or arthritis, or mumps – and then find out that only cuddyaks ever had it, or fire-breathers, or wise-hoofs. There weren't very many illustrations of internal organs – and when they were the internal organs of a small-tail or a vamprey, he was totally at sea. By sunset Betony hadn't made any more progress than he had. They made their way back to the lobby, and waited for Ironclaw. It was nearly closing time, but Felix suspected they would need force to prise their friend out of the mathematics section.

Then the female brazzle appeared, carrying a selection of history books under her wing. The ragamucky at the information desk waved a wand over them. As the brazzle turned to go she saw Felix out of the corner of her eye, and she stopped dead in her tracks. Felix had become so used to passing for a tangle-child by now that he wondered whether, unwittingly, he'd broken some library rule. Or maybe his nose was running.

The brazzle hesitated for a moment, then she came over. "Blue eyes," she said. Then, "Your roots are beginning to show, human child. You have brown hair, not blond." Then, quick as a flash, she seized his cap in her beak and pulled it off. "You really *are* a human being," she said, looking at his ears. "Well, well." She gave the cap back to him. "How did you get here?"

Felix looked at Betony.

"I asked you a question, boy," said the brazzle, pinning him to the spot with her fierce yellow eyes. "Have the decency to answer."

213

"It's a bit complicated," said Felix. She reminded him rather too strongly of a particular teacher at school.

"Complicated?" repeated the brazzle. "You think your explanation is going to be too complicated for me to understand? You have a very high opinion of your brain-power, boy, and a very low opinion of mine."

"No," said Felix, desperately, "I didn't mean it like that."

Suddenly there was a commotion behind them, and they turned to look. Ironclaw was arguing with a wise-hoof who was obviously a librarian, and protesting that he only needed just a little more time. His neatly preened feathers were in disarray, and he looked flustered and frustrated. Then he saw the other brazzle, and froze.

"Ironclaw," said the brazzle.

"Thornbeak," said Ironclaw, lamely.

There was a stony silence. Betony and Felix looked at one another. Betony shrugged.

"Still playing with numbers?" asked Thornbeak.

"I don't *play* with numbers," said Ironclaw. "I've done some ground-breaking work recently, as it happens. What about you? Still stuck in the past?"

"I've just finished my book on Flintfeather," said Thornbeak. "There's been a lot of interest in it. Seen anything of Stonetalon lately?"

Ironclaw looked blank. "Stonetalon?"

"Our son," said Thornbeak icily.

"Oh. No."

"Would you please continue this touching reunion out-side?" said the wise-hoof. "We're closing."

Felix and Betony followed the brazzles out onto the lawn.

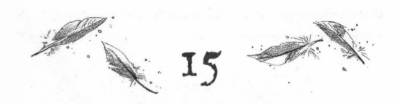

15

When Tansy hit the water in preference to being ripped apart by Architrex, she was surprised at how cold it was. Then she was going down, and wondering whether she should be pleased or sorry that she'd never learned to swim. She was going to drown. If she'd been able to fight her way to the surface the sinistrom would have hauled her out and sliced her up, bit by bit, until she gave him the information he wanted. This was better.

But it didn't feel better, not right at that moment. She couldn't just let the water fill her lungs – holding her breath was such a powerful instinct that it overcame everything else. She opened her eyes, expecting to see little, if anything, in the murk. The water was filthy, of course, but not so filthy that she couldn't see a yard or two in front of her. She felt that stupid lickit shoe come off her foot, and she watched it float lazily upwards, a few inches from her nose. Her eyes travelled along the wall until they came to a big black hole, where presumably a sewer drained into the canal. There was something *in* the hole – big, knobbly, long vicious snout and slitty yellow eyes. A shreddermouth. She was going to be ripped to pieces after all.

She watched it slither out of its retreat, its scaly legs scrab-bling against the lip of the hole as it pushed off towards her. Holding her breath was beginning to hurt, but she still couldn't make herself breathe in the scummy water, and get it over with. The jaws opened, and she felt herself seized around the waist. And then everything went upside-down, and round and round, and she didn't know which way the surface was. The swirling water raised a cloud of mud particles, and went opaque. She shut her eyes, tight. She felt her elbows hit some-thing hard, then her knees; there was a ringing in her ears, she was going to black out, let it be soon, let it be soon ...

Suddenly her head was above water, and she took the

deepest, loveliest breath she had ever taken in her whole life.

It was all a question of comparison, of course. It was only lovely because she wanted it so badly; the smell, when it filtered through, was vile. She took another breath, and then she was coughing and retching but she was alive. She opened her eyes, and after a little while they adjusted to the gloom and she saw the dark shape in front of her.

"And dare was me finking I'd got myself a lickit for dinner," said a gravelly voice. "But you're not a lickit, are you? You're a young tangle-person."

Tansy swallowed, gagging as she tasted canal water. "Who are you?" she managed.

"I'm a shreddermouf, aren't I?"

"I was afraid of that," said Tansy. He was going to keep her in his larder until he was hungry again, and *then* he was going to rip her apart.

"Dis is my lair," said the shreddermouth proudly. "It's de best lair in Tiratattle."

"Is it?" said Tansy.

"Oh yes. It's a drainage tunnel. Goes right up to de surface, it does. Lots of storage space. My name's Gulp."

"Tansy," said Tansy, deciding not to ask him what he kept in his storage space, and wondering whether introductions were quite the thing.

"Dare I was," said Gulp, "minding my own business, pretending to be a log of wood – I like doing dat – and suddenly dare *you* are, frowing yourself in de water. What a funny fing to do, I fink, and so I look up. And dare's dis sinistrom, watching." He made a sort of gulping noise, which seemed appropriate.

"When are you going to eat me?" asked Tansy. It was as well to know.

"I don't eat tangle-people," said the shreddermouth. "Whatever next? No, I'm a specific feeder I am, I only take lickits."

"Then I'm free to go?" asked Tansy, hardly believing she'd heard him right. She hadn't known that shreddermouths didn't eat tangle-folk – but then, she hadn't paid much attention to animal studies at school.

"Not *exactly* free to go," said Gulp. "Seeing as I've rescued you from certain deaf, I fink you owe me a little somefink in return, don't you?"

"What do you want?"

"I want to know what's going on up dare. Time was when lickit flesh was de sweetest, tastiest food ever. After it had been kept for a while, you understand, so dat it fell off de bone like jelly. But now – you never know what you're getting. Sometimes it's so bitter it's not even edible after a couple of moons' ripening time. It's as dough day've been eating somefink nasty, and de flavour of it's seeped right froo dem. I caught one a while back, left it in de storeroom de way I do, and what do you know – it turns to mush. All dat's left is its cloding, and a gourd of somefink called Snakeweed's cough remedy. So I sniff de stuff, and I fink –

disgusting. Sort of sharp and acidic, like fruit – well, dat's unpleasant enough in itself – but dare's somefink else, a sort of aftersmell. Now den. Have lickits changed dare diets, do you know? Or is it just some of dem like dis new-fangled stuff?"

"It's a medicine," said Tansy.

"Go on," said Gulp.

So Tansy told him the whole story, thinking how strange life was, and it took quite a while.

When she'd finished, Gulp went very quiet. Eventually, he said, "And you and dis Ramson are going to try and stop him spreading dis poison around, are you?"

"That's right," said Tansy.

"Good," said Gulp. "You see, it's not just you dis affects. De stuff's getting into de food-chain. I only eat lickits, and if I can't eat lickits … well. Me and my kind are going to become extinct, aren't we? Now, dare's some dat would fink dat a good fing, but dare's anudder side to it. Lickits have always frown dare dead into de canal, knowing day'll get recycled by a shreddermouf sooner or later. And to be perfectly honest, dat killing business takes up so much energy, and we all prefer de maturer sort of corpse …" He looked wistful for a moment, obviously remembering better times. "It's a good system," he went on. "Lickits don't have a problem wid it – day prefer it to your tangle-folk solution, which is to let dem rot in de ground – or de japegrin way, which is to burn dem. So if dare's no shreddermoufs left, dare won't be no lickit disposal system."

"I see," said Tansy.

"So you'll get even more diseases up dare, and need even more of Snakeweed's poison. Can I help in any way?"

"There's nothing I can think of, offhand," said Tansy. "Except for telling me the way out."

"Carry on up de tunnel, it'll branch two ways. Take de left-hand one. Keep going, until you come to a free-way split, and take de central one. Be careful; Gobble's up dare – my female – and she's got young. She may not wait to find out dat you're tangle-blood and not lickit flesh, she'll see de cloding and dat'll be dat. If she does spot you – run. She won't follow you far, because she won't want to leave de little ones. When you come to de end of *dat* tunnel, you'll find yourself on de surface, in de ragamucky quarter."

This was excellent news, because Ramson's room wouldn't be very far away at all. But she'd have to get there, first.

She said goodbye to Gulp, and made her way along the tunnel. Every so often there would be a drainage-hole overhead, so although there wasn't much light, there was some. The whole place stank. Tansy was still wet through, and she shivered constantly. If I get a cold after this, she thought, I'm not taking anything for it. It can just get better on its own.

She came to the branch, and continued along the left-hand tunnel. So far so good. She was trying to walk as quietly as possible, but it wasn't easy – the floor of the tunnel was littered with bones and scraps of clothing and shreddermouth droppings. There were lumps of rock as well, where parts of the tunnel were crumbling away, and she nearly turned her ankle on one. It wasn't easy walking with just one shoe.

She arrived at the three-way split. Everything was quiet; she couldn't see any sign of the shreddermouth, apart from its garbage, so she entered the central passage, and tiptoed along it. She was going to make it. Then the tunnel veered sharply to the right, and she couldn't see beyond the turn. She flattened herself against the wall, and edged forward. Just a few more steps.

Then she heard it. A scrabbling sound first; then a squeak with a sort of gurgle to it, and after that a thump. It didn't sound like a shreddermouth. She peeped around the corner. Something was playing with a bone, pouncing on it and worrying it, then patting it away and pouncing on it again. Then she saw its tail; long, scaly, a deep dark green. It *was* a shreddermouth, but it was a baby one.

It looked up, and their eyes met. She could see it assessing her; was this lickit too big for it, or should it have a go? It took a step forward, and its tail lashed from side to side. Tansy knew she ought to make a run for it, but it was between her and the eventual exit. It took another step forward, its eyes never leaving her face. Tansy bent down, keeping the eye contact, and picked up a stone. The shreddermouth didn't make the connection, and it gathered itself to spring. Tansy was just getting ready to throw the stone at it as hard as she could, when she heard the last thing she wanted to hear – a sound behind her.

A gravelly voice said, "Leave dat lickit alone, Sludge, you don't know where it's been."

Tansy turned round. Gobble was watching her with her slitty yellow eyes, and her snout looked horribly businesslike. "I'm not a lickit," said Tansy, "I'm a tangle-being."

"I can see dat now," said the shreddermouth. "I'm not stupid." She glanced at her offspring. "Get back to de lair, Sludge, before I wallop you wid my tail."

The baby slithered past Tansy, and disappeared.

"So what's your business down here?" asked Gobble.

So Tansy told her the whole story, the same way she'd told Gulp.

"A few years back," said Gobble, "assuming you'd been a genuine lickit, of course – I'd have left Sludge to it, and perhaps he'd have learned a fing or two. But times have changed. You can't trust lickit meat any more, so I have to test everyfink before I let de children at it. If you can stop Snakeweed, Tansy, we'll all be grateful. And if you ever need somewhere to hide, you're more dan welcome in de lair."

"Thank you," said Tansy, although the prospect of spending any more time in a shreddermouth lair turned her stomach.

She carried on along the tunnel with mixed feelings. Yes, the extinction of a whole species was a terrible thing – but shreddermouths fed on lickits, and lickits were very closely related to tangle-folk. It felt disloyal to help shreddermouths, and wrong not to. Why was life so complicated? Not that shreddermouths actually *killed* all that many lickits ...

At last there was daylight, and she emerged in the ragamucky quarter, leaving the sewer stench behind her. She realised she'd been away all night, and she was cold and wet and very tired. She found Ramson's room, and knocked on the door.

A diggeluck answered it. They've caught Ramson, thought Tansy, and the room's been rented to someone else. A part of her seemed to give up and sink; she did love her brother, despite the fact that he could be such a prat.

"Tansy?" queried the diggeluck. "You *are* Tansy, aren't you? Are you all right?"

Tansy shook her head and bit her lip.

And suddenly Ramson was there too. He took one look at her long nose peeking out from her lank wet hair, and burst out laughing.

"I hate you!" screamed Tansy. "I've been nearly ... and a sinistrom ... and then a shreddermouth ... and all you can do ..."

"But Dibber and me have been *busy*," said Ramson. "We've done twenty-one letters, and Dibber's spent a small fortune on buying up just about every sheet of paper in Tiratattle, and ..."

"Not now, Ramson," said Dibber.

"Oh," said Ramson, suddenly noticing that Tansy was crying.

Dibber picked up Tansy as though she weighed nothing at all, carried her upstairs, and filled a tub with hot water. She had a very welcome bath, after which she went straight to bed.

On the road out of Tiratattle, Architrex picked up Felix and Betony's scent quite quickly. So it *had* been them. What was he going to say to Snakeweed? In a few days' time they were *all* going to be in Andria. Andria was a big place, but a human child was going to be the talk of the town, and Snakeweed was bound to hear of it. However, Snakeweed still wanted Architrex to open negotiations with the brazzle, so he wasn't likely to juice his pebble just yet – but if he found out that Felix and Betony had survived *after* that was done, he might feel rather differently. Feeling cornered, Architrex decided to return to the conference centre and tell Snakeweed the truth.

Although Snakeweed looked very hard at the glass of fertle-juice on his desk, he didn't make any further threats. He merely suggested that Architrex resume his search for Ramson, and that Vomidor would assist him.

"Thank you, master," said Architrex, feeling that he'd got off lightly.

"And Architrex," said Snakeweed, "you'd better start

thinking of something else we can offer that brazzle. Tangle-children seem to be off the menu."

Grimspite had a long wait. He lay curled up in the shadows of the strange building with the bell tower, wondering about some statues he'd noticed in the alcoves. A man with wings, holding some sort of stringed instrument; a woman with a boy-child. How long would it be before their turn-to-stone spells wore off, and they came back to life? His mind started to wander. What were those cross-things growing in the grass? And then he was asleep.

The next morning someone did come, a human in a long black dress and a tangle-cap. Grimspite watched, his head on one side, as the man took out a big bunch of metal things, and pushed one of them into a hole in the door. It seemed a very complicated way of performing an unlocking spell, but it worked. The door creaked open, and the man went into the building. Grimspite stood up, stretched, yawned, scratched, and followed him.

It was cool inside, just one big room filled with rows of wooden benches, and there was a wonderful smell of wax everywhere. And yes, there were the candles – hundreds of them, some of them tall and white and new, others burnt halfway down, others just stubs. Grimspite trotted down the central aisle feeling quite light-hearted, his claws click-clicking on the stone floor. The man had knelt down – but he must have heard something, because he turned round.

His eyes widened. Then he stood up, and said something that somehow reminded Grimspite of the gobbledegook he'd seen on the sign by the Divide. The words didn't make sense. He stopped for another scratch, and made it a thorough one.

The man waved his arms and shouted. Grimspite realised that the man was asking him to go away, but not very politely. He lifted his lip to show the man the size of his left canine. The man picked up a stick, which was not a terribly good move when faced with a sinistrom. Grimspite showed him the size of his right canine as well. Instead of sensibly retreating, the man took a step forward and brandished the stick at him.

He's mad, thought Grimspite. Completely insane. He babbles nonsense, although he obviously thinks it makes sense, so there's no point talking to him and making a few threats. Do I really want to rip someone apart who won't fully appreciate it? He glanced towards the candles. He could just grab a couple of them, and make his exit. The man took another step forward, so Grimspite jumped over one of the benches, seized two of the candles in his mouth, and trotted back down the aisle and out of the door. Then he went all the way back up to the top of the hill, feeling as though he'd achieved something. His new masters would be pleased with him.

They weren't there. He searched the surrounding area; nothing. The bunch of flowers was still lying across the

Divide, although it had wilted. It was all a bit of a let-down, really. He went and lay down in the shadows, his head on his paws, and it was back to the same old problem: what should he do next? Sleep seemed the most sensible solution, so he curled himself up and closed his eyes.

Agrimony worked very hard at learning all the new dances, and Squill was pleased with her. They had a delightful lunch of squirtled seaweed and bumbled butterbugs at a very exclusive restaurant. During the afternoon she made equally good progress with the songs, and when she went back to her room at the conference centre she was feeling very pleased with herself, and more sophisticated by the minute. When Squill left, she decided to have another go at mixing the shreddermouth-lullaby. Everyone who was anyone drank them; she'd tried a proper one now, and she knew what it ought to taste like.

She sang *The Moon Wail* to herself as she squeezed things and measured things and poured them into the silver container that was used for the purpose. Then she shook them all up together, the way you were meant to, and tipped the result into a chalice. She tasted it rather tentatively, at first. But it wasn't bad. It wasn't bad at all. She finished it rather more quickly than she had the one in the restaurant. Then she made herself another, and drank that too. By the time she'd drunk five of them she was feeling a bit peculiar.

She lay down on the bed – but she'd forgotten to deactivate the spell. The bed started to go up and down, and it wouldn't stop. One minute the ceiling was zooming towards her, the next it was flying away from her. She began to feel sick. Eventually, she rolled off when the bed hit the floor for the seventeenth time, and she just lay on the plush green carpet, feeling thoroughly rotten. Her head was beginning to ache.

She crawled into the bathroom, and threw up in the disposal hole. After that she felt very slightly better, but her head still felt as though a couple of diggelucks were mining something behind her eyes.

"Oh dear," said the mirror, "you don't look too good."

"I don't feel very well," said Agrimony miserably.

"There are some medicines in the cabinet," said the mirror.

Agrimony opened the cabinet door, and found a sachet of Snakeweed's headache cure. She remembered telling Squill she didn't get headaches. Well, she certainly had one now. She emptied the sachet into some water, drank it down, and recited the words of the spell that were on the packet. At least by the morning she'd have one genuine recommendation to make concerning Global Panaceas. All in all, though, she'd rather have lied about it than gone through this. She managed to stop the bed going up and down by shouting at it; then she climbed into it, and went to sleep.

The next morning she felt ten times worse. When Squill arrived she told him she didn't feel well, and crawled back underneath the bedclothes. She heard Squill go into the bathroom, and start talking to the mirror. To begin with the voices were low and inaudible; then she heard Squill shout, "You *what*?"

The mirror's reply was too quiet to make out.

"Yes, I *know* it was my fault I left it there," she heard Squill say, "but you should have had more sense."

"How was I to know the remedy hadn't been tested on tangle-children?" snapped the mirror.

Hadn't been tested? Agrimony could hardly believe her ears. She'd lived in a herbalist community all her life; you just didn't *do* things like that.

"If we tested every spell on every being, we'd still be peddling the stuff on market stalls," said Squill. "This is big business – we have to cut corners, and it's only occasionally we get it wrong. We call it our negative-reaction risk factor; it's in single figures. The only way people are going to find out about it is by word of mouth, and in a big town people don't talk to one another much."

"Is she going to be all right?" asked the mirror.

"Who knows," said Squill. "It's a nuisance, though. She had exactly the right face – provincial, naïve, innocent. People would believe what she said. The chances of me finding another one like her with only three days to go is pretty remote."

Provincial? Naïve? Innocent? Agrimony lay there, feeling too ill to be as angry as she'd have liked. Everything seemed to be getting a bit distant – and then everything went black.

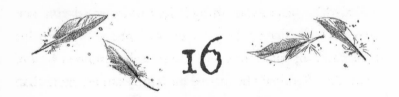

16

"You haven't changed," said Thornbeak, her immaculate feathers glinting gold in the late afternoon sun.

"Neither have you," said Ironclaw. He looked at Felix and Betony. "Shall we go?"

"Not so fast," said Thornbeak. "I want to know what you're doing here with a mythical being."

"We're looking for a cure for his illness," said Betony. She wasn't going to be put off by Ironclaw's attitude. Thornbeak probably knew the library inside out, and perhaps she could help.

"Illness?" Thornbeak softened very slightly.

"He'll die if we don't find it."

Thornbeak studied Felix for a moment with her bright yellow eyes. "Is this true?"

"Yes," said Felix, giving Betony a filthy look. He felt really annoyed with her, the way she'd just come out with it to a total stranger.

"Poor little chick," said Thornbeak. "It must be very hard for you."

Sympathy was the last thing Felix had expected from her. Unexpected understanding always brought a lump to his throat, and for just a moment Thornbeak reminded him of his mother. Suddenly he missed his family almost more than he could bear.

"What's the nature of this illness?" asked Thornbeak gently.

"My heart," said Felix miserably.

The brazzle stiffened.

Same old thing, thought Felix, there's nothing that can be done. Live each day as though it's your last, and then the following day's a bonus. Heard it, hated it, didn't buy the T-shirt.

"Meet me here tomorrow," said Thornbeak. "I'm not going to raise your hopes, boy, that would be cruel. But modern herbalists – they think the only worthwhile potions and spells are those that were invented yesterday. I'm an historian, and I don't assume that if something is old it's automatically rubbish. We'll do a bit of research, and see if we come up with anything." She looked at Ironclaw. "It was kind of you to bring him all the way over here. I know how you don't like interruptions in your work."

Ironclaw blinked with astonishment. Then he glanced behind him, to see if perhaps Thornbeak was speaking to somebody else. Then he said, as though trying the water with his toe, "The thing I've been working on – the ground-breaking work I mentioned – it's a mathematical spell to get Felix back to his own world."

"Well, well," said Thornbeak, "it's a pity you don't extend that sort of consideration towards your own son, but I suppose you've got to start somewhere. How close are you to a solution?"

"About a chick's dropping away," said Ironclaw, and then wished he hadn't.

Thornbeak ignored it. "As it happens, Stonetalon's in Andria as well. He's very good with figures, though I can't say I see the attraction myself. I could tell him you need an assistant. That's if you can bear to work with anyone else."

Ironclaw looked annoyed. "Of course I can work with other brazzles," he said. "Granitelegs and I collaborate all the time." This was a total lie; he would never have asked for Granitelegs's help, even if he'd been stuck on something for a year.

"I'll tell him to meet you here tomorrow as well, then."

Ironclaw looked seriously alarmed all of a sudden, but he didn't argue.

That night, Felix and Betony stayed in a lodging house close to the library. Ironclaw paid, although he examined the bill minutely and found a small error, which he pointed out to the proprietor. He himself went to a brazzle rock. These were situated just outside the town. They consisted of a series of stony outcrops arranged in an isometric grid, where each brazzle could be nicely isolated from the others, fifty metres apart. He spent the night with his head tucked under his wing, dreaming about solid geometry, which wasn't his thing at all. It was Granitelegs's territory, and he'd always considered it a bit beneath him.

Just before Felix climbed into the soft feather bed, he remembered it was time to take his brittlehorn potion. He picked up the gourd, tilted his head, and put it to his lips. A tiny little dribble found its way into his mouth – and then that was it. The potion had all gone.

The next morning they all met up outside the library, as arranged. Ironclaw was late. Stonetalon was a very handsome brazzle, a smarter version of his father, and he questioned Felix in great detail about exactly what had happened to him on the Divide.

Ironclaw arrived eventually, dusty and flustered. His claws were dirty again, and his feathers were ruffled. Thornbeak regarded him with something close to contempt, and he looked sheepish and had a quick preen.

"This calculation spell ..." said Stonetalon, and within a couple of minutes he and his father were throwing numbers at one another like snowballs, and squawking with excitement.

"Come on," said Thornbeak, "we'll leave them to it."

This time they made their way to the history section. Thornbeak indicated a set of shelves and said, "If it's any-where, it's there." Then she allocated them each a row of books.

It was, in many ways, harder than what they'd been doing the day before. The books weren't specifically about cures – there would be a chapter here, or a paragraph there, hidden amongst lists of kings and queens, or information about daily life. Felix was the first to come up with a reference to heart problems – and it was desperately disappointing, as it only said what he'd heard so many times already – that they didn't respond to magic.

Betony didn't seem to be making as much progress as Felix. By lunchtime she'd only got through half the material he had. "It's so interesting," she said. "I keep getting side-tracked." Then she saw the expression on his face and she said, "Oh, I'm sorry, Felix, I wasn't thinking. I'll really knuckle down to it this afternoon."

Ironclaw and Stonetalon had gone off to the beach, so that they could do some calculations in the sand. Betony had forgotten all about the sea; she looked decidedly envious for a moment, so Thornbeak said, "We'll go there after the library shuts, and we can't work any more." She made the word *work* sound like the most delightful activity there was.

They went back inside, and started on the next load of books. Felix was getting more and more depressed. They'd found half a dozen references to hearts now, and they all said the same thing.

"Never give up," said Thornbeak. "If I'd given up on Flintfeather, I'd never have got where I am today."

Betony was slowing down again, because she was reading

things she shouldn't. She noticed Thornbeak watching her. "I'm sorry," she said, "I'm not very good at this, am I?"

"On the contrary," said Thornbeak. "You're remarkably thorough. What are you going to do when you leave school?"

Betony scowled. "My family always assumed I'd follow them into the herbal trade. But it's so *boring*."

"Hmm," said Thornbeak. "Maybe you should think about doing something else, then."

"Anything."

"No," said Thornbeak, "not anything. Something that interests you, and gives you pleasure."

"I like doing this," said Betony. "But there isn't much call for it in Geddon."

"See if you still feel the same way after you've been doing it for several days," said Thornbeak.

Betony grinned.

By the time the library closed, they were no further ahead. But Thornbeak made them feel that the day hadn't been wasted at all; it had simply narrowed the research they still had to do.

They went down to the beach, but Ironclaw and Stonetalon weren't very good company. They couldn't tear themselves away from the scrawl in the sand, and they kept adding bits and rubbing bits out and jumping up and down and screeching when they agreed on something.

"I want to swim in the sea," said Betony, stripping off her outer garments and revealing a set of green underwear that had seen better days. There was a different smell in the air, and she loved the way the waves frothed and hissed as they travelled up the sand, changed their minds, and went back to the sea again. She turned to Felix. "Coming?"

Felix shook his head. Swimming in the sea was forbidden. If he passed out, he'd drown.

"Don't go too far," said Thornbeak.

Betony nodded, and skipped down to the sea. Felix sat on the sand and watched her, feeling jealous. Thornbeak lay down next to him, her bird-legs stretched in front of her, her lion-legs tucked against her body, and her tail curved tastefully beside them. "Tell me about *your* world," she said. "Do you have historians there?"

Felix nodded.

"And are they just human beings, or do other creatures take an interest? The long-nosed flap-ears, for instance? Humungallies."

"Elephants," said Felix. He laughed. "No. Human beings are the only animals that talk ... well, whales sing to each other, but they don't speak the way we do ... at least, we don't think they do."

"How extraordinary," said Thornbeak.

Felix was racking his brains for things he'd learned from natural history books. There hadn't been a lot else to do when he'd been in hospital, except read – and some of his hospital stays had been long ones. "Actually," he said, "the elephants are a surprisingly good example. They make noises that are below our level of hearing – infra-sound. And they do seem to communicate with one another, and they go back to places where friends of theirs have died, and they pick up their bones and stroke them ..." Back to the same old subject again; it seemed as though he just couldn't avoid it, whatever he did.

"But they don't write history books?"

He smiled. "No."

"But you do have history books?"

"Oh yes," said Felix. "Masses of them. There is a lot of history in my world, going back thousands and thousands of years. You start off with flint arrowheads and stone circles, and you end up with bombs and cathedrals."

"So you do learn from the past?"

Felix laughed. "That's a very good question. In some ways yes, in some ways no. All children learn history at school, and we have museums."

"Museums?"

Felix told her about the British Museum. He told her about the huge statues, the swords, the pots, the Rosetta Stone. He was going to tell her about the mummies, but that was death again, so he left them out. She listened intently, shaking her head in astonishment every so often.

"Tell me," she said eventually, "what would your world make of one of *our* creatures, if it crossed the Divide?"

Felix took a deep breath. "They'd capture you, and put you in a zoo. A prison. Then they'd study you, and write books about you, and try and find out how to get more of you. And when you died they'd dissect you, and write more books."

"I see," said the brazzle. "And supposing they discovered that the creature couldn't be captured, that its magic was too strong?"

"Then they'd try and kill you," said Felix, "because they'd be frightened of something they didn't understand." He suddenly felt very ashamed of his own world. It didn't sound like a nice place at all.

"I see," said Thornbeak again. "But you still want to return there?"

"It's my home," said Felix. A sudden picture of the house he lived in flashed into his mind; the kitchen, with its constant supply of food in the fridge; the hall, with its push-button telephone and instant communication; the sitting room, with the soft blue sofa he'd curl up on when he wasn't feeling too good and just wanted to watch a video. His bedroom, with its posters and model aeroplanes. The tug of the familiar hit him hard this time, and he made a face.

"You've let this illness dominate your life, haven't you?" observed Thornbeak.

"I haven't had much option!" snapped Felix.

Thornbeak sighed. "You allow your temper get the better of you. Even with those who are trying to help you."

Felix stared at her. It had never occurred to him how unfair this might be.

"Try seeing things from other points of view, Felix. You're a nice boy at heart, but you have given Betony a hard time on a few occasions. She's told me."

Felix felt himself go red. It was true, he'd used his condition to excuse himself for biting people's heads off, over and over again. "It's just ... well, it really *gets* to me when I wonder what I could have achieved if I hadn't been ill. I might have been good at football, or playing the trombone, or scuba diving ..."

Thornbeak looked blankly at him, and he realised she didn't have the faintest idea what he was talking about. After a moment's reflection, he realised it had all been *me me me* again. "I'm sorry," he said.

"I'm not the one you should be apologising to."

"I know," said Felix, wondering what on earth he could do to show Betony how much he appreciated her. She was the best friend he'd ever made. It would have been easy in his world; buy her a present, take her to a theme park, arrange a surprise party for her. He shaded his eyes with his hand, searching for her bright blonde hair amongst the waves. He couldn't see it. "Thornbeak," he said, "where is she?"

Thornbeak tilted her head, so that she could use her magnified vision. "There," she said. "But she keeps going under – I think she's in trouble."

Betony had been amazed to discover that the sea was salty, and the waves were a surprise too. She'd let herself be carried up and down on them, and it was the most incredible fun. Then she'd lain on her back for a while, looking up at the sky. There were big white birds she'd never seen before, wheeling above her, but when she'd turned over on to her front again she realised she'd drifted quite a long way from the shore. There was a strong current, and she didn't have the strength to fight it. Panic had washed over her with the next wave; the water was up her nose, in her eyes ... and suddenly there was a dark shape above her, and the rush of wings. She felt something seize hold of her underwear, and haul her out of the water and up into the air.

"I warned you not to go too far," said Thornbeak, as she carried Betony back to the beach in her talons. "If you're going to be my apprentice, you're going to have to do as you're told a bit more often. It's Felix who noticed you were in trouble, by the way," and she dropped Betony unceremoniously on the sand next to him.

Betony was amazed to see Felix wipe away a tear.

"I thought you were going to drown," he said.

"So did I," said Betony, and quite spontaneously they hugged each other.

"I'm really sorry I've been such a pain from time to time," said Felix.

Betony grinned. "Forget it. I daresay I'd have been even worse, if I'd had your problems." She turned to Thornbeak. "What did you mean, 'If I'm going to be your apprentice'?"

"I might consider taking you on, if you're still enthusiastic in a few days' time."

Betony's eyes widened. "*Can* tangle-folk become historians?"

"I don't see why not," said Thornbeak.

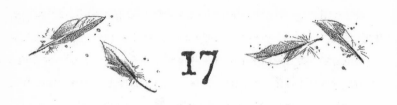

17

The following day's research was no better than the previous day's. Ironclaw and Stonetalon were very bouncy, however, and they reckoned they were extremely close to solving the problem of a spell that froze someone for the length of a heartbeat. Ironclaw *had* memorised the calculations he'd done on Tromm Fell, and the two brazzles were quite sure that a combination of the two spells would send someone back across the Divide.

"I did it once before, you see," Ironclaw told Felix. "I froze a sinistrom with bloodwort – I couldn't do that with *you*, it might kill you – and I packed him off to your world, just like that, with my number spell. It was very satisfying."

Felix blanched. "You did *what*?" he said.

"Sent a sinistrom across the Divide," said Ironclaw. "What's the matter?"

"My parents are there," said Felix. "On the other side of the Divide."

"Oh," said Ironclaw. He hadn't had much contact with his own parents after he'd grown up, but his father had been very good on transcendental numbers. Ironclaw had enjoyed meeting up once every decade or so, and thrashing out a few problems with an equally sharp mind. Since his father's death, Stonetalon was the best mathematician Ironclaw had encountered. He suddenly wondered whether his son would like similar meetings; it had never occurred to him to look at it the other way round before. Perhaps they could get together every decade or so from now on. It was a thought.

"A sinistrom needs a mission," said Stonetalon. "If it hasn't been told to hunt down your parents, it won't."

Felix looked at Ironclaw.

"I didn't tell it to do anything," said Ironclaw. "I just wanted to get rid of it."

"So it's over there in my world, waiting for someone to tell it what to do."

"That's about the size of it," said Ironclaw.

"I don't think a sinistrom can survive for very long without a master," said Stonetalon thoughtfully. "It would just waste away without anyone to tell it what to do. It's probably dead by now."

"Come on," said Thornbeak, "there's work to do." And once again, she made it sound like the most fascinating activity there could ever be.

When they finished that day, they went down to the beach once more, but Betony didn't swim in the sea again.

She and Felix went beach-combing, and poked around in the rock pools; even these were different from the ones in his own world. The starfish had seven legs, not five, and the sea-weed was rainbow-coloured. Betony was trying to keep Felix's mind off their failure to find anything in the library, and to some extent she succeeded. After a happy day on the beach, Felix presented Betony with a necklace he'd made out of some of the shells they'd found. It was quite beautiful; the colours had been carefully selected, and he'd taken a lot of trouble stringing them together on a silver chain that Ironclaw had paid for. She was really touched, and put it on immediately.

The next day she found herself entranced by yet another book. There hadn't always been candle-lighting spells – they were a recent discovery. Fire-breathers hadn't always been tame, and lickits hadn't always known how to make sweets. But there *had* been toadstool location spells; these days, you just had to go looking for them. The past *was* different to the present, but it wasn't all good and it wasn't all bad. When she put it back, she saw something at the rear of the shelf, almost hidden behind one of the wooden struts. A book's fallen down from the shelf above, thought Betony, and got stuck there. She wiggled her fingers behind the strut and eventually managed to pull it out.

It was a small slim volume about the maths behind medicines of the past. She flicked through it, and then she saw Flintfeather's name on the final page. I wonder if Thornbeak knows about this one, she thought. She looked at the entry, and saw that it was simply a booklist, referring to other volumes on the same subject. The book by Flintfeather was called *Strength in Feathers*.

She showed it to Thornbeak, and Thornbeak actually squawked with excitement. "I've never even *heard* of this work," she said. "How extraordinary. Let's see ... Flintfeather's book is mentioned because it gives further reading on the subject in chapter three." She turned back to chapter three. And there it was – one little sentence.

Although heart diseases are usually considered to be incurable, Flintfeather has done some important work in this area which should not be disregarded, despite its rather unorthodox approach.

They looked at one another. "It's almost beyond belief," said Thornbeak. "Flintfeather."

"We need to get hold of his book," said Betony.

"Well, it's not here," said Thornbeak. "Otherwise I'd have known about it. Unless it's fallen down behind a shelf, the same way that one had. I don't see how, though. Look – the entry in the index says that *Strength in Feathers* has over three hundred pages. It's going to be enormous."

"What do you think's happened, then?" asked Betony, feeling sick with disappointment. "Has it been lost?"

"I don't know," said Thornbeak. "But I wouldn't mention this to Felix, until we've got a better lead. I'll ask around, see if anyone knows of a private book collection anywhere. I've never heard of one, but that doesn't mean it doesn't exist."

When they left the library that evening, Andria was a very different place. The wide leafy streets were crowded, and there was an atmosphere of excitement and anticipation. A ragamucky was juggling lighted candles, and little stalls had appeared, selling drinks and bags of nuts. As it grew dark, Betony could see lights in the sky as fire-breathers circled above the terminal, waiting to land, and sending out jets of identification flame in little bursts.

"What's going on?" Betony asked.

"It's the dance festival tomorrow," said Thornbeak. "The place will be packed."

"Oh," said Betony. "Can we go to it?"

Thornbeak looked at her severely.

"Well, can *I* go?" asked Betony. "You'll be trying to find out about private book collections, I can't do that, I don't know who to ask."

Thornbeak softened. "I keep forgetting you're only a chick," she said. "You've done some very grown-up work in the library, and I think you'll make a great historian. If that's what you want."

Betony's face lit up. "It is," she said. "I'd love to be your apprentice, if you'll have me."

Thornbeak patted her on the head with her wing. "I'll have to ask your parents," she said.

"Ah," said Betony, feeling a bit guilty as it was a long time since she'd cleaned them, let alone polished them. She explained the situation.

Thornbeak remarked that she didn't think a few licks of polish would matter all that much. An aunt of hers had once been turned into a tree for a few years, and pruning her had been a nightmare. Then she said, "I think you deserve a day off. The library will be shut tomorrow, because of the festival. Take Felix with you; it'll be a distraction for him. Yes, you both go. It'll be good for you."

It had taken a couple of days for Agrimony to get over her reaction to Snakeweed's headache remedy. She had never been so ill; passing out had been a new experience. When she was up and about again, she felt rather differently about what Squill was asking her to do. To begin with, Tiratattle had seemed so glamorous. But the dances were actually a bit silly, and so were the songs. And shreddermouth-lullabies were seriously bad news. Was this really what she wanted to do with her life?

She went for a walk, and found herself in the ragamucky quarter. All of a sudden she felt a bit homesick, so she decided to go to one of the crystal ball parlours and find out how things were back in Geddon – but she couldn't find one that was open.

And then someone tapped her on the shoulder. She turned round. It was Tansy, still dressed as a lickit.

"I want to talk to you," said Tansy.

"OK," said Agrimony meekly, and she followed her upstairs to the poky little room above a shop.

"Sit down," said Tansy.

Agrimony sat down.

"I want you to realise exactly what you're publicising for Snakeweed," said Tansy.

Agrimony had a feeling she knew already, but she sat and listened as Tansy told her.

When she'd finished, Agrimony said, "I know you'll find this a bit hard to believe, but I've had a change of heart." Then she told her about the headache remedy, and the conversation she'd overheard between Squill and the mirror.

"You're more sensible than I'd realised, Agrimony," said Tansy. "You've had your taste of the high life, and it wasn't as wonderful as you expected. Now then. Do you have enough of a conscience to want to do something about all this?"

Agrimony took a deep breath. "What exactly did you have in mind?"

"I want you to take as many as you can carry of the newspapers we've printed to Andria; we'll distribute the rest here, whilst Snakeweed's away. And when you get up on stage to do your promotion, I want you to do just the opposite. I want you to tell the truth."

This was scary. Agrimony hadn't met Snakeweed, but she was sure he would try and stop her the moment she started saying things that weren't in the script.

And then she thought – if I travelled there on my own firebreather I'd have a means of escape. She suddenly felt brave and grown-up, but grown-up in a totally different way to the way she'd felt in the conference centre. This was serious; clothes were just clothes, and dances were just dances. When she went back to Geddon – and she *did* want to go back to Geddon, in the end – she'd have a story to rival anything the elders told. Fame. She still wanted it, but now she wanted to earn it. Properly.

"All right," she said, and she told Tansy about her plan to take Sulphur.

"I think that's a very good idea," said Tansy, "and you'll be able to take more newspapers that way. But you must stick to the flight path, and remember to wear your harness."

Snakeweed was a little disappointed that he hadn't been able to meet Squill's protégé before the festival, but he trusted Squill to have found the right face. He sat on the saddle of his fire-breather, the sinistrom pebbles in his pocket. He'd summon Architrex and Vomidor when they got there. Ramson hadn't been found, either, which was annoying. Snakeweed had commissioned another set of posters, but the artists told him that there was a sudden shortage of paper in Tiratattle, and they couldn't oblige. Some diggeluck or other had bought the lot, for what reason he couldn't imagine.

But his sales initiative was going well. He'd sent a lot of potions out a couple of weeks beforehand, by cuddyak, so they ought to be able to flood the market. Andria was the biggest target Snakeweed had ever attempted – and it was a port, as well. With a base at Andria he could start to export his spells and potions to other lands, across the sea. And once he'd got a brazzle in his employment, surely the dimension question was just a matter of time. He rubbed his hands together. Science. There would be no end to the things he could do.

The only bribe Architrex had been able to think of was a curious one, but it might work. Male brazzles were fascinated by mathematics. Perhaps, Architrex had suggested, there might be books on that subject in the other world. Snakeweed had told him it was up to him to make this sound like a certainty, not a possibility, and Architrex had taken his point.

As they approached Andria, Snakeweed looked down and saw the strange mosaic of the landscape. He'd heard about farms, and they interested him a lot. You could save a lot of money if you didn't have to pay herb gatherers. Grow them all in one place; it was a fantastic idea. He pictured fields and fields of peribott and vamolin; they could cut down some of the forest around Tiratattle, and grow them there. It's a changing world, he reflected, and I'm going to change it more than anyone.

Felix and Betony were among the first to arrive at the palace grounds for the festival so they got good seats, right at the front, on the grass. The perimeter was lined with stalls selling sweets and flowers, and scores of little braziers, which smelt of burning charcoal and roasting nuts. The palace itself wasn't open to visitors, but it had all the right things — towers and turrets and trellises. "I don't understand what that roof's made of," said Betony, pointing to one of the pale green ones. "Is it a new strain of moss?"

"It's metal," said Felix, who'd seen roofs like that before.

"Copper. It goes green with age. I wonder how they refined it?"

"Same way they do gold, probably," said Betony. "A puri-fying spell."

The king and queen made their entrance, and sat on the wooden thrones at the front. There was very little ceremony at their arrival, apart from someone blowing a horn. They looked just like the other tangle-folk – except for their crowns, which were filigree silver and gold, and sprinkled with gems that sparkled with every colour of the rainbow. A wise-hoof stamped his hoof for silence, and introduced the first dance troupe – some tangle-children. The king and queen got up, and joined the children on-stage. The children curtsied to them; a band of pipe players struck up a tune, and the dance began.

Felix couldn't follow it at all. The children twined in and out of one another, and made little jumps and stamped their feet and yelled when he least expected it.

"They're really good," Betony whispered.

The music was full of discords and sudden key-changes, and the rhythm seemed to fluctuate. Halfway through the dance the king and queen sat down again, their duty done. After that there was some singing which sounded more like wailing to Felix, but Betony was entranced and sang along from time to time. Then there was a juggler, and some acro-bats, and then some more dancing. The scent of roasting nuts wafted by, mixed with the perfume from the flowers that people were wearing in their hair. Everyone seemed to be in high spirits; it was a day to enjoy yourself, and forget about digging for gold or mixing potions.

People were still arriving, although they waited for breaks in the performances before they sat down. Then a party of japegrins and lickits walked in. They took a long time to settle down, and the audience became restless, telling them to be quiet and have some consideration. Felix turned round to look.

He felt the hairs on the back of his neck rise. "Betony," he hissed, "it's Snakeweed. He's got those traders we met in the mountains with him."

Betony turned round to look. "Are you sure?"

"Of course I'm sure," said Felix. "What are we going to do?"

"He won't spot us in this crowd," said Betony, with more confidence than she felt. "If we get up and go, he'll see us for certain."

They sat there, trying to be as inconspicuous as possible. The dancing went on, but neither of them could concentrate any more.

There was a short break, when people moved around and bought more drinks and said hello to friends. Felix and Betony stayed where they were, but no one came by and tapped either of them on the shoulder, and they began to think they were going to be all right. Then a bright red bird with iridescent blue wings and a crest on its head landed on the grass in front of them. There was a stir; a flame-bird was a most unusual visitor to something like this.

"Thought I recognised you," said the flame-bird. It was a

young one, only just old enough to fly – there was still some yellow at the edge of its beak. "You helped me build my reincarnation nest. As you can see, it worked. I'm back. Where are the brittlehorns?"

Felix glanced over his shoulder. Snakeweed was still there, but he was deep in conversation with someone; the arrival of the flame-bird hadn't seemed to interest him.

Betony started telling the bird everything that had happened. When the next act started she just carried on, although she lowered her voice to a whisper. When she got to the bit about finding the reference to Flintfeather's book, she turned her back to Felix so that he couldn't hear.

The flame-bird listened – and then it said, "But there *is* another library in Andria."

Betony's mouth dropped open. "Where?"

"There," said the flame-bird, pointing a wing at the palace. "It's an amazing place. I took a little fly round it before the festival, and had a peek through the upstairs windows. The king and queen don't appreciate what they've got in there, you know. There's a room full of books. I've seen it."

"Could you see the titles?"

"I wasn't looking," said the flame-bird. "But a lot of the spines are facing the window, I could have another go. Do you want me to?"

"Oh," said Betony, "that would be wonderful."

"One good turn deserves another," said the bird. It had to wait until the end of the next act, so as not to attract too much attention to itself. The small-tail's solo finally came to an end, with a complicated trill on a set of pipes. "Not enough definition between the notes, and far too fast," criticised the flame-bird, before departing.

Two more acts passed before the bird returned. "Well?" said Betony, the second the bird landed.

"It's there all right," said the flame-bird. "*Strength in Feathers* – that's the one, isn't it? It's a big book. Now all you have to do is get in there."

Betony seized Felix by the hand. "We didn't tell you before, because we didn't know where it was."

"Where what was?"

"Flintfeather's book. I found a reference to it, and Thornbeak realised how important it was."

"Will you please tell me what you're talking about?"

"I'll try and remember it word for word." Betony closed her eyes, and screwed up her face. Then she said, "Although heart diseases are usually considered to be incurable, Flintfeather has done some important work in this area which should not be disregarded, despite its rather unorthodox approach."

"You found something? You actually *found* something?"

Betony nodded. "But the book isn't in the library at all, it's in the palace. Somehow or other we've got to get in there."

"Couldn't you just ask?"

Betony stared at him. "What? Ask the *king and queen*?"

"Why not?"

And then everyone gasped as a jet of flame lit up the sky

overhead. Felix looked up. A fire-breather was going to land in the grounds. He could tell from the crowd's behaviour that this wasn't allowed, despite the fact that it seemed to be a very *small* fire-breather – Betony had told him they were enormous.

A space for it was cleared very quickly indeed, and the fire-breather landed. A wise-hoof cantered over to it, looking stern. Felix could see that Snakeweed had got to his feet, along with another japegrin next to him. They were both smiling broadly. Snakeweed's got something to do with this, thought Felix, I just know it. He nudged Betony.

Betony, however, had gone quite rigid. A tangle-child was getting off the fire-breather, wearing a very expensive outfit. The beads in her hair glittered nearly as extravagantly as the jewels in the queen's crown. She smiled, and waved at the crowd, and then she walked to the front and stepped up onto the stage.

"*Fangs and talons,*" swore Betony, "I don't *believe* it. It's Agrimony."

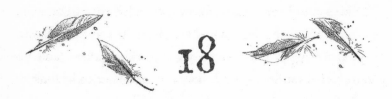

18

Ramson, Tansy and Dibber had given Agrimony the first newspapers off the press.

Tansy was delighted with them. She'd written about the brittlehorns and the flame-bird, and Agrimony had told all about the effects of the headache cure. There was an obituary to Progg, and an interview with Dibber which recounted the events leading up to his friend's death. The full story of Ramson's arrest was there too, and the true murderers of the ragamuckies revealed, with the shocking news that Snakeweed employed sinistroms to do his dirty work.

The piece she was least certain about was the one she'd written about the shreddermouths, but she felt they were entitled to tell their story too. She finished by explaining what Snakeweed was setting out to achieve; the way he wanted to expand his horrible business all over the world, and the fact that he was in Andria at the moment, putting it into practice. On the back page was a list of all the potions and spells Snakeweed produced, and the words: *Let's stop buying these products, and put this japegrin out of business for good.*

Dibber hired some carts, and they loaded the newspapers onto them and took them to all the shops. It was harder than Tansy had expected to get people to stock them – a lot of people relied on Snakeweed for their livelihoods these days, and they didn't want trouble.

The ragamuckies were the first to react – they were furious to find that Snakeweed had been behind the murders in the crystal ball parlours. The diggelucks were the next to get angry; a lot them had coughs themselves, and were worried. The tangle-folk had a great respect for brittlehorns and flame-birds, and before long they, too, wanted action.

The lickits were in two minds when they read the shreddermouth piece. Much as they feared shreddermouths, they didn't want to exterminate them – for who knew what the knock-on effect might be? Shreddermouths had their own predators – parasites which would have to look for new hosts, the way the creepy-biters had when the brittlehorns left the Tiratattle province because it became too crowded.

There were even a few japegrins who agreed with Tansy – more than she might have expected. Not all of them were Snakeweed's employees, and not all of them lived to make a profit out of others.

It took a while for the newspapers to circulate effectively amongst the population of Tiratattle, but by the evening of the second day everyone was talking about them. Ramson's

WANTED posters were all torn down, and a few shops stopped displaying Snakeweed's remedies. The ones that carried on promoting them hit back with hastily scribbled signs on bits of wood, saying that Ramson was only trying to clear his name. There was no paper anywhere in Tiratattle, which made further written action difficult.

Then things took an uglier turn. One of the shops that refused to withdraw Snakeweed's products burnt down. Then another. When the third one went up in flames, two japegrins died. This wasn't what Ramson, Tansy and Dibber had foreseen at all, and as the violence increased they began to wonder what they'd done.

Snakeweed settled back into his cross-legged position on the grass; Architrex and Vomidor were in lickit form on either side of him, and Squill had an expression of eager anticipation on his face. Snakeweed was feeling pleased. His potions had arrived by cuddyak, as arranged, and it appeared that there were at least three brazzles in Andria at the moment. He watched Agrimony take the centre of the stage, and heard the wise-hoof introduce her as a singer.

"I had a headache the other day," Agrimony said, "and I took something for it. This song is about someone else who did something similar."

Snakeweed glanced at Squill. Squill was looking very pleased with himself indeed.

The pipe band started to play, and Agrimony began to

sing. She had a lovely voice, and the notes rose and fell like birds on the wing. Good move Squill, Snakeweed thought; entertain us first, then the hard sell will be twice as effective.

There was a sudden rustling to his right and he glanced across, annoyed. A diggeluck had some sort of book – only the pages were much larger, and it didn't have a cover. The writing was extraordinarily neat and even. Snakeweed felt that this wasn't the time to be reading; the pages made a lot of noise as the diggeluck turned them, so he nudged Architrex, and Architrex asked the diggeluck to have a bit more consideration. The diggeluck ignored him for a moment – then Architrex's powerful smell must have made some sort of impression, because the diggeluck looked up suddenly, and paled. Architrex smiled his death's head smile, and the diggeluck folded up his book, and put it in his pocket.

A few seconds later, there was a rustling from the other side. A ragamucky was reading an identical book. Snakeweed scanned the audience. There were hundreds of the books, and each one was exactly the same; how was this possible?

Agrimony was really getting into her stride now, and those who weren't reading were listening intently. Snakeweed looked at Squill. Squill was no longer smiling. He was sitting as still as a stone, with an expression of horror on his face. For the first time, Snakeweed started to listen to the words.

That moonlit night would be her last, Agrimony sang.

Snakeweed started to pay real attention – this wasn't the popular song they all knew and loathed – those with any taste, anyway.

The drink was drunk, the spell was cast, Agrimony continued.

Sounds like she wrote it herself, thought Snakeweed. The drink was drunk? Dreadful.

Agrimony's voice grew more powerful, she was really belting out the lines now.

Untested remedies can kill,
So don't buy stuff from those like Squill.
The tangle-child of this sad song
Would learn too late the spell was wrong;
Her body wracked by dreadful pain
She realised she'd not dance again –
And as she took her dying breath,
She knew the cure had caused her death!

Squill had gone very white. Architrex and Vomidor looked at Snakeweed – should they take to their four-legged forms, rush the stage and rip the tangle-child apart?

For once, Snakeweed didn't know what to do. He shook his head. When you couldn't make a decision, no action at all was the best bet.

The band played its final note, and there was absolute silence for a moment. Then a diggeluck started to clap – then another, and another.

Agrimony held her hand up for silence, and they stopped. "I was sent here to promote a whole new range of potions and spells," she said, and Snakeweed's heart sank. "I can see that some of you have been reading the newspapers I brought with me."

"Get one," snarled Snakeweed.

Architrex snatched one of the book-things from the nearest ragamucky, and punched her in the stomach when she protested. The punch was nicely disguised, and no one saw.

Snakeweed looked at the headline, and his mouth narrowed to a thin vicious line.

Global Panaceas Are Pure Poison, it said.

"Snakeweed must be stopped," Agrimony was saying. "None of his products have had proper trials. Don't buy anything, and tell everyone else not to buy anything, either. There are stalls here selling them – pass on by. Shopkeepers – don't stock them. Progg died, the brittlehorns died, I thought I was going to die myself when I took one of his headache remedies. So that's what I really came here to do – warn you all. Thank you."

There was an explosion of applause, which drowned out the buzz of voices beneath as people showed each other the newspapers, pointing out things.

"You're dead," said Snakeweed to Squill.

Architrex looked thrilled, and stood up.

"Not *here*," said Snakeweed. "I think we should make a quiet exit."

"That's him!" yelled Agrimony, over the hubbub. "That's Squill, over there!"

Snakeweed and the sinistroms elbowed their way through the crowd, and left Squill to his fate.

Felix and Betony sat there, stunned.

"I thought you said Agrimony was a pain?" said Felix eventually.

"She was," said Betony. "She seems to have changed completely. That was a really brave thing to do."

Felix stood up and scanned the crowd, but he couldn't see Snakeweed anywhere. Squill, however, had been trussed up and seated on a wise-hoof; as he left the grounds, two more wise-hoofs fell into step on either side, looking grim. Wise-hoofs seemed to be very good at looking grim.

"I'm going to get hold of one of those newspapers," said Betony. She darted off, and returned with one a few minutes later. "They did it!" she exclaimed, really excited. "Ramson and Tansy actually did it. Look, it's brilliant, it tears Snakeweed to pieces. Tansy wrote it all, and Ramson and some diggeluck made all the copies, goodness knows how."

"Let me see," said Felix. Then he laughed. "They made a printing press," he said. "Of course, you left my book with Ramson, and it explained all about printing. How clever of him."

Betony wasn't used to hearing her brother described as clever, and she felt at a bit of a loss. So she said, "I'm going to go and see Agrimony."

She pushed her way to the front, where Agrimony was surrounded by people. She was talking to the king and queen, who had apparently invited her back for dinner. When she saw Betony her face broke into a huge smile.

"Bet!" she called. "Come and meet the king and queen! If it wasn't for you none of this would have happened, and it's been the most exciting week of my whole life!"

Betony gulped, and went over. She suddenly felt terribly shy in front of royalty; she didn't have Agrimony's self-confidence in situations like this.

"Hello, tangle-child," said the queen. "Any friend of Agrimony's is a friend of mine. Would you care to dine with us this evening as well?"

Everything's coming right, thought Betony. I've even been invited into the palace. If I can summon up the courage to ask, I'll probably get to see Flintfeather's book. "Yes please," she said to the queen. She wanted to ask if Felix could come too, but she didn't quite have the nerve.

Snakeweed had realised very quickly that his sales initiative was now a lost cause. He wondered what was going on back in Tiratattle, for that was obviously where the book-things had come from. Then he thought – if I could reproduce that number of pages of writing in a similarly short space of time, there's no end to what I could achieve. Overseas, where no one's heard of me. Or in another world.

"Architrex," he said, "I want you to sniff out a brazzle for me."

"That's easy, master," said Architrex, pleased that he could do something right for a change. It was clear he wasn't going to get the opportunity to dispose of Squill, not now the wise-hoofs had him. "There's a wind blowing in from the sea," he said, "and I can smell brazzle quite plainly. I think we should head for the beach."

They changed direction, and started to walk towards the sea.

"I'm not sure how much longer I can maintain my lickit form," said Vomidor after a while. "Can I go back to my four-legged state, master?"

"No," said Snakeweed. "If a brazzle sees me with a sinistrom, there's no way it will agree to work for me."

Architrex looked smug, as he'd realised this already. It *was* hard to stay a lickit for this long, though, and he was looking forward to getting back to his old self. It would be particularly hard to remain in character on a beach, where there would be sand to roll in, and waves to bite. Maybe he could slip behind a rock, have a few minutes break, and then change back once more.

When they reached the beach, sure enough, there was the brazzle, scratching in the sand. He was quite a young one – forty or so – and he was a handsome creature. Architrex felt a little apprehensive.

"Off you go, the pair of you," said Snakeweed. "I'll just sit here in the shade for a bit."

Architrex and Vomidor approached the brazzle with caution. The creature didn't notice them until they were just a few yards away – he was thoroughly engrossed with whatever it was he was writing with his talon.

"Hello," said Architrex. "My name's Architrex, and I've been at the festival. But that looks much more interesting." He couldn't make head nor tail of it – it was a mess of numbers and symbols that didn't seem to make any sense at all.

"Stonetalon," said the brazzle vaguely.

"Pleased to meet you," said Architrex. "You're calculating something quite intriguing, by the look of it."

"It's all a question of division," said Stonetalon. "Addition, subtraction, multiplication – start with integers, and you end with integers. But division – it's division that leads to all the interesting numbers, in the end."

"What's an integer?" asked Vomidor.

"A whole number," said Stonetalon, with a look of total astonishment that someone could *not* know a thing like that.

"And why is one number more interesting than another?" asked Vomidor.

"Because of the things it does when you use it with other numbers, of course," said Stonetalon.

"We've been working on a tricky little problem of our own," said Architrex.

Stonetalon gave him a patronising look. This stated quite plainly that he didn't think a lickit capable of adding two and two together, let alone doing anything interesting.

"It's a dimension problem," said Architrex.

The brazzle looked astounded for a moment – then he glanced down the beach, and Architrex saw another brazzle flying towards them, carrying a rump of something.

This brazzle was older, and altogether more disreputable. He landed on the sand next to them and said, "Lunch. How's it going?" Then he noticed Architrex and Vomidor and said, quite rudely, "What do *you* want?"

Architrex suddenly had a feeling that this brazzle wasn't the one he wanted to deal with at all – he needed the other one.

"You'll never guess what," said Stonetalon. "They're working on a dimension problem as well."

"Really," said Ironclaw.

"But we need help," said Architrex.

"Sorry," said Ironclaw. "We're busy."

"But it sounds as though you may be working on the same thing," said Architrex. "A spell to send someone to another world."

"Who sent you?"

"No one," said Vomidor nervously.

"So you're working on this thing on your own – two lick-its? I don't think so."

"We've just got a bit stuck," said Vomidor.

Shut up, thought Architrex. He'll ask you a question you can't answer if you don't watch out, and then you'll be in trouble.

"Have you tried any trifles?" asked Ironclaw.

Architrex winced. Even he knew that trifles were weird numbers, but Vomidor was shaking his head and saying, "I don't like sweet things."

"Neither do I," said Ironclaw. "And it's only the fact that lickit flesh is meant to be on the sweet side that's stopping me pecking your eyes out."

It was too much for Vomidor. He couldn't maintain his lickit shape any longer, and he transformed back to his four-legged one.

"Blazing feathers!" squawked Stonetalon. "It's a sinistrom!"

Vomidor snarled.

Don't be a fool, Vomidor, thought Architrex, and he changed back himself. Four legs were a lot faster than two. The older brazzle looked at him warily – perhaps he'd had dealings with sinistroms in the past, and he knew that several brazzles had met their ends in the jaws of a sinistrom. But Architrex also knew that rather more sinistroms had been killed by brazzles.

I don't think we'll stay and face it out, thought Architrex, and he turned and ran, expecting Vomidor to follow his lead. When he reached the safety of the rocks – they were full of little hollows and caverns, big enough for a sinistrom, but too small for a brazzle – he turned to look for Vomidor. But Vomidor wasn't there – he was still on the beach, his hackles raised, snarling. Vomidor really isn't very bright, thought Architrex, and that young brazzle is full of bravado. It's going to be an interesting contest.

Stonetalon lifted into the air and dived down on to Vomidor, who feinted to the left, and then ran to the right. It was clear that the brazzle wasn't an experienced fighter; the creatures he hunted weren't intelligent, and were unlikely to have complex evasion strategies. The second time Stonetalon dived, Vomidor rolled over on his back and seized the brazzle's front leg in his jaws. Stonetalon rose into the air again, Vomidor hanging on. He flew up until he was high enough for Vomidor to break his neck if he fell, and then he tried to scrape him off with his back legs. Vomidor was prepared for this, and he kicked back with his own hind legs, which were armed with equally fearsome claws. They struggled for a while, and then the effort of hovering at the same time became too much for the brazzle, and he landed once more on the sand. The blow knocked Vomidor loose, and the two creatures separated again and faced one another.

"Architrex!" yelled Snakeweed.

Architrex had forgotten his master was watching.

"*Architrex*. Are you just going to sit there, or are you going to help Vomidor?"

I'd rather like to just sit here, thought Architrex. And I think I'll interpret what you've just said as offering me a choice of actions.

To make sure there weren't any further instructions he *couldn't* ignore he turned his head on one side and lifted his hind paw to scratch his ear, as though he had sand in it. Then he shook his head to look convincing, and became conveniently deaf.

Vomidor launched himself at Stonetalon once again; this time it was Stonetalon who side-stepped. As Vomidor tried to brake, sliding along the sand with his forepaws stretched out in front of him, the brazzle landed a sharp peck on his flank. Vomidor yelped, somersaulted, and got to his feet again. There was a streak of blood on his fur now. Stonetalon followed it up by spreading his wings and leaping into the air, scoring a hit on the sinistrom's back with his talons. There was more blood. That young brazzle learns fast, thought Architrex. I don't fancy Vomidor's chances, to be honest. Particularly if the other one decides to join the fray.

This didn't look terribly likely, however. The older brazzle was more concerned about trying to protect the calculations in the sand, and he shielded them with his wings and screeched every time the scuffle got too close.

And then the positions reversed. As Stonetalon swooped in for another strike, Vomidor seized his leg again – but this time the brazzle overbalanced, and landed on his back. Vomidor let go of the leg and went for his throat, but the brazzle was trying to rise, and he swiped at Vomidor with his wing. Vomidor ducked, and then he grabbed hold of the wing and worried it. Stonetalon backed away, limping and dragging his wing. Vomidor launched himself at the brazzle once again, sensing victory. Stonetalon side-stepped him for the second time, not as badly injured as he'd made out, and

271

Vomidor came away with a mouthful of feathers.

As Vomidor tried to brush the feathers from his mouth with his paw he swallowed one. He coughed, and then he coughed again. Stonetalon just stood there, watching, his head on one side, his ears pricked. Vomidor looked as though he were trying to be sick; his flanks were heaving and his head was nearly touching the sand. The brazzle swished its tail, but made no move to attack. Vomidor seemed to be having trouble breathing now. And then, quite suddenly, he collapsed on the sand. He lay there for a moment, until his flanks stopped heaving. And then he vanished.

He's dead, thought Architrex. That's what happens when you kill one of us shadow-beasts – we just disappear. For ever. He glanced at Snakeweed. His mouth was one thin line of annoyance. He beckoned Architrex, and Architrex got up. He couldn't ignore a visual command. He trotted over, and the two of them left the beach.

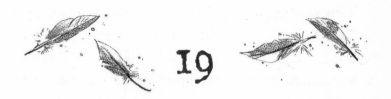

19

Betony and Agrimony sat on one side of the long polished wooden table, and sipped their silver chalices of rainbow-juice. Night had fallen, and the room was lit with hundreds of candles. The king and queen sat at opposite ends of the table, and had to shout to one another to be heard. They didn't seem to object to this in the slightest, and Betony assumed it was some sort of royal custom, otherwise – surely – they'd have sat closer together. Then the soup arrived, and everyone fell silent and got on with it.

The room itself had a high ceiling, which was painted dark blue and covered with stars that had some ghostly light of their own. The walls were panelled with a rich dark wood, and the floor was paved with a pale pink stone that glittered. The chairs were carved in a similar style to the thrones, and there were a lot of statues standing in little niches.

A stone replica of a humungally caught Betony's eye. An elephant, that's what Felix had called it. The next alcove held a dog, and the one after that a boy. She cleared her throat and said, "I like the statues."

"What?" shouted the king.

"The statues," said Betony, somewhat louder. "They're really nice."

The queen was a little closer to her, and she said, "Mythical beasts, Betony, all of them. I think they're quite ridiculous, myself. I've no idea what they're all called, and I have no intention of learning." She laughed her tinkly little laugh, and poured herself another drink. Agrimony started to talk to the king about herbs. Betony felt envious of the ease with which she then slipped from one subject to another, making him smile from time to time.

The tangle-cook came in with the main course. It was a frothy soufflé, full of different toadstools, and it was served with a rich spicy sauce. There was an assortment of vegetables, baked in honey, and a variety of peppery herb-breads. There was a sugary fruit thing for dessert, covered with nuts, and after that there was cheese and pancakes. By the time Betony had finished she was really full.

Taking her courage in both hands she said to the queen, "It's such a lovely palace. Is there any chance we could look round it before we leave?"

The queen looked surprised. "Why would you want to do that?"

"Well," said Betony, "you've got an art collection, and an armoury ... and a library."

"And you want to see those? How extraordinary."

"What's that about arm or reel?" shouted the king. "Is it a new dance?"

"Armoury!" yelled the queen. "She wants to see the armoury!"

The king looked nonplussed, and turned back to Agrimony.

"May I visit the library?" asked Betony. "I love books."

"Do you read a lot, then?"

"When I get the chance."

"I don't," said the queen. "Don't you want see the ballroom, though? I could understand you wanting to see the ballroom. We have such dances there, you must come to one."

Betony smiled politely. They got up and left the table, and for a moment she thought the queen had forgotten all about her request.

"Coming for a turn on the grass then, Pointy-ears?" asked the king. "A little bit of the old midnight wriggle?"

Pointy-ears?

The queen's face lit up, and it looked as though she were going to agree. Then she said, "Oh! Nearly forgot. Got to show Betony the ballroom."

"Ah," said the king. "Right."

Betony followed the queen along the long winding corridors. There were the most beautiful paintings on the walls, portraits of previous kings and queens, paintings of dancers.

The queen completely ignored them, ushered her into the ballroom and stood there. "Nice, isn't it?" she said. It was painted a horrible shade of pink.

"Lovely," said Betony. "Where's the library?"

"Oh, that's upstairs," said the queen. "Are you sure you want to go up all those steps?"

"Quite sure," said Betony. "Why do you and the king sit at opposite ends of the table? If you sat closer together, you wouldn't have to shout."

"What a clever idea," said the queen. "We'll try it tomorrow."

They went up the staircase, which seemed to take for ever, their footsteps echoing in the stairwell. They turned right at the top, and went along another corridor. This was hung with the most exquisite tapestries, and, like everywhere else, was awash with candlelight.

"More myths," said the queen, indicating the delicately embroidered leopards and hippopotamuses and zebras. Betony realised that she had remembered all the names, and felt very pleased with herself. "They're so *boring*," said the queen, and Betony recalled saying exactly the same thing about herbalism. People are so different, she thought. I wonder what Felix wants to be when he grows up? If he grows up. No, not if. He *will* grow up, I'm going to make it happen for him.

At long last they came to the library. Betony stepped inside, holding her breath. There were shelves and shelves of books, and a big desk with writing materials on it. It was nothing like as big as the other library, but it was going to take a while to find what she wanted.

"Shall we go, then?" said the queen.

"Oh," said Betony, "not yet. Please."

The queen sighed, went over to a window seat and sat down. Betony started to think quickly. The flame-bird had seen the title from the window. Therefore, the most logical place to start looking was directly opposite it. She ran her eyes along the middle shelf. *Horns, Antlers and Hoofs. A Directory of Opening Spells. The History of the Chalice.* They were all muddled up, there was no system at all. She cast her eyes down to the shelf below. *Diggeluck Dialects. The Cuddyak Question. Sailing for Beginners.* She began to feel desperate. She tried another shelf. *The Song of the Flame-Bird. Strength in Feathers.* That was it! She pulled it out. It was very heavy; the cover was made of dark blue leather, and the writing was in gold. She opened it, and flicked through. There were drawings of the insides of creatures, strange twisted shapes with lots of worm-like structures sprouting out of them like branches. She'd never seen a picture of a stomach before, or a heart ... *a heart.* She started to read.

When I examined the prince, I noted that his lips were tinged with blue, and his breathing was laboured. When I listened to his heart, the reason for his lethargy was all too apparent. I told his father my findings, and he groaned aloud ...

"I think it's time we went now," said the queen. "I can see

the king waiting for me, out there on the grass. It really is the most delightful moonlit night. You can join us if you like."

"I really wanted to carry on reading this book," said Betony.

"Oh, we can't stay up here," said the queen. "Not on a night like this."

"It's very important," said Betony desperately.

"How can a book be more important than dancing?"

"It can," said Betony, greatly daring.

"Oh well, you'd better have it then," said the queen off-handedly.

"Sorry?" said Betony, thinking she must have misheard.

"Take it," said the queen. "No one here is going to read it, I can assure you of that." She laughed. "Can we go now?"

"Of course," said Betony, clutching the book to her chest.

When they got downstairs she made her excuses, and left. Agrimony was staying overnight, and flying back to Tiratattle on her fire-breather the following day.

Betony went back to the lodging house. Felix wasn't there, so she went looking for the innkeeper. Eventually she found her, sitting at the kitchen table, peeling fruit.

"Oh, it's you," she said. "There was a bit of a crisis here earlier."

"What do you mean?"

"Your friend the tangle-child. Taken queer, he was."

"Queer? How queer?"

"Very queer indeed."

That was no help at all. Betony felt her heart start to beat faster. "Where is he now?"

"Down on the beach, if he's still with us. Keeled over he did, just like he'd been hit with something. Well, I didn't know what to do, did I? So I goes off looking for that brazzle you came with, and I finds another one and I asks her where your one is ... well, to cut a long story short, she comes back here. Gets very officious, says he's got to have some air, and the beach is the best place. So she flies off with him, and that was the last I saw of him. Now, about the bill ..."

"I'll be back," said Betony, and she ran out of the lodging house.

When she got to the beach her legs were aching and she was completely out of breath. It *was* a lovely night, and the moonlight threw the figures into sharp relief. She could see the three brazzles, and Felix's body lying stretched out on the sand. She took a great gulp of air, and ran the last couple of hundred metres flat out. Thornbeak looked up. "He hasn't come round this time," she said, and for the first time there was something close to despair in her voice. "He's still breathing, but his lips are slowly turning blue."

Betony was panting too hard to say anything, so she just handed Thornbeak the book.

Thornbeak's eyes widened. "You brought it with you? What did you do, steal it?"

Betony shook her head.

Thornbeak flicked through the thick creamy pages until she came to the picture of the heart. Then she started to read, getting more and more excited and nodding every so often and muttering things like, "I see," and, "The prince. Of *course.*"

Betony stood there for a bit, getting her breath back and trying to think of something other than Felix dying. She noticed that Stonetalon had an injury to his wing. She pointed to it. "What happened?"

"He killed a sinistrom," said Ironclaw, with considerable pride.

Stonetalon told her the whole story. Betony couldn't concentrate to begin with; she kept looking at Felix, and then back to Thornbeak to see how far she'd got. After a while she realised that Stonetalon was trying to take her mind off it, so she paid a bit more attention. Then she told him how Vomidor had sharpened his claws in preparation for killing *her*, and she praised Stonetalon to the skies for his heroism. Stonetalon looked embarrassed, and gave himself a quick preen. Thornbeak was still reading, so Betony forced herself to carry on talking and told them what had happened at the festival.

"Yes, we heard a bit about it," said Stonetalon. "All the potions have been destroyed, and the japegrins and their cuddyaks have gone back empty-handed."

At long last Thornbeak looked up and said, "We've got everything we need right here, on the beach. The spell is simple, it's the standard healing incantation. But it needs to be recited by someone who really cares about the outcome. We all care, of course, but I think you care the most, Betony. So you shall read the words, although I suspect you know them already."

Betony did. "What about the herbs?"

"There are no herbs," said Thornbeak.

"Well, what's the other ingredient? There must be something else."

"Oh yes," said Thornbeak, "there most certainly *is* something else."

"Well, what is it?"

"A brazzle feather," said Thornbeak.

Betony was speechless.

Ironclaw wasn't, however. "Do you mean to tell me we've had the remedy all the time?"

Thornbeak nodded.

"Oh," said Betony. "The flame-bird's death-song. It sang something about brazzle feathers. Why didn't it tell me when I saw it at the palace, if it knew the answer?"

"It was just a chick," said Thornbeak. "It takes time for it to remember everything it knew before. Now then. We need to take off Felix's top, and lay the feather over his heart."

Betony stripped off Felix's top. His body looked frail and white in the moonlight, and his breathing was shallow. Thornbeak bent her head, and plucked a feather from her golden breast.

"Hold on," said Ironclaw, "I think it ought to be *my* feather."

"And why is that?" said Thornbeak icily.

"Well, I got involved first." He plucked a feather from his own breast, as red as blood.

"I did the research," said Thornbeak.

"And I did the transportation," snapped Ironclaw.

"You stood by and watched our son nearly killed by a sinistrom."

"I was protecting the calculations. Stonetalon was doing extremely well on his own."

"So well that his wing needs at least three spells and some ointment."

"I still think it should be *my* feather," said Ironclaw grumpily.

"Your reasoning is unsound."

"Don't you dare accuse me of shaky reasoning, Thornbeak."

"At least my feather's *clean*," said Thornbeak.

There was no answer to that. They glared at one another.

"Please get *on* with it!" Betony shouted in sheer frustration, and Stonetalon lashed his tail in agreement.

Thornbeak laid the feather gently over Felix's heart, and Betony knelt down beside him. His lips were very blue now, and his breathing was barely visible. She recited the standard healing spell, exactly the way she'd learned it at school, her voice a little wobbly, her eyes a little wet. Then she sat back on her heels, and waited. The half-silence just seemed to go on and on for ever; her own breathing, and the gentle lapping of the waves on the shore.

After a while she began to wonder whether there was just a suspicion of colour on Felix's cheeks. It was hard to tell in the moonlight, so she lit a candle-stub that was lying on the sand and looked at him more closely. It was still hard to tell. Was his chest rising and falling slightly more noticeably? She wasn't sure. The wait dragged on. His face looked very peaceful. And then, quite suddenly, Betony saw that the blue had gone from his lips – and yes, there really *was* more colour on his face. She looked at Thornbeak, her eyes shining.

Thornbeak nodded. "I think it's working."

"Oh good," said Ironclaw. "Because Stonetalon and I have been throwing everything into that dimension spell, and it would have been such a waste if Felix couldn't ... ouch."

Thornbeak had trodden on his foot, hard. And she had some very formidable talons.

They turned their attention back to Felix. And after a moment or two, very slowly, he opened his eyes. He blinked a few times, and gave them a weak smile.

Betony didn't know whether to laugh or cry.

"I nearly went that time, didn't I?" said Felix.

Betony nodded, too choked to speak.

"What brought me round, the brittlehorn potion? I thought it had all gone."

Betony shook her head.

"What then?" His voice was a lot stronger now.

Betony glanced at Thornbeak.

Thornbeak shook her head very slightly. "Let's wait a little bit longer," she said.

"Wait a little bit longer for what?" said Felix, and he sat up.

"How do you feel now?" asked Betony.

"Fine," said Felix. Then, "That's strange. I usually come round really slowly, much more slowly than this. And I never feel kind of ... connected to things. It's always a bit dreamy, I have to think my way round my body to make sure it's still there. And it takes a while to remember what happened just before I passed out – but I can remember it all quite clearly. I was standing in the entrance hall of the lodging house ... then I felt the dizziness start, so I grabbed hold of the window-ledge. But I sort of knew straight away it wasn't going to do any good because the dizziness was the worst it had ever been, and I started to get frightened, really frightened, and then ... nothing." He looked round at them all. "Why do I feel so different this time? What's been going on?"

"Do something for me, Felix," said Thornbeak. "Run to the edge of the sea and back again, as fast as you can go."

Felix looked surprised. The sea was quite a long way out,

and the beach stretched for several hundred metres, flat and smooth, getting shinier and shinier as it neared the water's edge. He shook his head. "I can't run that far."

"Try."

Felix shrugged, and set off at a jog.

"Faster!" yelled Thornbeak, so Felix speeded up. Then he seemed to get into it, because he speeded up even more until he was running flat out. When he reached the sea he stopped, and turned round. Then he jumped right up into the air, and shook his fist in triumph.

"I think that's fairly conclusive," said Thornbeak drily.

Felix sprinted back, his feet barely seeming to touch the ground. "You found the book, didn't you?" he said.

"Yes."

"What did you have to do?"

"Betony recited the standard healing spell, and we placed a brazzle feather over your heart."

"A *brazzle* feather?" said Felix. He looked thoughtful. Then he said, "When I met the leader of the brittlehorns, he said that as I crossed the Divide, I died for a moment. And then something must have jolted me back to life. We use electricity to do that in my world. When I came to, I remember brushing a feather off my shirt ... And when I was really cold, on the mountaintop, and the brittlehorn potion had frozen, I snuggled up to Ironclaw, and I recovered. That all makes sense now, doesn't it?"

"It does," said Thornbeak.

"And ... did it ... was there ... is this temporary, or is it for ever?"

"Nothing is for ever, Felix," said Thornbeak. "One day your heart will decide it's had enough, and stop beating. But not for another seventy years or so."

Felix stood there, not knowing what to feel. He'd fantasised about this moment so many times, but not with any real expectation that it would ever happen. It was a shock, as much as anything. He looked at Thornbeak. "Do you mind if I take a walk down the beach?"

Betony jumped to her feet.

Thornbeak put a restraining wing on her arm. "I think Felix wants to be on his own for a bit, Betony."

"Oh," said Betony. Then, "Why?"

"You may be a very grown-up historian, Betony," said Thornbeak, "but you still have a lot to learn about people."

Felix walked off towards the rocks at the far end of the beach. What had happened to him was so enormous that he could hardly take it in. One moment he felt like crying, the next moment like laughing out loud. He tried imagining being able to do some of the things he hadn't been able to do, like swimming in the sea. That was a small thing. Then he imagined the dream scenario he'd fantasised about for years – the doctor at the hospital looking at his scans and his X-rays and saying, "It's a miracle, Mr and Mrs Sanders, I can't explain it. But there's nothing wrong with him any more. Nothing whatsoever." He imagined the incredulous expressions on his parents' faces, then the smiles and the tears – and then he remembered that it still wasn't certain he could get back there. And then he did cry, great racking sobs that smoothed away some of the shock. When he reached the end of the beach he turned round and walked back again. He felt more composed now, as though he'd got something out of his system. A fierce joy was working its way through him, inch by glorious inch; he could hardly bear it, he was so happy. The stars had never been so bright, the sea so silver, the brazzles so *lovely*. He wanted to hug them, feel their soft silky feathers against his face, smell their distinctive oily smell, tell them how wonderful they were. And Betony. Could any of this have happened without her? He hadn't been able to have many friends; as soon as he did make one, he'd go back into hospital again, and when he came out they'd be going round with someone else. They were pleased to see him again, certainly, but he wasn't reliable. There one day, gone the next. Betony was the best friend he'd ever had.

When he got back to the little group they were all sitting on the sand, talking about the future. The *future*. The word wasn't a bad joke any more.

"We need another day to finish the spell," said Ironclaw, "that's all. Then we fly back to Tiratattle, and see what's happened to Snakeweed's business. After that we pick your brother and sister up, Betony, and all fly back to Tromm Fell. And then we send Felix back to his world."

Betony didn't like the idea of saying goodbye to Felix one

bit, so she put it to the back of her mind and wondered instead what Ramson and Tansy would say when she told them she wanted to be an historian. They wouldn't be able to see the point of it. It was something she wasn't quite sure about herself, yet – but Thornbeak would undoubtedly have an answer. She glanced at Felix. "That's something you can think about now," she said. "What you want to be when you grow up. Any ideas?"

"Oh yes," said Felix, suddenly knowing exactly what he wanted to do.

"What?"

"I want to be a scientist."

"I thought you already were?" said Ironclaw.

"No, I'm just a chick," said Felix. "But give me time."

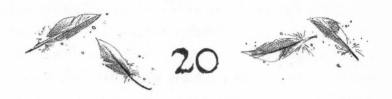

20

There was only so long you could sleep. Grimspite stood up, yawned, stretched himself, and looked round. It was dusk, and there were funny little things flittering through the air. They looked a bit like vampreys, although they weren't anything like big enough. Although he'd killed a few things they hadn't been very big either, and he was hungry. Mythical beasts tasted just as good as the creatures from his world, but they weren't terribly sustaining; it was time he hunted for something larger. He started off down the track again. There weren't any humans around, and he felt rather disappointed about the candle episode. He'd done his best, and they hadn't even waited.

Then something ran across the path. Grimspite was on to it in a moment – but it rolled itself up into a ball, and appeared to be armour-plated. He turned it over with his paw, but it stayed curled up and impenetrable. He wondered if there were some sort of spell he could recite to make it

uncurl and turn into dinner, but none of the ones he tried
made any difference. After a while he gave up.

When he reached the candle-building he had a good sniff
– but the door had been shut with the closing spell, and
there probably wasn't anything to eat in there anyway. He
carried on down the road, until he came to a patch of grass
surrounded by a fence. There was something in *there*, all
right. He jumped over the fence, and found a herd of big
brown-and-white creatures that made a strange mooing
sound. That'll do, thought Grimspite. Instead of forming a
defence circle the way cuddyaks would have done, these animals took fright immediately and galloped over to the other
side of the enclosure. Grimspite selected his dinner, and
killed it with the minimum of fuss. He was too hungry to
torment it. The meat turned out to be quite delicious.

After that he had a little sleep, and when he woke up it
was back to the same old problem – what to do next. He had
a few more mouthfuls of moo-beast, and then he wondered
whether *that* was something he could investigate – the range
of food on offer. He could try out all the different animals,
and if he ever got back to his world, he could write a book.
Dining Out on Mythical Beasts. It had a nice ring to it. Perhaps
he could do a chapter on torture – mauling, partial disem-
bowelling, selective amputation. Grimspite was a very
junior sinistrom, and the idea of taking the initiative and
making a name for himself was rather appealing. It would be
a good career-move. Then he thought – I really *have* made a

proper decision now, haven't I?

It felt good – as though his life had reached a dividing-point, and he was moving on to the next chapter of it. He had a goal of his very own, and he'd created it himself.

Agrimony's flight from Andria was uneventful – but just before Sulphur landed, she realised there was something very wrong in Tiratattle. From the air she could see countless fires, and people rushing around in the streets. The terminal was in chaos, as two fire-breathers had tried to land at the same time – they couldn't stay up there indefinitely, but there hadn't been any puff of smoke to give them the all-clear. They'd decided to risk it, run into each other, and were lying winded on the runway.

Agrimony stabled Sulphur herself, and started to make her way to Ramson's room. She was dying to tell him what a success her song had been, and how well his newspapers had done their job. When she reached the ragamucky quarter, she hardly recognised it. Half the buildings were smoking ruins, and Ramson's place simply wasn't there any more. She just stood there, feeling gutted. Then a diggeluck came by, carrying his entire set of spades, and she decided to ask a few questions. She discovered that there had been riots after the newspapers had done their work, and the conference centre had been totally destroyed. Feelings were very mixed. Half the population thought Ramson, Tansy and Dibber were heroes; the other half thought they were troublemakers of the worst sort. The three of them had gone into hiding, apparently, and no one knew where they were. There was no doubt that Snakeweed's business was finished, but what was there to put in its place? People were unemployed now, they'd left their old trades behind and taken up new ones. The source of their income had gone up in flames; they'd forgotten most of their old ways of making a living, and didn't feel they knew enough to take them up again. Agrimony kept quiet about her part in the whole affair and decided to return to the terminal, get Sulphur, and fly back to Geddon.

She took the canal path, to save time. It was very quiet along there, compared with the activity there had been in the streets. She picked her way through the piles of rubbish, wishing she were wearing more sensible shoes. Eventually she came to a bridge, which she suspected led to the street she'd stayed in with Tansy. It didn't look very safe, there were slats missing and the handrail had broken off halfway across. She glanced down into the water below. It was covered with green scum, and there were logs of wood floating in it. At least, she hoped they were logs of wood. She stepped on to the bridge, holding tightly to the handrails on either side, and made her way very carefully to the middle, trying out each slat before she put her weight fully on it. So far so good. She glanced down again. One of the logs of wood was directly below her now ... and it had eyes.

She felt herself break out in a cold sweat. The next few metres didn't have a handrail at all; she would have to step from slat to slat, with nothing to hold on to if one gave way. Perhaps she should go back, and find another way. She turned round, and retraced her steps. And then one of the slats did snap, and it fell into the water with a loud splash. The gaping hole in the bridge was in front of her, so there was no going back. She would have to turn round again, and cross the bit without the handrail. When she was back where she'd stopped before, she glanced down again. The log of wood was still there, and the eyes were still watching her. It had to be a shreddermouth, there wasn't anything else it could be. She hadn't paid as much attention to animal studies as she had to plant studies at school; animals were a minor subject, and didn't carry all that many marks. What did shreddermouths eat? She wasn't sure.

She edged her way forward, one step at a time. The other bank was looking a lot closer now, she was going to make it … no she wasn't. The slat beneath her just seemed to crumble away. She teetered alarmingly for a moment or two, and then, just as she thought she'd regained her balance another slat handed in its resignation, and both she and it dropped through the resulting hole and landed in the water.

Agrimony was a strong swimmer, and she struck out for the bank as though a sea-monster were behind her. Then the shreddermouth was in front of her, and it was *speaking* to her. She trod water, not knowing what else to do.

"Hello," said the shreddermouth. "I'm Gulp, and I fink you must be Agrimony."

The fact that the creature knew her name surprised her so much that she forgot to keep her head above water, and she went down. Quick as a flash the shreddermouth was beneath her, and then she was on the surface again, lying across its back.

"Tansy asked me to keep a look-out for you," said Gulp. "She and Ramson and Dibber are hiding out in Gobble's lair. Day want to get back to Geddon, but day can't take a public fire-breeder. Day were hoping you'd take dem on your one."

Agrimony burst into tears with relief.

"Dare dare," said Gulp, and he took her to meet the others.

Snakeweed also saw the devastation as he circled above Tiratattle on his fire-breather. Landing didn't seem like a good idea at all, but the fire-breather needed feeding and watering. He decided to go down and refuel, and then take off again as quickly as possible. But where should he go? Architrex had told him that the brazzles were working on the dimension problem already; they must be doing it for the human child. So what would they do, once they'd cracked it? They were natives of Tromm Fell, and that was where Felix had appeared in the first place. It seemed like a logical destination. He told the fire-breather to go down.

The fire-breather shook his head; he hadn't had the signal.

"Just do it," said Snakeweed.

The fire-breather wasn't terribly happy, but he was hungry and thirsty and just a teensy bit tired. He swung round to make the approach, and just as he was about to lower his legs he saw another fire-breather galloping down the runway towards him. It was too late to abort the landing, so he veered to one side and the other one took off just as it came level.

Snakeweed got a very good view of the passengers on the other creature. Agrimony, Ramson, Ramson's sister, presumably, and a diggeluck. Then they were gone, and his own fire-breather was making a very shaky landing indeed, staggering from side to side and only just keeping his balance. Snakeweed turned round and looked up into the sky. The other fire-breather was just a speck now, but the speck was heading in the direction of Geddon. And Geddon wasn't very far from Tromm Fell at all.

Well, well, thought Snakeweed, looks like we're going to have a party.

He had to see to the fire-breather himself, as there wasn't anyone on duty. He kept his head down, hoping no one would recognise him, and Architrex stayed in his pebble. Food and water were in short supply, but Snakeweed nicked a bucket when no one was looking, and before long the fire-breather was ready to go, although he was still a bit tired and grouchy.

As Snakeweed took off he felt he'd handled things rather well. He pointed the fire-breather in the direction of Tromm

Fell, and they settled down to long slow wing-beats that wouldn't beat any records, but would certainly get them there.

"That's it!" squawked Ironclaw. "The last bit of the Cross-the-Divide puzzle! I knew it was all to do with division. You can divide a creature's physical body, but you can't divide its self. We knew that. We knew that when the pressure to divide became too great, the self shot off into the other dimension, and the body followed, because it had to. But what you have to do is freeze the two halves separately to get the numerical stability, not freeze the whole being in one go, and if you get an odd number you have to destroy one itty-bitty to even it up. Felix's case was unique, a chance in I don't know how many million ..." He looked thoughtful.

"No," said Stonetalon, "we don't have time to work that one out now." They'd lost a little bit of time that morning because Thornbeak had insisted on taking Stonetalon to a brazzle-doctor, and getting the spells and the ointment to heal his wing.

Ironclaw sighed. "I suppose so. But what must have happened is that the bloodwort froze the sinistrom in two halves, without us realising," he said. "I wonder how it did that?"

"Bloodwort has been used in fertility spells for fire-breathers," said Stonetalon knowledgeably. "It enables the body-grains to divide more easily."

"Does it?" said Ironclaw. "That's interesting."

Stonetalon flapped his right wing experimentally, and was pleased to note that it was as good as new. "I think we ought to take Felix back to Tromm Fell," he said, "and send him home."

Thornbeak was having trouble tearing herself away from *Strength in Feathers*. It threw new light on her research, and she would have to write an appendix to her book. She was really looking forward to it.

"Are you coming back with us?" asked Ironclaw bluntly.

"Of course I am," said Thornbeak, not even looking up.

"Oh," said Ironclaw. "Right."

Felix was still on top of the world. He had never felt so well, not ever. He had so much more energy. The colours all seemed brighter, somehow, the air sweeter, the sounds sharper. And now he was going home. He climbed on to Stonetalon's back, and Betony scrambled up on to Ironclaw's. They took off, and started the long journey back to Tromm Fell.

They crossed the mountains the first day, and camped on the other side, in the foothills. Betony lit the fire, and the brazzles found some suitable rocks, tucked their heads under their wings, and went to sleep.

Betony bit her lip, and looked at Felix. "I'm going to miss you," she said.

"I'm going to miss you too," said Felix. It sounded a bit lame, and it didn't begin to express what he really felt. He'd made the most fantastic friend, and now they had to part — probably for ever. The two worlds didn't fit together, the divide between them was truly enormous. It was nice to fantasise about Thornbeak joining the British Library, or Ironclaw giving a lecture at the Royal Institution, but he couldn't really see it. And it was delightful to imagine coming here for holidays, but he couldn't envisage his parents allowing it. Once they'd got him back they wouldn't let him out of their sight.

"What are you thinking?" asked Betony.

Felix told her.

Betony pulled at her silvery hair, and made a face. "It won't be like that for ever, you know. You'll grow up, and then you can do whatever you want. The same is true of me. I'd really like to visit your world."

"You'd attract too much attention," said Felix.

"Even if I wore a hat the whole time?"

Felix laughed. "I think it's easier for me to fit in here than it is for you to fit in over there. You see, we have such rapid communications. If someone tumbled to the fact that you were an elf from another dimension, the news would be everywhere in no time at all."

"I expect we'll get that sooner or later here," said Betony. "I can't see anyone *forgetting* about printing, now it's been invented, can you?"

"No." Their world will go the same way as ours, now, thought Felix. And it's all my fault.

"We *will* meet again," said Betony. "Even if I have to cut the tops off my ears."

"Maybe someone knows a spell that will change them — just for a few weeks, long enough for a holiday."

It was a comforting thought, but he still couldn't see it actually happening. "Talking of spells," he said, "let's have one last go at the candle."

Betony handed it to him. As Felix recited the words in his head and waved his hand, he was vaguely aware that this time he had the energy to concentrate a lot harder.

The tip of the wick glowed red for a moment, and then faded. Felix wiped his mind and tried again. The wick burst into flame, showered them with sparks, and set fire to the leaf litter.

Betony stamped it out. "Eleven out of thirteen," she said. "Try and control it a bit more next time, will you?"

When Agrimony and the others arrived back in Geddon, Grisette met them with a face like thunder.

"How *dare* you go off like that!" she shouted. "You were only meant to be away for a day." She turned to Tansy. "I should never have trusted a teenager. You were meant to be in charge of my daughter, and now she's missed her toadstool test, and she looks like a ... well, I've never seen clothes like it. Jade? What is the world coming to. And her hair ... you can take tangles too far, you know, and Agrimony has definitely taken hers way beyond common sense. And my husband needed that fire-breather to go to Tiratattle ..."

"Tiratattle's in ruins," said Tansy.

Grisette blinked. "What?"

"It's a long story," said Tansy, "but I think you'll find that Agrimony is twice the person you thought she was – and I know you had a high opinion of her already."

Grisette looked astonished. Tansy had never had a good word to say about Agrimony before. Then she said, "Betony never turned up, you know. Have you heard anything?"

"Betony's fine. Agrimony met her in Andria."

"*Andria?*" Grisette had to sit down. "You've been to Andria?"

"Not only that," said Agrimony, "but I stayed with the king and queen in the palace."

Grisette's mouth dropped open.

"I've got loads to tell you," said Agrimony.

"I think we just want to get home now," said Tansy, and they all said their goodbyes.

"Well, that wasn't too bad after all, was it?" said Ramson. "I thought she'd be a lot more upset about not getting the fire-breather back on time." He looked wistful. "*We'll* never be able to afford one."

They crossed the yard to the rope ladder.

"You can't be that hard up," said Dibber, "those statues must be worth a bit."

Ramson looked thoughtful, spat on his handkerchief and wiped some birdlime off his father's shoulder.

"Don't even think about it," hissed Tansy. "When they came back to life we'd be in real trouble."

"Actually," said Dibber, "the idea of putting my gold into a printer's business is quite appealing. You could write books about your remedies, and we could sell them."

Ironclaw, Stonetalon and Thornbeak circled high over Tiratattle, watching the scene below with their magnifying vision. Felix and Betony could see the smoke rising, but little else.

"I don't like it," said Thornbeak. "I think we ought to fly on to Tromm Fell."

"But Betony wants to meet up with her brother and sister," said Ironclaw. "And we could give them a lift back."

"How are we going to find them?" asked Thornbeak. "It's absolute chaos down there."

"We could try a crystal ball parlour," said Stonetalon.

"You never know if they're genuine," Thornbeak pointed out. "The ragamuckies often give out false information just for fun."

"Have you got a better idea?" asked Ironclaw.

"No," Thornbeak admitted. "But brazzles don't usually visit Tiratattle — we're going to attract a lot of unwelcome attention."

"Well, let's land somewhere relatively deserted," suggested Stonetalon. "The airstrip looks like a waste of time anyway, there are far too many fire-breathers down there waiting to take off."

"That canal path looks pretty empty," said Ironclaw, "let's

try that." He turned his head and said to Felix, "One of the best things about brazzles is the vertical take-off and landing facility."

The brazzles touched down one after the other, and folded their wings.

"I know where we are," said Felix. "If you want a crystal ball parlour, they're that way."

"We'll wait here," said Thornbeak. "You go and find out what you can."

The children started to make their way to the ragamucky quarter, feeling distinctly uneasy. There was smoke everywhere. When they reached the main road they just stood there, aghast. "There *aren't* any crystal ball parlours any more," said Betony. "What on earth has happened?" She started to ask passers-by what had been going on, and got a rough picture of the events. But she had no idea where to look for Ramson and Tansy at all now.

"Maybe they've gone back to Geddon," said Felix.

"And if they haven't? If we go back, and they're not there? Supposing they're in real trouble, and we were here, and we didn't help them?"

"Well, we're not getting anywhere here," said Felix. "Let's go back to the brazzles."

They walked back to the canal, and as they turned the corner Betony stopped dead.

"What?" said Felix.

"Look. On the bank."

Felix looked. A long green knobbly creature not unlike a crocodile was lying there, talking to Thornbeak.

"What is it?"

"A shreddermouth. I think they eat lickits."

"Well, we're all right then, aren't we?"

"I only said I *think*," said Betony.

"Thornbeak seems quite happy."

"Thornbeak's a brazzle," said Betony.

Thornbeak glanced over, and saw them. "It's all right," she called. "This is Gobble. She hid Tansy and Ramson until Agrimony arrived. They've all gone back to Geddon by fire-breather. We can go now."

"Thank goodness for that," said Betony. But she gave Gobble a wide berth, and climbed on to Thornbeak's back very quickly indeed. Then the three brazzles took off again, and they were on their way.

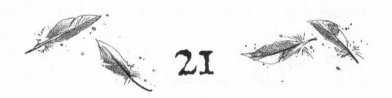

21

By the time Felix and Betony reached Tromm Fell, Felix was feeling very nervous. Supposing there was something just a tiny bit wrong with Ironclaw's spell – would he die as he crosses the Divide? One part of him wanted to say, look, I've changed my mind. I want to stay. It was easy to justify it, as well. His parents must think he was dead by now – he'd been away for a month. They'd have got used to the idea. After all, they'd been preparing themselves for it for a long time. But he did miss them, and he knew how happy he could make them by returning fit and well. On the other hand, there was so much he could do here. He knew enough about science to get things moving, even if he didn't know the finer details – but did he want to? He understood the internal combustion engine, electricity, how to make a microscope. Were these things this world really needed? Perhaps he wasn't old enough or experienced enough to know. It all hung in the balance – the reasons to stay, the reasons to go.

A fourth brazzle flew over and joined them as soon as they landed.

"Granitelegs," said Thornbeak. "I haven't seen *you* for a few decades."

Granitelegs glanced at Ironclaw. Thornbeak had always intimidated him, she was so fearfully *decisive*. Surely they weren't going to mate again? It had only been forty years since the last time.

"Hello," he said, and then he couldn't think of anything else whatsoever to say.

"I hear you and Ironclaw have been collaborating," said Thornbeak.

Granitelegs couldn't help it; he laughed. "Ironclaw? Collaborate with *me*? He thinks solid geometry's for pullets."

Thornbeak cast Ironclaw a withering look, and Ironclaw studied his feet and said nothing.

"Oh, by the way Ironclaw," said Granitelegs cheerfully, "your calculations got wiped out by the rain."

"It doesn't matter," said Ironclaw. "I memorised them."

Granitelegs looked irritated. He couldn't have remembered that amount of work himself, and to be honest, he was downright jealous of Ironclaw's ability to do it.

"Right," said Thornbeak, "let's get to work."

"There's one thing I want to ask," said Felix. "Once I'm back in my world, can I ever return here?"

"Only if you've got the spell," said Ironclaw.

"Well, can I write it down?"

"If you need to," said Ironclaw, "although, personally, I always find my memory the best storage facility." He cast Granitelegs a superior look.

Felix retrieved his notebook, and wrote down the spell after all his vocabulary entries. "And that's all I need?" he asked.

Ironclaw nodded.

Felix gave Betony his compass, and the biro. He'd thrown the torch away once the batteries had died, and Ramson still had his book. All he would take back was his notebook.

"Here," said Thornbeak. "Take this as well," and she gave him one of her feathers.

Ironclaw looked annoyed, as though he should have thought of it first.

"Write down the healing spell as well," said Betony. "It's very short."

So Felix took back the biro, wrote it down, and handed the pen back again.

Then it was time to say goodbye. Felix hugged each of the brazzles in turn – apart from Granitelegs, who looked totally perplexed at this demonstration of affection.

When it came to Betony, he found he had tears in his eyes, and so did she. Prolonging the goodbye didn't seem like a good idea, so he went over to the Divide – and that was when he heard a sudden leathery flapping of wings. He looked up; a fire-breather was approaching far too fast – and then it landed, every muscle stretched to the limit as it tried to brake. It couldn't quite stop in time to avoid colliding with Granitelegs. The brazzle swore, and the two of them rolled over and over before regaining their feet and glaring at one another.

And there, a few yards away, was Snakeweed. He'd jumped off at just the right moment and was standing there with his hands behind his back and a big smile on his freckled face.

"What do *you* want?" said Ironclaw rudely.

"I want to go to Felix's world," said Snakeweed. "I know you have the means to do it."

"No way," said Felix.

Snakeweed smiled faintly. "What's it to you?" he asked. "You haven't got long to live anyway."

"Wrong," said Felix. "Thornbeak has cured me. At the moment I feel as though I could live for ever."

"Really," said Snakeweed. "Well, that is good news. Perhaps you could send a little joy my way, too. There's nothing for me in this world any longer. I think your world would be an ideal alternative. A totally untapped market for magic. We could go into business together."

"You've got a nerve," said Stonetalon, taking a step towards him.

And then Felix realised why Snakeweed's hands had been behind his back. He'd been rubbing the sinistrom pebble. Architrex stepped out from behind him – and then, so quickly that Felix hardly had time to draw breath, the sinistrom sprang. Felix fell to the ground, the wind knocked out of him, with Architrex on top of him – and a split second later he felt the creature's teeth close around his neck.

It had all happened so quickly. Everyone just stood there, frozen.

"Send me across the Divide," said Snakeweed, "or Architrex will rip the boy's throat out."

The brazzles looked at one another.

"Do it," said Thornbeak.

"I want Architrex to cross over as well."

Felix could feel the sinistrom's breath hot on his face, feel the needle-sharp points of Architrex's fangs against his jugular.

"Do it," repeated Thornbeak.

"One foot either side of the Divide then, you canal-scum," said Ironclaw. "And Architrex and the boy have to be in that position as well."

Felix swivelled round so that he was lying across the Divide. Architrex stood above him, so that they made a perfectly symmetrical pattern. Then Architrex let go of Felix's neck, although he didn't raise his head. He lifted his lip into a half-smile and whispered, in the most malicious way imaginable, "What makes you think that a magical cure from *this* world will have the slightest effect in *yours*?"

Felix only had a moment for the implications of what Architrex had said to sink in – then Ironclaw began to recite the spell. After that everything went black.

* * *

When Felix came round he sat up straight away, but there was no sign of Snakeweed or Architrex. They must have regained consciousness faster than he had. The heat struck him full in the face like a hammer-blow – he was back in Costa Rica, and the air was full of insects and humming-birds.

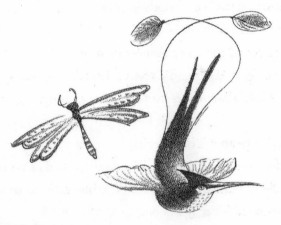

He remembered Architrex's parting words, and something inside him sank like a stone. How did he feel? He stood up. Sick and dizzy was the answer, so he sat down again. This wasn't so good. Perhaps it was the heat. He felt in his pocket, and there was his notebook. He took it out, and opened it. The pages on which he'd written the spells were blank.

He suddenly wanted his parents really badly. It's all been a dream, he thought, I just fell asleep up here and dreamt it. But his compass wasn't round his neck any more, and he didn't have his bag, or his book, or his biro. And when he looked down at himself, he was still wearing the green tangle-child clothes.

There was one more thing he could try. He tore up a handful of dried grass, concentrated on it, waved his hand and said in his head: *Don't fight; ignite; flame, light; burn bright*. But the grass didn't catch light, nor did it turn into anything else. That was it, then. Magic didn't work over here.

He tried standing up again, and this time it was a little easier. He started to make his way back down the path, stopping every so often for a rest. When he came to the stream he had a drink and peered at himself in the water. He still looked healthy, and his hair had returned to its normal brown. But he felt sick, deep down inside; he knew he didn't feel as well as he had the day before. For the first time, he really felt like giving up and throwing himself off a cliff somewhere. The hope had grown from a little nugget to something quite extraordinary – a reality he'd really believed in – and now it had been taken away again. This was the worst time *ever*.

He carried on down the path, dragging his feet, looking at nothing except the track in front of him. When he eventually reached the Study Centre there was a crowd of men on horseback in the humming-bird garden, talking animatedly. Felix spotted Miguel and went over to him. Miguel glanced down at him. He stared as though he couldn't believe his eyes.

"It's me, Felix," said Felix.

"*Sweet Mary, mother of God,*" said Miguel. He shouted to the others in Spanish, and they all turned to look.

"You hadn't given up, then," said Felix. "Are my parents here?"

"They have gone back to England," said Miguel.

Felix looked at all the men on horseback. They were carrying rifles. He turned back to Miguel, an expression of incomprehension on his face.

"We think a jaguar has killed one of our cows," said Miguel. "This is a hunting party." He dismounted. "But this – you – this is amazing. No European has survived that long in the jungle before, not here. How did you do it?"

Felix thought very quickly. "I don't know," he said. "I think I must have lost my memory, or something. I just found myself wandering up on the Divide, so I came back here."

"We must contact your parents immediately. They will be overjoyed. Come, you must need a drink – something to eat – a bath, clean clothes, a lie down."

Felix was ushered into the Centre, and a lot of telephone calls were made. Eventually, it was decided that it would take too long for his parents to come over and collect him, and it would be better if he flew back by himself. Miguel's wife was to take him to San José, and put him on the plane.

* * *

Architrex felt as though someone had tried to cut him in two with a blunt blade – and then squeezed him as hard as possible. He looked round. No sign of Snakeweed, but the human boy was still out cold. What should he do? Go and look for his master, probably. He trotted off down the path, following Snakeweed's trail. There were a lot of insects here – in which case there ought to be things that fed on them. He stopped for a drink. That was odd – he was sure he could smell sinistrom. He must be mistaken, surely? He carried on down the path, feeling slightly uneasy. He was beginning to feel hungry, though. He took a detour into the jungle, and caught a very tasty bird. After that he had a sleep. When he woke up, he thought he'd better start looking for Snakeweed again. It was irritating – Snakeweed should have waited for him. Surely a master owed a sinistrom that small courtesy, at least? But then, Snakeweed came fairly low in the top twenty list of masters Architrex had had over the centuries. He went back to the path, and continued on down, following the scent.

After a while, he could smell humans. He wasn't as naïve as Grimspite, so he circled round, and came to a patch of grass enclosed by a fence. He could smell blood. Something had been killed here, and killed recently. He found a depression in the grass, small shreds of flesh, slivers of bone – and he could smell sinistrom again, far more strongly. He didn't like it. He didn't like it one bit.

And then he heard something. Voices, and hooves. He

glanced round. He was out in the open here, it wouldn't do at all. He loped back to the trees for cover, in the opposite direction from the voices.

And then he saw another man, coming towards him, mounted on one of the brittlehorn things that didn't have horns. The man shouted something, and there was an answering cry of, "Are you sure, Miguel? Where are you?"

The man raised some sort of stick to his shoulder.

Architrex smiled to himself. A stick? A knife would have been better, and a lance better still. A stick wasn't going to be much use. He moved forward, gathering himself to spring.

Bang!

Architrex felt a searing pain in his shoulder, like fire. But they don't *have* magic here, thought Architrex, staggering back a couple of paces. That's the most powerful wand I've ever encountered, what on earth does it do, harness lightning?

There was a second bang, and after that … nothing.

Miguel rubbed his eyes. He'd hit it, he was sure he'd hit it. But it just seemed to have vanished. He rode over to the spot where the creature had fallen, but there was no blood, nothing. He widened his search, and then widened it still further in case he'd only wounded the beast – but there were no tracks, no blood-trail, no evidence of anything whatsoever. Eventually, he gave up. As he went back to tell the others what had happened he shook his head, and crossed himself. Perhaps the padre had been right, and it hadn't been a jaguar at all, but a devil-beast from hell.

Two days later, Felix found himself circling above Heathrow. It was cloudy and grey, and it was drizzling. The trip had been exhausting, although he didn't feel as tired as he might have expected. I suppose the holiday's done me good, he thought. The plane's engines changed tone as it prepared to land. He was wearing new clothes now, and apart from his memories, the trip to Betony's world might never have happened. He opened his notebook. The pages were still blank. He turned them over one by one, fighting back the tears. And there, in the middle, were his two pages of vocabulary notes – he'd missed them the first time he'd looked. And what was more, pressed between them, was the brazzle feather. He lifted it out, and looked at it. The shaft was snow white, as was the downy part, but the plume itself shone pure gold. He turned it around, watching it gleam as it caught the light. And then the plane touched down, and he was home.

His father smiled the broadest smile possible and his mother started to cry the moment they saw him emerge from Customs. He hugged them, and fended off their questions with the same story – he'd lost his memory, he had no idea what had happened.

"Someone must have taken him in, and looked after him," said his mother. "There's no way he could have survived otherwise. Tribesmen, maybe."

"There are no tribesmen in Costa Rica," said his father.

"Well, some hermit or something. *Someone*, anyway."

"You look surprisingly well, Felix," said his father. "Remarkably well, under the circumstances."

"I feel OK," said Felix. But he didn't. All he felt was the most overwhelming despair.

"Hospital visit tomorrow," said his mother. "Just to check you over."

And then she was crying again and Felix thought – I wonder if it's the same for her? She'd started to get used to losing me, and now she's got to go through it all over again.

They drove home, and he went up to his room. He wasn't as pleased to see it as he'd expected – all the old emotions came rushing back, the *what's the point of anything* feeling. That night, he cried himself to sleep.

Snakeweed hadn't been too bothered about leaving the other two to recover. He had no more use for Felix, and Architrex would track him when he woke up. He followed the path down the hill, planning his next move. He needed to set himself up in business; his magical remedies would be a sensation. Science couldn't possibly cure snick-pox and ear-rot as quickly as the tangle-charm he'd bought for next to nothing. And they wouldn't know about illusion spells. He could use a simple children's party trick to convince people they were ill when they weren't, then sell them the remedies. And then he could market potions under a different name to counteract the inevitable side-effects. There were plenty of promising-looking plants for his infusions, and with a bit of advertising ...

When he got to the Study Centre he decided he wasn't quite ready to meet humans *en masse* yet. So he pulled his hat down harder over his ears, nodded politely, and continued on his way. He needed to get to a town where he would be less noticeable until he'd learned how to fit in.

Transport was the priority. Perhaps he could steal one of those no-horns that the men rode. He carried on down the road, looking with interest at the houses he passed. They were very luxurious, with lots of rooms and a wonderful transparent substance covering the windows. He crept up to one of the windows and peered through. A woman was watching a box of light that seemed to have people in it. *Science*, thought Snakeweed. Perhaps it *is* more powerful than magic. Who would have thought you could make people really tiny and imprison them in a box? There's no end to the things you can do over here. He could hear a sort of rumbling sound in the distance, so he went back to the road. A metal box with wheels went past, belching smoke. There were people sitting inside, but it had no animal pulling it. *Fangs and talons*, thought Snakeweed. So all the old stories are true. There really are machines that propel themselves. Presumably humungallies and river-fatties exist as well, and the humans light their streets with gas-lamps and fly from country to country by balloon.

He left the houses behind, and saw fields to either side. Eventually, he spotted a small herd of no-horns, grazing. One of them raised its head and neighed, just like brittlehorns did when they were excited. After that they all wheeled round, and galloped away. Snakeweed swore to himself. Then he realised that something was stalking them, in the bushes at the edge of the grass. He looked closer. It's Architrex, he thought. How dare he put his dinner before looking for *me*.

"Oy, sinistrom!" he called, feeling too annoyed to even give Architrex his name.

Grimspite stopped what he was doing, taken completely by surprise. Then he saw Snakeweed. A japegrin, he thought. Well I never. I suppose he's got some sort of mission for me. He trotted out of the bushes, and went over.

"I don't want you to kill one of those creatures, I want you to capture one for me!" shouted Snakeweed. "Alive!"

Grimspite thought about it. He'd been rather looking forward to trying one of them out for *Dining Out on Mythical Beasts*. He wasn't quite sure how he felt about taking orders any more. It wasn't as though this japegrin had summoned him by rubbing his pebble. If the brazzle on Tromm Fell had suddenly appeared and started bossing him about – well, that would have been a different matter entirely.

"Architrex," said Snakeweed dangerously, "I'm warning you."

Architrex? It was a nicer name than Grimspite. Oh all

right, he thought, just this once. But don't you push me too far, japegrin, because I might just disembowel you. They'd have juiced my pebble for that back home – but there's no chance of that here. My pebble's in another world. I'm free.

"Architrex!" yelled Snakeweed.

Oh dear, thought Grimspite, you're not going to last very long if you carry on using *that* tone of voice. He pictured himself rearranging Snakeweed's intestines – something a bit arty, with a strong composition and a touch of symbolism. Then he grinned and trotted off after the herd, a picture of dutiful obedience.

Snakeweed smiled. He could rely on Architrex.

Hospitals. The familiar antiseptic smell, the whirring metal machines, the too-kind nurses. Felix had his usual battery of tests – and to his astonishment, his peak-flow reading was good.

"Curious," said the doctor.

His parents sat and waited with him for the rest of the results. They waited far longer than usual. Felix heard his mother whisper, "Do you think that maybe … just maybe … he's gone into remission again?"

The doctor called them all into his consulting room, and looked at them a little oddly. He put the tips of his fingers together, and cleared his throat. "I don't quite know how to say this," he said. "It's never happened before, you see. But … well, it's quite extraordinary. I can't explain it. If I believed in miracles, I'd think I'd just seen one. But I've checked everything out with my colleagues, and there are no errors. There's nothing wrong with him any more, Mr and Mrs Sanders. Nothing whatsoever."

"*What?*" gulped Felix's father.

His mother went very white and clung on to the edge of the doctor's desk.

Felix pinched himself to see if he'd drifted off to sleep. It hurt. Then he muttered, "*Bingo,*" under his breath. He didn't wake up. This time, his dream scenario was no fantasy. This was reality.

The doctor turned to Felix. "Tell me," he said, "can you remember any of the plants you ate when you were in the jungle? There might be some sort of lead there ... We're doing research all the time into rainforest plants, with a view to making drugs out of them ..."

But Felix wasn't listening any more. He had felt the weight fall off him for the second time, and this time was best of all. Architrex had been wrong; the sinistrom hadn't had any basis for what he'd said – nothing except pure spite. And as for the ignition spell, was he really certain he'd remembered the words correctly? Maybe he'd got the order wrong, or put in a word that wasn't meant to be there, or left one out. The evidence of a cure was here, the *scientific* evidence, right in front of his eyes. He had felt ill back up on the Divide because he'd just been sent from one dimension to another. Perhaps crossing over always had a debilitating

319

effect. And once he was back in Costa Rica, he'd *thought* himself back into his illness. Become so depressed that he had actually made himself sick. And now ... now he really was better, for good. Magic *did* work over here, after all. It was as powerful a force as anything science had to offer, and presumably with sufficient study you could understand precisely how it worked.

And then, with a sickening jolt, he remembered that Snakeweed was out there somewhere. Magic had got rid of Felix's affliction, so Snakeweed wouldn't have lost any of his powers either. And, even worse than that, he still had Architrex ...

Felix took a deep breath. Things were going to be a little more complicated than he'd anticipated. No one else was going to realise what a menace Snakeweed was. But perhaps he could do something about that, because now he had a future. *Blazing feathers!* He was going to *live*.